THE DOGS MAY BARK

BUT THE CARAVAN MOVES ON

J. Russell & Gertrude Morse on their wedding day

THE DOGS MAY BARK

BUT THE CARAVAN MOVES ON

GERTRUDE MORSE

EDITED BY HELEN M. MORSE

Acknowledgments

The editing of this book would not have been possible except for the fact of having access to old letters and newsletters.

Pictures were taken from family collections of photos taken by J. Russell Morse, and his sons Eugene, Robert, and LaVerne, as well as from old newsletters. Pictures were enhanced and preapared for printing by Tom Silkwood, of Freedom Films.

Thanks also go to:
My husband, Eugene, and my children for their encouragement during the editing process.
Eugene for the hours of proofreading and correcting typos.
Janet Dittemore Bemo for access to her mother's papers and letters.
To Daryl Williams, who designed the cover.
To Chris DeWelt and Steve Jennings at College Press for their help and kindness.

About the title

In China there used to be a saying that went something like this: "The dogs may bark, but the caravan moves on." The reference was to the horse caravans which traveled from China up into Tibet. As they passed through a village, the dogs barked furiously, but the horses and mules in the caravan ignored them and kept moving on their way.

This is something like the way the Morse family faced the many trials and difficulties which beset them during their years on the mission field. In spite of political uprisings, opposition of local officials, sickness, loss of their mission station and supplies in a flood, the problems of being cut off from the outside world due to snow-blocked mountain passes, or the dangers of World War II, they continued unflinchingly in their determination to serve the Lord among the people to whom God had called them.

Yes, the "dogs" of difficulties barked, but the "caravan" of their family's devotion to the Lord's work moved on.

Table of Contents

Contents

Preface

It was in April, 1948, at a Missionary Convention in Springfield, Illinois that I first met Gertrude Morse, briefly. It was at that same convention that I met her son, Eugene, and two months later, he and I were married. Although we spent three weeks in California with his parents before they sailed for China in August, it wasn't until we, too, reached China that I had an opportunity to really get to know his mother.

I had heard much about Gertrude Morse, first from Isabel Maxey Dittemore, who was their co-worker, and then from Eugene, so when I arrived on the field I stood in awe of her. But as I heard from Gertrude of some of her experiences in the Salween Valley, and learned more about living in an isolated and primitive part of Asia, my awe was replaced with appreciation and affection. I began to realize that the difficulties she had met had been learning experiences, and that God had used them to make her the person that she was, a "tool" in the Master's Hand which He used to accomplish His purposes. I also realized that He was using Gertrude to teach me much that I needed to know. She was a tireless teacher — and a good one. Not only did I learn about mission work, but I also received many practical tips about living and working in the backwoods of Asia. However, the one message that came through above all else was this: When we trust in God and are fully yielded to Him, He is faithful to supply all our needs, and to do for us "far above what we can ask or think".

The months following our arrival in China were full of
political turmoil, as the Communists gradually took over all of
China. Eugene and I tried to travel to the former mission station in the Mekong Valley, but had to return to Kunming.
Then, in November, 1949, together with Drema Esther, we
left China and went to Hong Kong. Gertrude Morse joined us
there in December, 1949, leaving her husband, J. Russell, in
Kunming. There he subsequently spent two and a half years
under the Communists, the last fifteen months of which were
in solitary confinement in a Chinese prison. When the way
opened for all of us to move from Hong Kong on into Burma,
Gertrude never hesitated, but entered into the work with
tremendous zeal. Her quiet bravery during those trying and
stressful years of separation when she received no word from or
about her husband, were an eye-opening witness to me of the
true meaning of trust, for her faith in God never wavered. It
was also a demonstration of true dedication to God and His
work, as she put aside her own feelings and emotions in order
to serve the Lord.

For twenty-three years I had the privilege of being with
Gertrude Morse on the mission field. I saw how she gave
unstintingly of herself in order to teach and train Christian
leaders. I saw how she endured discomfort and weariness, traveling on foot, through rain and shine, to scattered villages to
hold schools for women; and how she disregarded her own
poor health (she suffered from chronic anemia) in order to help
others. I saw, too, that she considered one inquirer worth as
much effort as fifty or a hundred. She was a dedicated missionary, whose life was devoted to sharing the Gospel with those
who had not heard, regardless of difficulties, inconvenience, or
personal discomfort.

Gertrude Morse was a humble person who never considered her life or her accomplishments anything to boast about,
and she was always careful to give God the glory for any victo-
ries. She firmly maintained her principles and her standards of

right and wrong, and never hesitated to speak out against wrong-doing. Keep these things in mind as you read her story, and try to "read between the lines" to understand what kind of a person she had to be to do the things she did. She endured and persevered in circumstances which would have caused many people to become discouraged and return home, yet her faith in God remained steadfast.

This is Gertrude Morse's story, as she recalled many incidents from her years of experience. Hesitant to rely solely on memory, she supplemented that with reference to and excerpts from personal letters and newsletters of the time. The editing of this book has been a labor of love. Although I have clarified details of some incidents and have filled out the accounts of some events from recently available historical material, the basic story is as she wrote it.

As you read her story, may it bless you as her life blessed me and so many others.

Helen M. Morse

Chiang Mai, Thailand
June, 1997

Introduction

God's plan and pattern for the lives of individuals may not always be readily discerned by the finite mind of man. It is only in retrospect that we can see clearly how certain incidents, though seemingly unimportant at the time, set in motion a series of happenings which affect many lives. For example, a preacher in a small country church in South Dakota prayed that God would grant a young woman's earnest prayer for a son who would be dedicated to Christian service. Who could foresee, or even imagine, that years later that preacher's grand-daughter would marry a son of the child born in answer to his prayer.

When Ruth MacKenzie was growing up, she wanted to be a missionary, but was unable to fulfill this desire. Instead, at the age of 16, she married Frank E. Morse, and by 1897 they had four children, the youngest of whom was thirteen. Still, Ruth Morse longed and prayed for a son, whom she would dedicate to the Lord, one who might grow up to serve Him as a missionary in a foreign land.

God heard her prayer, and on February 4, 1898 Justin Russell Morse was born in Alexandria, South Dakota. In 1900, when Russell was still very young, the family moved to the Indian Territory (later to become the state of Oklahoma), near what later became the city of Tulsa. There Frank Morse developed a successful and prosperous real estate business, and was able to provide well for his family.

At the age of eleven, Russell accepted Christ as his Savior, and was baptized. After his high school graduation in 1916, Russell wanted to become a preacher and missionary. His father was opposed to this, and refused to help him in his desire. To make it possible for him to go to Bible College, his mother bred and sold registered, pedigreed bull dogs to earn the money to help him attend Phillips University in Enid, OK.

✝

Another pioneering family in Oklahoma was that of George and Margaret Howe. George Oliver Howe had studied under Dwight L. Moody, had attended the Baptist Bible School at Ottawa, Kansas, and later became a traveling evangelist. In 1880 he married Margaret Anne Filbert, and they became the parents of four boys and three girls, one of whom died in infancy. Gertrude Erma Howe, born December 19, 1896, was the youngest daughter and baby of the family. From her parents and also from the older children, little Gertrude learned about Jesus, and His sacrificial death for the sins of mankind. At the age of four she heard a missionary from India tell of the thousands in that land who had never heard about Christ, and even then felt that some day she must go and tell them. At the age of nine Gertrude publicly accepted Christ as her Saviour and was baptized. Her sister Helen was nine years older than she, but they were very close. When Helen decided to be a missionary, this served to strengthen Gertrude's desire to devote her life to serving the Lord in a foreign land.

George Howe, too, had staked a claim in the Indian Territory, near the small town of Rankin, on the edge of the "Black Kettle" grasslands. In 1902, when Gertrude was five years old, he moved his family from Ottawa, Kansas to Sayre, Oklahoma. In later years Gertrude told how she and her brother went with their mother to meet her father and older brothers and sister, who had gone ahead to "get things ready" in their new homestead. They traveled on a train with a wood-burning engine, over an old-fashioned narrow-gauge railway.

As they left the familiar farm country, with its well-cultivated fields, they were filled with awe and excitement over the new sights, and expectations of what lay ahead. But as they journeyed on into the wild, untouched wilderness and prairies of Indian Territory they began to have fears and misgivings, for they had heard many tales of the wild land to which they were moving. The neighbors had even warned that they would probably all be killed by either Indians or rattlesnakes.

"As we approached Sayre, where we were to meet Papa," Gertrude recalled, "I remembered all the warnings we had been given, and I thought it was funny that we had come all this way and hadn't seen either a snake or an Indian."

Her father and the rest of the family were waiting for them when they got off the train. They found that Mr. Howe had bought a big covered wagon to take them from the end of the railway line on to the homestead. And there Gertrude saw her first Indians.

"I can still remember sitting in an Indian tepee," Gertrude reminisced, "waiting while Papa and my brothers made arrangements for some Indians to guide the wagon team across the river because they knew how to avoid the quicksand beds."

After arriving at the homestead, they set up the cook-stove outside, and used the wagon for sleeping quarters until their one-room "dugout" or sod house was completed. Gertrude described how crowded it was, and how the children slept in double bunks. She also recalled how frightened they were when at night the coyotes jumped on top of the sod roof, just above their heads, and howled. "Anyone who has heard a coyote's eerie, quavering howl knows how frightening it can be," she said, "especially to children." And she admitted how disappointed she was when a long-anticipated birthday cake turned out to be only "johnny-cake" (corn bread).

After living at the homestead for four years, when Gertrude was about nine years old, the family moved to Norman, Oklahoma, where she completed her grade school and high school education. She went on to attend Oklahoma University at Norman, where she graduated with honors, and was elected to Phi Beta Kappa.

✝

While Gertrude was in the University she joined the Christian Student Volunteer Movement for foreign missions. In 1918 she attended a state convention in Enid, Oklahoma, and there she met J. Russell Morse, who was a student at Phillips University, located in Enid. Since both were officers in the C.S.V.M., they were assigned to the same table at the banquet. Later, a certain amount of correspondence was required with regard to Student Volunteer matters. This led to closer acquaintance, and then romance. They agreed, though, that both of them should finish college before they married. Gertrude graduated first, and taught school for a year in Tonkawa, OK. On May 26, 1920, after J. Russell graduated, they were married by A. A. Profitt, minister of the First Christian Church in Tonkawa.

Because both Russell and Gertrude had commited themselves to missionary service while in their teens, they decided to take a year of post-graduate work in the Bible Department of Phillips University. They knew that life on a mission field could be both difficult and dangerous, but they were challenged, and at the same time comforted and reassured, by the words of Matthew 28:19-20: "Go ye, therefore, and teach all nations, baptizing them in the name of the Father and of the Son and of the Holy Ghost, teaching them to observe all things whatsoever I have commanded you; and lo, I am with you always even until the end of the world." They took that as their own personal "call", or commission, and also as a personal promise that Christ would be with them, to lead, guide, and uphold them in all circumstances.

They both had read about the work of Dr. Albert L. Shelton in Tibet, and were thrilled when Dr. Shelton spoke at one of the chapel services. When he called for volunteers to go to Tibet with him, Russell and Gertrude looked across the chapel room, smiled, and nodded to each other, and at the close of the service they volunteered to go back with him. From then on, every spare moment was spent in assembling and packing those possessions and supplies they needed to take with them. When school was out, they were ready to go. Another special event in their lives that year, second in importance only to their decision to go to Tibet, was the birth of their first child, Eugene Russell Morse, on April 18, 1921.

At the close of the school year, both Russell and Gertrude were ordained as missionaries at the College of Missions in Indianapolis, IN, together with Marion and Louise Duncan, of Hiram College. The Duncans had also responded to Dr. Shelton's call for volunteers to go to Tibet. In the few months remaining before their departure, Russell and Gertrude visited with parents and other relatives, and spoke in churches as they traveled to the west coast. It was at that point they decided never to ask for money in the churches, but only for prayer. While there were many who encouraged them in their new undertaking, there were also those who considered it wrong to take a small baby (four months old) to "a wild, robber-infested country."

"If anything happens to that baby", they warned, "God will hold you responsible and bring judgment on you."

But Russell and Gertrude had faith and confidence in Him Who had told them to "go...into all the world and preach the Gospel" and had promised "Lo, I am with you always, even unto the end of the world." They just smiled and replied that they were trusting God to take care of both them and their baby.

☩

The following chapters contain Gertrude Morse's recollections of how God honored their faith through the years, gave them a great ministry, and preserved them in times of danger. For fifty-six years the Lord used Gertrude and Russell in remote areas of Tibet, China, and Burma, to win tens of thousands of souls for His kingdom, and to encourage thousands more in the United States and elsewhere through their testimony.

☦

On February 6, 1977, Gertrude and Russell went out for an afternoon walk. As they walked, arm in arm, they reminisced about the many ways God had blessed them through all their years of working together. They rejoiced in the fact that their children, grandchildren, and even great-grandchildren were continuing the work on the mission field. As they talked, they kept walking, until they were almost home. As they neared their house some of the neighbor children who were playing greeted them.

"Russell," Gertrude suggested, "why don't you go ahead to the house and put the teakettle on, so we can have some tea. I want to talk with the children for just a moment, then I'll be right along."

"Will you be all right if I leave you?"

"Yes, I'm fine. You go ahead."

Russell unlocked the door, and went through the house, turned on the lights, and filled the teakettle. He was still in the kitchen when he heard the door open, then a thud, as of something falling.

"What was that? Did Gertrude fall?" he wondered, and rushed to see. He saw Gertrude lying on the floor, just inside the door, but when he reached her side he found she no longer needed help from him or anyone else, for she had "gone Home".

Gertrude had mentioned one time that she had prayed that when it was time for the Lord to call her Home, it would be suddenly, without a long illness. The Lord answered that prayer. A neighbor child expressed it well: "She thought she was opening the door to her house, but she was opening the door to heaven." Gertrude was 80 years old.

J. Russell continued to live in Tulsa, OK, and to witness to everyone he met, telling of God's mercy and faithfulness. One of his favorite sayings was, "Without a battle, there is no victory. The greater the battle, the greater the victory." Then he would hold up his hand in the "V for Victory" sign, and emphatically say, "Victory in Jesus!" As he lay in the hospital in January, 1991, his last words to his last visitors were, "Victory in Jesus!" J. Russell went to his eternal rest on January 27, 1991, just a few days before his 93rd birthday.

J. Russell and Gertrude in Tulsa, about 1976

George O. & Margaret Howe (Gertrude's parents)

Frank & Ruth Morse (Russell's parents)

J. Russell Morse at 19 years of age   Gertrude Howe (Morse) at age 18

J. Russell & Gertrude with baby Eugene

1
Introduction to Asia

I was in our stateroom, getting things settled, when Russell returned from his self-appointed errand to try to find out the details of our sailing. I could tell from his expression that he was troubled about something.

"Russell, what is wrong?" I asked.

"Oh, nothing, really. They just told me that we won't be sailing until day after tomorrow."

"Oh, Russell!", I exclaimed. "Why not? What reason did they give?" After all our anticipation, this was a let-down, and I was disappointed.

"Well," he said, "this is a British 'Royal Mail' ship, and the mail hasn't arrived yet from England. Until it does, we'll just have to sit here and wait."

This seemed to be the Lord's way of introducing us to the fact that any missionary going to the Orient has to learn patience. We had arrived in Vancouver, B.C. and had boarded our ship, "Empress of Japan", about 11:30 a.m. on August 11, 1921, right on schedule. Now we found we were to be delayed two days and wouldn't sail until August 13. So there we sat at the dock, with a ship full of passengers eager to be on their way, but not going anywhere. The delay had some good points, though. For one thing, while we were waiting, meals were served just as if we were sailing, so we had no added expense. Another good thing was that the delay gave us extra time with our friends, who came and took us out on Friday evening.

We were a party of seven: Dr. and Mrs. Albert Shelton, Mr. and Mrs. Marion Duncan, Russell and Eugene and myself. When we finally did set sail, it was very early in the morning on August 13, 1921, while we were still sleeping, so when we awoke we were actually out on the ocean. Our first stop was in beautiful Hawaii where we spent several days. On Sunday we attended a church there which was so beautifully decorated with small palm trees, and vines and flowers that it looked like an outdoor garden. The memory of it remains with me even after more than fifty years.

☦

The next stop was Japan. In Tokyo we visited with Mr. and Mrs. W. D. Cunningham, some of the first independent missionaries to Japan from the Christian Church in the United States. We soon learned that local custom required us to remove our shoes before entering a church, a temple, a Japanese home — or even a restaurant. One time, though, when we went to a restaurant we forgot to remove our shoes. Although we took only a step or two, they came right away and mopped the floor. It was rather embarrassing. We ate in real Japanese style, sitting on the floor and eating from a small table only about 2 ½ ft. high. It was in Tokyo that we had our first experience of riding in a ricksha. There, too, for the first time in our lives, we saw people worshipping idols and sacrificing to them. This made a very deep impression on us, as we were faced with the reality of their spiritual darkness, and their deep need to know the love of the true God! As we sailed through the inland sea, we could see the mountains on the island, covered with rice field terraces, and looking beautiful and green. We stopped in Kobe and also Nagasaki, where we went ashore in small boats, while the ship was taking on coal for the onward journey to Shanghai and Hong Kong.

☦

As we were approaching our next stop, Shanghai, we learned that our ship would have to anchor quite a distance out in the harbor, because Shanghai is up the Yangtze River. To get there, we had to go about 14 miles in a small boat. It was raining, but I took Eugene and went anyway, because I wanted to see this city I had heard so much about. Going that distance up the Yangtze River took quite some time, and then I had only about 15 minutes to get out and look around. At least I got to look up and down a few streets, enough to learn that the city was an immense shipping center.

It was at Shanghai, too, that Mrs. Shelton left us. I have come to realize since then how truly brave they both were, and how totally dedicated to the Lord's work. As she and the doctor bid each other a tender farewell — she to travel alone to India, and he to proceed on into the isolated interior of China and Tibet — they could not know that this was their final good-bye until they would be reunited in heaven. In the light of later events, I couldn't help but wonder if perhaps they had some sort of premonition that they might not meet again. She and Dr. Shelton had compiled what was to our knowledge the first New Testament ever translated into the Tibetan language, and she had to go to Delhi to supervise the printing of it. At that time the only two places where the Bible could be printed in Tibetan were at Delhi and in Germany.

A few days later we arrived in Hong Kong, where we said good-bye to the "Empress of Japan" and transferred all of our baggage to a smaller ship in preparation for going on to Haiphong in French Indochina (now called Vietnam). There we also bought canned foods and other supplies which would not be available as we went farther inland. It seemed we were buying a lot of everything, but we were trying to get a sufficient amount of each thing without being extravagant, because we knew it would have to last us through the next five years. We just hoped we hadn't forgotten anything important. We then boarded the small coastal steamer which was to take us to Haiphong.

Arriving in Haiphong after the 5-day trip on the coastal steamer (a small freighter), we stayed at the "Grand Hotel Du

Commerce", a French hotel, while our possessions went through a very careful inspection at the customs office. The proprietor of the hotel, who could speak English, talked to the customs officials, and told them that we were missionaries just passing through. This helped us a great deal in getting through all the formalities. We had to wait there several days because the little French railway to Yunnan-Fu was having continuous trouble, due to heavy rain which caused mud slides and washed out parts of the tracks. We took advantage of this delay and went sight-seeing, taking some ricksha rides around the city. The French-controlled section was very nice, with broad streets and many trees, but the other sections were quite squalid. The French ladies loved Eugene, who now was almost six months old. He smiled a lot, and because of his happy disposition they begged me to bring him to their homes in the afternoons.

✞

From Haiphong we traveled by narrow-gauge railway to Yunnan-Fu, which is now called Kunming (pronounced Quinming), the capital of Yunnan Province. The scenery was beautiful as we went through the many rice fields. Rice fields are all flooded, although you wouldn't know it, just looking at them from a distance. The rice was the most brilliant green imaginable. Here and there were banana and palm trees. We learned that plowing in these fields was done with water buffalo. From the train we could see people working in the fields. They wore big hats to protect them from the sun, and because we were above them we couldn't see the people. So when they moved around it looked almost as if big birds were moving along on top of the rice. Houses were up on stilts, and had straw roofs. Because of the moisture, whenever the sun came out, the steam rose from the houses and made them look as if they were on fire. The steamy, hot weather made our clothes feel sticky, and if we put anything away even a tiny bit soiled it molded. Even our suitcases rusted and molded.

By the second day we began to leave the marshy lowland, and started up into the area of high mountains and deep canyons. This part of the country was so rugged it was too dangerous to travel at night, so we traveled only in daylight, and at night we stayed in French hotels. We went through 104 tunnels the second day, and 66 on the third day. In the tunnels the gas and smoke from the train were unpleasant, and made Eugene cough, so we had to close the windows. In between times we had to keep the windows open because of the extremely hot weather. Just opening and closing the windows kept Russell and Marion Duncan busy during the whole trip, . We crossed over one bridge, built by the French between two very high cliffs, which at that time was classified by the Book of Knowledge as one of the seven wonders of the modern world. Really, the engineering of the whole railway was a wonder. It was said, though, that one Chinese coolie died for every tie of the railroad track. We were shocked to learn that on the lower class cars there were no toilet facilities . We were warned not to look up and down the tracks when the train stopped, lest we be embarrassed by the seeming lack of modesty of the passengers in those cars

✞

On September 23, 1921, we arrived in Kunming, the end of the railway. We stayed at the China Inland Mission boarding home for about a month while we repacked all of our supplies so they could be carried on the backs of pack animals. Of course we wanted to explore our new "homeland", so went out walking and were appalled by what we saw. When we returned to the mission home, one of the older missionaries asked, "Well, what do you think of the city?"

"I never expected the provincial capital to have such very narrow, cobblestone streets," I said, "or to be so terribly unsanitary. There were pigs, and dogs, and even uncared-for children running loose!"

"We really had to watch where we stepped, to avoid animal droppings and other kinds of refuse," Russell commented. "Also, there were many beggars who approached us, and a lot of lepers, too.

25

"We saw many women with bound feet, too," I added. I'm certainly glad I grew up in America instead of China!"

Buddhism was the main religion, so we saw many temples and idol worshippers. Yunnan Province was noted for its copper supply, and one temple, known as the "Copper Temple" contained five hundred copper idols. Copper was also used extensively for making teakettles, cooking pots, and other utensils. All over the city we could hear the coppersmiths hammering out their wares.

While waiting in Kunming, the family with whom we were staying took us on a little picnic. We went by boat down a canal, then out onto a lake, and after a while went ashore for our meal. Our cook and a coolie had gone ahead and were waiting for us at a Chinese inn, with our meal all prepared. They had taken our own tablecloth, dishes, and food, because they thought we would not want to eat the food in the Chinese inn.

"The inn here is about like what you will find along the road," one of our friends told us. "They are all about the same, with dirt floors and dirty walls!"

To us that inn seemed worse than an American barn! The chickens and dogs had free access to the place, which shocked us. I remember there were about twenty Chinese standing nearby watching our every move, because it was quite a sight for them to see foreigners eat! After we finished eating, we returned to town again by boat.

In 1920, while traveling from Batang to Kunming with his wife and two daughters, Dr. Shelton had been kidnapped by a band of robbers who demanded $25,000 ransom for his release. The Chinese government troops which were escorting the family did not resist when the robbers attacked, but retreated to the nearest village. Dr. Shelton rushed forward to protect his wife and two daughters, but was no match for such a group, of course, so he was captured and taken into the mountains. Although badly frightened, the women were unharmed. Soon the government troops returned to take them back to the village, to await word of their husband and father.

Dr. Shelton was held captive for seventy-two days. During the entire time he steadfastly refused to offer himself for ransom saying, "You can kill me or whatever you wish but I will not be ransomed." He knew if he or the family met the demands for ransom, it would only encourage the capture of other missionaries.

While he was held prisoner, Dr. Shelton was very kind to his captors. When they were ill or wounded he treated them, and they began to think of him as their friend. After 72 days of captivity he was suffering from lack of sufficient nourishment and became too ill to stand. The robbers left him by the side of the road where they knew he would be found by the government troops who had been following them.

Now, a little more than a year later, we were preparing to make that same dangerous journey from Kunming to Batang. You can imagine our feelings when we received a report from our American consul that this same band of robbers was waiting to recapture Dr. Shelton. This time, however, they did not plan to ask for ransom, but intended to keep him to be their doctor.

☦

While our party was waiting in Kunming, two sedan chairs (known as *"jou dzi"*) were constructed. One was for Louise Duncan who was expecting her first child the last of December, and the other one was for Eugene and me. Each of the four corners of the sedan chair had a loop attached. Through these loops were put two 12-foot bamboo poles, by which the chair would be carried by four men at a time. There were six carriers for each chair, and they would change back and forth every few hours. The chairs had thin wooden floors, walls of woven bamboo, two windows, and a roof of strong, stiff rainproof material. The windows and door could be protected in time of rain, snow or cold wind by lowering rain proof curtains. The arm rests were four inches wide, and they made the ones on my chair extra long to accommodate the basket in which my baby would ride. The basket was woven from bamboo, about 14"×24", with a back rest and partial cover similar to a perambulator (pram, or stroller). The basket, which I had completely lined, had a cotton mattress and pads, and rested on the arms of the chair, just above my lap, so I could keep at least one hand on the baby or the basket at all times. This was necessary because 6-month-old Eugene was very alert and active. There was space under my seat for baby necessities.

While still in Kunming, we used any spare time to study Chinese and learn simple phrases, so we could ask for such necessary things as hot water. We also were making preparations for our long overland trip to the mission station. We bought what we called "road food", to be used on our two-month trip, and such things as sugar, soap, candles, and other staple articles to be used at the Batang mission station during the next five years.

Since Dr. Shelton had made this trip a number of times, he knew that in November and December it would be bitterly cold, because the road led through the Himalaya mountains, over passes at least 12,000 feet high. He insisted that those of us who could not get out and walk should order long coats lined with lamb's wool, and even thought to have us order a "baby bunting" of the same material for Eugene. We were indeed fortunate and blessed to have such a fine, considerate leader and guide, who tried to make as much provision as possible for our comfort as well as our safety.

Between Haiphong and Yunnan-fu we traveled on a train
with a wood-burning engine.

We sailed for China/Tibet on August 13, 1921

Dr. Shelton insisted that I get a warm, lamb's wool Chinese-style gown for traveling. He even thought to suggest getting a bunting of the same material for Eugene.

Eugene (6 mo. old) and I in Yunnan-fu

The chair (called *jou dzi*) in which Eugene and I traveled.

How the caravan traveled, with pack horses, along the narrow trail.

We had to go on dangerous trails, with wooden props holding flimsy wooden flooring, which formed part of the pathway.

One of the bridges we had to cross. The floor was loose planks, not nailed down, but with wooden cross pieces tied in place. The whole thing was propped up with wooden poles braced on the rocks below. With no sides, and a clear view of the raging river below, it was a frightening experience to cross such a bridge.

2
Caravan Journey

On October 31, 1921 our caravan left Kunming at sunrise with one hundred pack animals besides the saddle horses for Dr. Shelton, Mr. Duncan, and Russell, and our two sedan chairs. In those days there was no central government in China, but each province was governed by opposing "war lords". It was the policy in each province that all foreign caravans must be escorted by whatever number of government troops the officials ordered. The first two weeks of our journey were quite dangerous, and we had to have a large escort, ranging somewhere from fifty to one hundred men. Each day we were required to furnish "tea money" for each member of the troop. We had been advised not to expect much protection from these troops as some of them were former robbers. They were poorly clothed and very much underpaid.

From the very first day of travel we were aware that our chair carriers were opium smokers. Every few hours, when we came to a rest stop, they would go in, lie down on a straw mat and smoke their pipes. Even so, riding in a chair was not uncomfortable, although it was rather tiresome, because of the constant swinging or shaking. There were dangerous times too, especially on the mountain trails when it rained and made the path slippery. One time a pack mule ran against my chair, and knocked it down, and another time a mule ran against my chair when we were near a precipice, but God protected, and the chair stayed firm.

At night we usually stopped at a "horse inn". In these places the horse stables were on the ground floor, and travelers stayed on the second floor over them. The beds had no mattresses, but had only straw mats spread on boards. These we covered with oiled sheets to protect our bedding from lice, bedbugs, and other unwelcome "visitors". Sometimes we had to sleep in the family idol room. There were no beds in these rooms, so we could set up our own cots. In these places, the women of the house would bring in incense sticks each morning and evening, and after sounding a gong, would burn them before the idols.

✟

When we were traveling, one of the hardest things to get used to was meal time. It wasn't just the food, although that was different from what we were accustomed to. We usually had some kind of meat — fresh if available, and if not, then we had canned salmon, sardines, or dried beef. Occasionally we had potatoes, but they were very hard to get along the road. We had some canned vegetables — corn, tomatoes, and beans, which we used sparingly. One thing that was hard to adjust to was the fact that our cook did not know how to fix things very well, and the smoke was so bad we couldn't stay in the kitchen room ourselves. Fortunately, most of our food did not need much fixing. Sometimes we had canned fruit for dessert — Del Monte peaches, pears, apricots, plums or pineapple. This saved the day for me, for if nothing else seemed fit to eat, I could at least eat fruit. We seldom had bread, or if the cook did attempt to make bread, it wasn't fit to eat. Sometimes we could buy eggs.

Another thing which made adjustment difficult was the fact that most meals were eaten under conditions which did not tend to inspire one's appetite. We were usually surrounded by an assortment of chickens, dogs, cats, cattle, and mules, and always there were crowds of insatiably curious spectators. This was very hard to get accustomed to, especially for us who had just come from America and were used to having our privacy.

But the hardest thing to bear was the complete lack of cleanliness. For instance, the cook would take the dish towel to wipe off a table covered with thick dust, where cats, dogs, and chickens had slept or roosted. Then he would use this same cloth to wipe the dishes, or perhaps he would wrap up some bread or meat in it. Sometimes he would put this same cloth around his head for safe-keeping. Mrs. Duncan and I both tried to have things different, but it would have been possible only if we could have watched the cook constantly, and we just were not able to do that. The cook always traveled ahead on his mule, so as to get things ready, then we'd stop only long enough to eat. Sometimes we were very hungry, then we'd see how the cook used (or misused) the dish cloth, and we'd feel almost too ill to eat. Sometimes pigs, dogs, and chickens (China's scavengers) would run between our legs while we were at the table. At other times we would be surrounded by children with runny noses, and adults whose clothes were stiff with dirt, and faces so filthy it was impossible to tell their color. At such times we often lost our appetite. It was always a relief to get out on the road again, into God's pure mountain air, even if we had been unable to eat most of our meal except for a few bites which we had forced down. However we gradually got somewhat accustomed to such things and managed to eat a little more.

Eugene was between six and eight months old on this trip, and it was hard to find things he could eat. Most of the time he barely had enough to eat, and sometimes was still hungry. I fed him a little tea, cocoa, fruit juices, and once in a while a soft-boiled egg. We had no dried cereal, or other prepared baby foods in those days. We didn't have disposable diapers either, and it was very hard to keep his clothes washed, and to get them dry. Sometimes I had to dry them over a small charcoal fire built in a cast-iron pot.

On the ninth day it rained all day long. That morning the Doctor had said, "We'll be going through a really dangerous area today. Thank God it is raining, for the robbers won't move out of their hiding place when it rains." Having been a captive in their hands for such a long time, he knew their habits.

Each morning when we left our camping place we never knew whether we would all be together that night or not. We felt sure that if the bandits were able to successfully kidnap Dr. Shelton, they would also try to take Marion Duncan and Russell. We prayed often, both privately and together.

☦

After a month of travel from Kunming we arrived at Likiang (pronounced *lee-jahng*) where we stayed with an English missionary family. While there we were invited to a Chinese wedding feast which consisted of **thirty-two** courses, and included such "delicacies" as sea slugs, shark fins, devilfish, bamboo sprouts, etc. Dr. Shelton was well-known and liked in this area, and because of this our whole group was entertained.

In Likiang Dr. Shelton hired a young married man recommended by the missionaries, named Hsien Ming Liang, as a helper for the three families for the rest of the trip. We did not know then how important this man and his wife would be in our lives.

About six days out of Likiang we came to Wei Hsi (*way-shee*) where there was another English mission station. The missionaries, Mr. and Mrs. Lewer, were very friendly and invited us to spend the night at the mission. We had a good visit, and heard about their work. It was such a relief to be in a nice clean house again.

The last part of the journey was over narrow horse paths, around sharp mountain curves, usually overlooking the Yangtze or Mekong Rivers. Both rivers have their headwaters in that area. The path was so narrow that sometimes the packs on the horses scraped against the outcropping rocks, and the animals fell off the cliff. Occasionally, several feet of the narrow road had fallen away, so boards were put down with rocks on the ends to hold them. Underneath they were supported by nothing more than a pole or two stuck in a crevice, but this was considered enough to prop up the boards and provide a "safe" road.. Mud and rock slides also had to be contended with, and this made our progress even more difficult.

This narrow path was not only dangerous for the horses, but for the riders in the sedan chairs also. If one of the carriers happened to stumble, as they occasionally did, the chair would tip badly. When that happened I held on tightly to Eugene. Sometimes the path was so narrow the chair had to be tipped. Then I would get out and walk, and either Dr. Shelton or one of the guides held my hand while Russell carried Eugene. It was also very frightening when the lead carriers were on one side of a crevice 100 feet to 500 feet deep and the rear carriers were still on the other side, while the chair was suspended over it. I would breathe a prayer and look toward the mountainside instead of down into the deep chasm below. The danger of robbers, although somewhat less this second month, was still with us. We prayed very, very often during the entire two months of travel. We were sustained and comforted on the whole trip by our "special promise" from the Bible: "...and lo, I am with you always, even to the end of the way". We repeated this over and over, and trusted God to watch over us.

✞

One very interesting thing we saw was rope bridges, used by the local people to cross rivers, especially those in deep canyons such as the Mekong and Salween. These bridges were used by the Tibetans, but perhaps were adopted from the jungle people of the river valleys near them. Such a bridge consisted of a "rope", made of bamboo which had been split into narrow strips which were then twisted together with the smooth side out. This "rope" was fastened on each side of the river to a pole or tree set firmly into the ground and braced by large rocks. The pole, usually cypress, was buried for half its length, with the upper part notched to hold the rope in place. The starting point would be about 50-100 feet above the river, while the landing on the opposite side would be only about 25-50 feet. There were two rope units for each crossing, one for going and one for coming. A semi-cylinder of very hard wood, with a groove in the center, and a slot at the top for leather straps to go through, was made to fit over the bamboo rope as a slider. The traveler would be tied into a rawhide strap or sling, in which he sat as in a swing. The swing was fastened to the slider through the wooden slots. The rider must hold the slider tightly (a matter of life or death) with both hands, elbows out, as he is shoved gently a few feet, suspended for a moment over the tree-tops on the steep bank, then given a hard shove by someone on the bank and sent out into space over the swirling, foaming river. If fortunate, the rider would land with a jolt on the opposite bank. However, if the shove was not hard enough, or if the slant was insufficient, he might stop in the middle of the river and have to pull himself the rest of the way, hand over hand. These bridges seemed a novelty to us at that time, but when it was necessary for us to use them later, we found them extremely frightening.

We were treated very well by all of the people along the way. When there were no inns we were always invited to the home of the main officials, although these usually were very little better than the inns. Many times presents were brought to the Doctor, and sometimes to all of us. These consisted of such things as English walnuts, Chinese pears, Chinese oranges, honey, dried persimmons, and pomegranates.

At last we arrived in Atuntze (*Ah-den-dzi*), at an elevation. of 11,000 feet. It was quite cold, and we were happy we had our lambskin coats to keep us warm. I still remember how hard it was to get up in that cold place at night to take care of my baby.

We saw many lamas (Buddhist priests) along the way, praying over and over "Om mani padme hom", the widely used but practically meaningless Tibetan prayer. Some writers say it means, "Oh, hail to the jewel in the lotus blossom." We also saw many villages in ruins because of the constant warfare between the Chinese and Tibetans.

At Atuntze, the official told us he could not guarantee our safety if we went on by way of the Tsali Pass. This was partly because of the ice and snow, but also because of the Tibetan robbers. He told us we must go by way of the Mekong Valley, which would take four days longer. We hardly knew what to do, because this road also was dangerous, with many places where the "road" was nothing more than "bridges" made by bracing small poles on rocks, putting tree branches across them, and rocks and dirt on top. Just a little knock could destroy the props and let you fall a thousand feet below. However, the longer route proved to be the wisest choice after all. On the third day out from Atuntze, just when we would have been climbing Tsali Pass on the shorter route, a great snow storm came. Had we gone that way we would have had to turn back and take the longer route anyway. Also, by going the longer way, through the Mekong Valley, we bypassed the Tibetan robbers who were waiting near the Tsali Pass to attack us.

On the way to Yengin, which was about five days' travel from Atuntze, a group of Tibetans came one evening with their musical instruments to greet Dr. Shelton and entertain us with songs and folk dances. They were very friendly because the Doctor had formerly befriended them. He had treated their wounded, and was also instrumental in helping make peace between them and their enemies, for which they were very grateful. Afterthe singing and dancing, Dr. Shelton gave them a little gift of money, according to Tibetan custom.

We came at last to Yengin, a village of salt wells. Women carried the salty water in buckets to be dried in red clay vats. We learned that this was the kind of salt we would be using for the next five years. Before it could be used, however, it had to be processed by dissolving it in a small amount of water, then straining it, first through a cloth, then several times through porous paper. However, after the water evaporated, and it was dried, it was nice and white. While in Yengin we were invited to another Chinese feast.

After leaving Yengin we crossed another very high pass of 15,800 feet before entering the lovely Bamutang Valley between the headwaters of the Mekong and Yangtze Rivers. Here there were many sheep, herded by the Tibetan shepherds, which entertained and amused our baby. We were again serenaded by the Tibetans, and afterward gave them gifts. Somewhere in this area we left Yunnan Province and entered Szechuan Province, in which Batang is located.

On December 19, only a few days before we were to reach Batang, we were just finishing breakfast when Dr. Shelton again demonstrated how kind and thoughtful he was. He came from the "kitchen" area, where the cook had been preparing the food, carefully carrying a plate which was covered with another plate.

As he uncovered the plate he said, "Happy Birthday, Mrs. Morse." Imagine my astonishment at seeing a plate of fudge! I could scarcely believe my eyes.

"Dr. Shelton!" I said. "Where in the world did you get THAT?" Then he told us he had had it made specially for my 25th birthday. How we did enjoy that treat! I wondered afterward if he had realized I was feeling rather homesick, and missing my family on my birthday.

☧

The night before our arrival in Batang we sent a runner on ahead to announce that we would arrive the next day. My chair carriers started out first that morning of December 23, 1921 with Russell on his horse beside us, so we were the first to see Batang. We were very glad to see Mr. R. A. MacLeod, an evangelist, and Dr. W. H. Hardy, the doctor in charge of the mission hospital, who came out several miles to meet us. Their faces meant home to us after more than four months of traveling. After the two men, came the children — Billy and Mollie Hardy, Laura and Duncan MacLeod — on their donkeys, with

40

the servants leading them. Then came the children of the orphanage, soldiers, friends of all descriptions, Dr. Shelton's adopted son Lee Gway Gwang, and even some Tibetan lamas. Many of the orphans, seeing Eugene's friendly face, followed my chair the rest of the way, always trying to keep him in sight. And so we were welcomed to Batang!

Russell and I ate lunch at the home of Dr. and Mrs. Hardy and supper at the home of the MacLeods. The nice, clean homes of the missionaries were such a relief, and the meals were delicious. Imagine!! We even had strawberry ice cream! Snow had been brought down from the mountain to use in making it.

☦

The mission grounds were located outside the town gate on a hill across a beautiful mountain stream. This complex, called Jop-o-ding, contained two residences with lovely grassy lawns, the hospital, and combination school and orphanage. There was a large garden spot on the mountain slope just above the residences. Each missionary family planted and tended their portion of this garden.

Our house and the Duncan's were on the opposite side of the city, right among the Tibetan houses, but only about a fifteen minute walk from Jop-o-ding. What a wonderful feeling it was to take baths in our own folding, rubberized bath tub and to sleep in our own house that night. All of the buildings had clay walls and flat mud roofs, with the exception of the mission properties in Jop-o-ding. Those had tin roofs.

The ground floor of our home was used for storage. There were two small rooms on one side, one used for storage of general supplies that was kept locked, and the other for keeping milk and butter, as we had no refrigeration and this was the coolest part of the house. The space on the other side of the house was used for storing cut stove wood.

The upper floor had six rooms. On one side was Russell's large study where men guests were received and where we both studied with our teachers. Adjoining that was a dining room, and beyond that a kitchen. On the other side was a small room which became my study, a nice large front room, and a nice large bedroom with three windows. Adjoining this was a small room where we could unfold our rubber bath tub. This room had an old-fashioned "drum" heater, and a nice long seat with drawers underneath to hold children's clothes. The roof was flat, with a small room for storing vegetables. Our floors were of wood, sanded and painted to look like polished floors. All this had been specially renovated and prepared for our use, as the truly Tibetan homes were very primitive.

All of the mission properties, including the Duncan's house and ours, were white-washed inside and out. We later learned this identified mission property and was protection from the marauding bands whose quarrel was not with the missionaries, so they were not disturbed.

Eugene was now eight months old and he had not been sick even once on the long journey from America. Because he was so good-natured and always smiling the carriers and others called him "smiling Mr. Morse". He was the youngest white child ever to have made that trip. Surely God had taken care of him and all of our party. As He said, "Lo, I am with you always."

Just six days after we arrived in Batang, Herbert Franklin Duncan was born. This had been a very hard trip for dear Louise Duncan, and there was some doubt about the baby's survival for a while, but in a few weeks he began to gain strength.

We were very happy that the caravan road cook, Hsien Ming Liang, liked us and wanted to stay on with us in Batang. His wife, Duje, who had become very attached to Eugene on the road, continued to help us and look after him.

✞

We were eager to start on our language lessons, so just as soon as we settled into our new home we began studying,

42

under the supervision of Mr. MacLeod, who was serving as language director while Mr. J. C. Ogden was on furlough. We studied Lhasa or standard Tibetan, as well as Batang Tibetan dialect (Khamba), and later Western Mandarin, the main Chinese dialect. Our Tibetan teacher Gigin (meaning "teacher") Atrin was a higher-class, educated Tibetan who, like most of the Tibetans in Batang spoke both Chinese and Tibetan. Although we were living in Tibet, we studied Chinese because it was necessary for traveling throughout China, and for dealing with the Chinese officials.

Russell studied the first two hours each morning, from 8-10:00, while I took care of the baby, fed him, and put him down for his nap. Then I studied from 10-12:00. We had a fenced yard where Eugene played under the supervision of a Tibetan girl while we studied.

Batang village had a population of about 4000, and was located at an elevation of 9400 feet. Most of the streets were from six to eight feet wide, with human and animal filth every few steps. Dead animals could often be seen along the paths. Flies, vultures, and vermin swarmed. As in Kunming, we had to be very careful where we stepped.

Since all the houses were made largely of clay (somewhat like the adobe walls made by American Indians), thieves could just dig a hole through the wall and crawl in. If they wanted to steal a cow or donkey they dug a larger hole. I often thought this must be like what is referred to in the Bible as the place "where thieves dig through and steal." If a clay wall surrounded the house, they would bring their ladder and climb over. Tibetan ladders were made of one small log notched for steps. We had one in our house by which we could go up to the roof.

It was common for young Tibetan women to put honey on their faces to keep them warm. Then when the dust and dirt settled in the honey, it made them look as if they had used black paint. In that culture, they thought the blacker a woman's face, the greater her purity. A clean-faced woman was regarded as unchaste. All Tibetans used butter on their hair, too, and the odor of this was almost overpowering.

You might say there were no middle-aged women in that part of the country. After a girl married, she soon was like an old woman in looks, in health, and in attitude toward life. Poor food, scanty clothing, no beds, and no care in childbirth, plus carrying heavy loads and other hard work, all combined to age them quickly. Men considered it beneath their dignity to carry heavy loads of wood and buckets of water from the river. Only women and girls did such work.

The Tibetans were neither moral nor immoral, but rather were a-moral, for they had no clearly defined moral standard. The mountain peaks pointing heavenward with pure white hands, and all the beauties of nature could not make goodness natural to these people, or draw them into loving communion with the Heavenly Father.

Sometimes the trail was only a narrow path around the side of the mountain. In places like this I just closed my eyes and prayed we would all get through safely.

Yengin was a very interesting sight, with all the "drying flats" for the salt. I had never seen anything quite like that before.

Our house in Batang, where we lived for five years. The roof was flat, for drying grain.

A Batang street scene. We learned to watch where we walked, and to "look before we stepped," lest we step in a pile of refuse.

Dr. Albert L. Shelton, our mentor and guide. He was killed by bandits only a few weeks after our arrival in Batang.

Russell saw to getting the tombstones for the graves of Dr. Shelton and Dr. Loftis, another missionary who had died.

3
Tragedy in Batang

When we arrived on the border of Tibet and China, the
political situation was quite unstable. During the Chinese-
Tibetan war of about 1915, the Chinese had taken over rule in
the Batang area, and the result was periodic warfare and almost
constant skirmishes at the very walls of the cities. Some of the
Chinese troops in Batang were quartered in the Tibetan homes
and dominated native village life. The number of Chinese soldiers protecting Batang changed almost daily, depending on
how many were out fighting the robber bands which infested
the country.

The district of Shang Chen was about seven days east of
Batang in the province of Szechuan. The Shang Chen men
were very fierce warriors, almost without fear. Nearly a year
before our arrival, about one thousand of them had attacked
the city of Batang for two days. They were repulsed only by the
use of several small cannons which apparently awed them. The
Tibetans were by nature liberty-loving and militant. They hated
and distrusted the Chinese because of many, many years of
oppression and persecution. Dr. Shelton even told us of one
case where the people skinned alive one unpopular official,
tanned his skin, and hung it up in the lamasery! Like the
American Indians, whom they resembled in many ways, they
knew how to be either friend or foe to the death. We were glad
that they were friendly to us missionaries, and not foes.

✝

47

Most Tibetans lived in houses which seemed to us worse than American barns. Those who could afford a two-story house kept the animals on the first floor and the family lived on the second floor. If there was only one floor, the family and animals lived together. Manure was very valuable as fertilizer and it was kept right in the house so it wouldn't be stolen. When there was no more room the owner carried it out to the fields. When our next-door neighbors cleaned their house we couldn't stay in our yard, and we had to keep the windows closed on that side of the house. These people had no soap, tubs, or wash boards and very few pans. There were no window panes in Tibetan houses, and, with few exceptions, no beds. An old sheep skin or a rug served as bedding. Clothes were washed in the river where the water was always cold. They slept in their clothes which they wore for months, with no underclothing. The women usually had one nice dress, which was worn only on very special occasions, such as the Chinese New Year celebration. Most of the children were nearly naked, winter and summer, but didn't seem to be adversely affected by the cold.

Once a year, about mid-year, the Tibetans produced a historical play for the people in Batang and surrounding countryside. Tibetans seem to have a natural talent for dramatization. They had no written history, and the plays, which lasted several days, were the only means of teaching children about their country's past. They were presented in tents put up on a smooth, level meadow, and thousands of people would gather to watch this event..

According to some estimates, one-seventh of the population of Tibet were lamas. Each family was expected to give one son to the priesthood. Some cities consisted almost entirely of lamaseries (or monasteries) housing thousands of members. Most of the wealth was in the hands of the lamas, (or priests). They obtained their wealth from the common people whom they held in bondage of both body and soul. Whenever the lamas went to the homes and prayed to keep the home free from pestilence, or to cast out the demons, there was always a "fee", and in this way they became quite rich. With this wealth they acquired land, which they rented to the poorer families. Sometimes they loaned money to people, and charged high interest.

✞

Tibetan food was very monotonous by American standards. All year they lived almost entirely on just two things: "tsamba" and "buttered tea". Tsamba is made of parched barley ground into a very fine flour. It is a good emergency ration also, for because it is parched, it requires no cooking, and it can be kept quite a long time. The tea is made by boiling the coarse green Chinese tea until it is very strong. This is strained into a churn, and to it is added a lump of yak butter (more or less stale, and often containing a few of the yak hairs), and a handful of salt. The mixture is then churned into an emulsion.

The typical meal began with drinking two or three bowls of buttered tea, continually blowing back from the rim of the bowl the film of butter that rose to the top. After several bowls had been drunk, there was a considerable accumulation of butter. The bowl was then half filled with the tea emulsion, the tsamba was poured in, and then, using the fingers, it was kneaded into lumps and eaten.

The marriage customs of the people of Tibet were a peculiar combination of monogamy, polygamy, and polyandry. The latter was practiced more by the nomadic tribes in the outlying districts. Under this system, when the oldest son of a family married, the woman became the common wife of himself and his brothers, — usually three or four, but sometimes as many as six. Usually, one husband would take care of the uplands; another might be a trader taking care of the caravan, and each of the others would have their special area of work, but all shared the one wife..

In such families, the children usually were not numerous, an average being from three to five. The oldest brother was

49

considered the father and the other brothers were uncles. If a family had only daughters, one of them would be kept at home and a husband brought in for her to carry on the family succession. The remaining daughters were normally given to other families. In a few cases where there were just two daughters, one husband was brought in for both, and a polygamous household was established.

✟

The dream of Dr. Shelton's life was to found a Christian hospital in Lhasa, the Forbidden City of Tibet. He finally received an invitation from the Dalai Lama,* the high priest of Tibet, to come to Lhasa to start preparations to fulfill that dream. In February, 1922 he started on that trip, with three Tibetan companions, but before reaching Gartok he received orders to return to Batang to await further instructions. On the afternoon of February 16, a runner came to the mission with the stunning news that a band of about twenty bandits had ambushed and shot our beloved Doctor about 2:00 p.m. at a low pass just six miles south of Batang — almost home. He was ahead of the others and fell with the first shot.

Taking a number of Tibetan companions, Dr. Hardy and Russell hurried to the pass and found the doctor unconscious. He had given himself an injection of morphine for the pain. Through the darkness, over that awful mountain road, they carried him back to Batang. Everything possible was done for him, but in spite of all efforts he died at 12:45 the morning of February 17.

His death was a great blow, piercing the very heart of the mission. He was truly an outstanding evangelist, and a tireless physician and surgeon. But more than this, he was our encourager, our joy, our constant inspiration. We remembered his tender good-bye (God be with you) to Mrs. Shelton in

---

*Note: See National Geographic Magazine of September, 1921, article by Dr. Albert L. Shelton, entitled "Life Among the People of Eastern Tibet."

Shanghai, and we wondered if she somehow felt she would not meet him again in this life. The funeral service was conducted on February 18, 1922, by Lee Gway Gwang, the Chinese-Tibetan evangelist whom Dr. Shelton had adopted nineteen years earlier, when he was just a poor orphan boy.

✝

There was a small tribe of Tibetans called "Geh-mo" who in some way had offended the powerful Shang Chen Tibetans. The Shang Shen, in revenge, took all they had except life. Then the Geh-mo burned all their sacred books and drank the ashes, thereby giving themselves over to the Devil. Some thought that Dr. Shelton was slain, as was Jesus, by some of those perverted souls for whose salvation he gladly gave his all. However, because he was so well-loved and also because he had dressed in typical Chinese clothing, there were some who doubted that the bandits realized his true identity until it was too late.

When the news of Dr. Shelton's death reached the United States, newspaper headlines blazed with the account of his assassination, and there was much concern about the fate of the rest of the missionaries. In those days, it took from three to six months for a letter from Batang to reach America and the families of the missionaries were very worried about their safety.

At the time of Dr. Shelton's funeral, Russell realized the deplorable condition of the mission cemetery and mentioned his concern to the other missionaries. At the next board meeting, Russell was assigned the task of restoring the cemetery to a more presentable condition. Since "planting and growing" had always been a favorite form of relaxation with him, he was very happy to accept that responsibility. He was also asked to obtain tombstones for both Dr. Shelton and Dr. Z. S. Loftis, a missionary who had served and died at Batang before our arrival. One day Russell and Lee Gway Gwang were on an evangelistic trip in the surrounding countryside, and found two suitable stones at an abandoned lamasery, probably two hundred years old. Each heavy stone was lashed to two strong bamboo poles and carried by four men in the same way hunters carry large game. Finally, after many days of smoothing and polishing, the inscriptions were engraved in English, Tibetan, and Chinese.

4
Settling In

One year and three months after our arrival in Batang, on April 8, 1923, we welcomed our eagerly-awaited second son, Robert Howe Morse. Dr. and Mrs. Hardy cared for me in our home. Robert was a lovely, strong 8-pound baby, and Eugene was so proud of his baby brother.

After my recovery I studied harder on the Chinese language and visited the Tibetan women in their homes more often. Some of them were quite superstitious, and it took time and patience to gain their confidence. By that time Russell and I spoke the language well enough that we could both teach classes in the Tibetan Sunday School. Russell had a nice class of teen-age boys, and I taught teen-age girls on Sunday mornings and women's class on Sunday afternoons. When Robert was old enough to sit alone, I would take him with me when I taught and he would sit very quietly on his high stool.

On December 7, 1923, after completing two years of Tibetan and Chinese language studies, Russell and I passed our tests with excellent grades. One of the requirements at the end of the two-year course was to prepare and deliver a sermon in Tibetan. My first sermon was "God, Sin, and Salvation".

☦

The MacLeods had applied for their furlough and had hoped to leave by the first of January, 1924, but the Chinese officials asked them to delay their departure because of the continuous fighting, robbing, and killing in the area. In fact, the overall political condition around Batang during the latter part of 1923 was very tense and disturbed. The road between Batang and Yengin, which they would need to travel, was particularly dangerous, and the corrupt, opium-smoking Chinese military commander made little or no attempt to control the tribal feuds.

When Mr. and Mrs. J. C. Ogden left on furlough, Mr. Ogden was in poor health, and Mrs. MacLeod had assumed the duties at the orphanage in Mrs. Ogden's absence. Mr. Ogden's health had improved, and now they were on their way back to Batang. With the MacLeods now planning to go on furlough, I was to be in charge of the orphanage from January 1, 1924 until Mrs. Ogden returned. At that time there were thirty-nine orphans, many of whom were babies or very small children requiring close supervision. I loved the children, and enjoyed working with them. Because our house was some distance away, it was decided that, until the Ogdens arrived, we should move into the house vacated by the MacLeods, so as to be closer to the orphange in case of emergencies, which might arise day or night. This made it easier to take care of my own home and children, but it was hard to have to move things out of our house, and then move back again, especially so because our own house got so very dirty and dusty while we were away.

The MacLeods were finally allowed to leave January 19, 1924. All of us took a holiday the day they left. If you could have seen the demonstration along the road, there would be no doubt about the place a real missionary wins in the hearts of those people. People were lined up along the road all the way to Ko-ee-la Pass, about five miles south of Batang. Mrs. MacLeod rode in a sedan chair carried by four Tibetans. The three children — Laura, Duncan, and Shelton — rode in another chair carried by three Tibetans, and Mr. MacLeod rode a horse.

Sixty soldiers lined up in ranks near the mission compound, ready to escort the caravan. Half of the soldiers marched off in advance, and the other half took up their position at the rear.

The going was slow for a while, as all along the road small parties of well-wishers waited to say goodbye. Many offered small bowls of milk for them to drink. The Tibetans would say only a few words, then break down weeping. A few hundred yards from the officers' tent all the little school children were lined up with the school flag at the end of the line. As the MacLeods passed, they all stood at attention, saying "goodbye", then broke into tears. Many of those children were in our orphanage, and since the MacLeods had been in charge of it for the past two years, they regarded them almost as parents. Dr. Hardy rode out about two miles, and looked so sad at their departure. Russell and I rode horses, carrying our children in the saddle in front of us, and accompanied them on a few more miles. We were very sorry to see them leave.

Russell and I worked very hard the next few months. He was in charge of evangelism after Mr. MacLeod's departure. Besides my duties at the orphanage and my home, I taught several women, including two who were blind. I told them Bible stories when visiting in their homes, sometimes twice a week, and sometimes every day. I also was happy to accept any other invitations to visit in the homes where the women were becoming interested in our work.

I had picked up an obstinate and hard-to-cure case of malaria which caused me great difficulty those first two years, because it recurred again and again. Then, too, from September, 1923 to April, 1924, our baby, Robert, suffered with eczema, which itched terribly and made him so miserable he had to be held almost day and night. We tried everything available from the clinic to relieve that aggravation, and finally, after about eight months, it cleared up.

While the MacLeods were experiencing delay in starting their furlough, the Ogdens were having difficulty returning. After numerous delays along the way they finally arrived in

Batang May 14, 1924. With them were some new missionaries: Dr. Ivan Wohrley, Leland Emerson, and Raymond Peterson, with their families, and Grace Young, a single lady. Miss Young was a nurse, and also had a very good singing voice, which helped in our church services.

They said that during their whole trip they neither saw a bandit nor heard a gun shot. Until they had been there a few days, they did not realize just how narrowly they had missed it. Some bandits from a place called Den-bo, four or five days' travel from Batang, had heard that some foreigners were coming to Batang with a big caravan loaded down with many wonderful things. About eighty of them had gone to the pass where Dr. Shelton was killed, to wait for the Ogden party. Most of them went off to a ravine to rest, eat, and sing, leaving only two or three with the horses. About that time a Chinese captain and twenty-four soldiers happened to be coming to Batang and had somehow learned of the robbers and their plans. The soldiers took the robbers' horses and brought them into Batang, just as Russell was returning from an evangelistic trip with his "boys". The Tibetan bandits were indignant with the Chinese for their "dirty trick" and demanded the return of the horses, but their demand was refused.

A few days later, in retaliation, the bandits captured about one hundred twenty Batang people who had gone to the mountains for a Buddhist religious fast, some from quite wealthy and influential families. The bandits released all the prisoners except for a few of the more prominent ones, and several girls, who were forced to carry the loads. The robbers took all of the people's possessions, including their clothing.

The soldiers finally agreed to give the horses back if the people of Batang would pay them (the Chinese) 1500 rupees. Although the horses were returned, the bandits would not release the last five hostages until the Batang Tibetans had paid 500 rupees for each of them. Such was life on the Tibetan-Chinese border.

My Sunday School class of girls in Batang

Russell's Sunday School class of boys.

I visited in individual homes to present the Gospel message.
Often I took my two sons with me.
(Eugene standing in front of Tibetan helper, and Robert being carried.)

Whenever there was a baptism, we all gathered around to sing and pray.

5
Exploring New Areas

After Dr. Shelton's death, the churches in America established a memorial fund in his name. They raised over $100,000 for the purpose of founding new mission stations in the Tibetan territory that he had so loved and for which he gave his life.

Some of us at the Batang Mission felt that another mission post should be established at Atuntze or Yengin. With that in mind, the mission sent Russell, Marion Duncan, their two Tibetan teachers, five students, our native evangelist Lee Gway Gwang, and a medical student Lee Gway Yuin, on a preaching trip to survey the area between Batang and Atuntze. They left Batang on July 24, 1924. Lee Gway Gwang wrote an excellent account of that trip, which J. Russell Morse translated, as follows:

"On the morning of our leave-taking, many members of the church, students and relatives came out to bid us good-bye.... We prayed together that strength would be given us to accomplish the work, and that a spirit of love for mankind might so fill our hearts that all men might see clearly that we were disciples of Christ.

"Before going far we came to the place where Dr. Shelton had been martyred. Here we stopped a moment to pray and rededicate ourselves before going on. With us were Captain Wang and about thirty soldiers to escort and protect us over the most dangerous part of the road.

We soon came to Drubalong and neighboring villages where many places had been burned the previous year by some rebellious

Tibetans. We tried in every way to show them the kindness of Christ and also to comfort them and to heal their sick. We went on to many other such places where we preached about Christ and ministered to the sick.

"Bamutang Valley is a crossroads for Batang and Yengin, Eastern Tibet and Yunnan.....A few of us made a circuit of the valley from morning until night, preaching from house to house and doctoring the sick. That night we used the stereopticon to show them the pictures of the 'Life of Christ'. People from all parts of the valley came to see.

"In Dzongen, a place of several hundred families the people heard the Gospel with gladness and quite a number asked for tracts to take back to their relatives and friends. In this way, the Gospel would go to many places where we ourselves were unable to go at that time.

"We went to Yengin, one of the most important places in all of the Tibetan frontier land because of the extensive mining of salt. There were about a thousand families in the Yengin district, most of whom were quite poor, and their living conditions were miserable. They had salt enough and to spare for their bodies, but no salt to save their souls. All of them still believed in the lamas and were in bondage to them.

"We stayed there three days and went out every day to preach and give medicines. Our hearts ached when we saw these people and their suffering, for they were truly as sheep without a shepherd.

"At the end of the three days we left for Atuntze with Lieutenant Chen and five soldiers to escort us. All of the villages where we stopped from now on were under the authority of the Yunnanese government.

"The city of Atuntze, which is high up in the mountains, has a population of over 2000 (and) is a trade center between eastern Tibet, Batang, and northern Yunnan. About half of the people are Chinese and the other half a mixture of Chinese, Tibetan, and Mosu. We stayed three and a half days in this place, preaching the Gospel in the streets to a total of nearly thirteen hundred people.

"While we rejoiced over the hospitality of many, our hearts were grieved that others could not realize that Jesus is their Lord.

We prayed that Jesus would strengthen us, that we might not cease to care for those blind ones whom Christ died to save.

☦

For Marion Duncan, this trip was interrupted by a tragic event. His son, Herbert, who was not quite two years old, became critically ill on August 10, and Mrs. Duncan immediately sent two runners to notify her husband. On August 12, 1924 Herbert died. It was August 17 before Mr. Duncan received word of his son's illness and three days later, as he was hurrying home, he received the sad news of his death. It was an unhappy homecoming for him, but the great love he and Mrs. Duncan had for Jesus enabled them to bear the loss. It was hard for Eugene to understand what had happened to his little companion. When he went to say good-bye to Herbert he picked a flower out of our garden and put it in his little friend's hand. Eugene and Herbert had played together so much that our home, too, felt lonesome after his death.

Although Mr. Duncan had to return to Batang, Russell and the others continued on their evangelistic trip. For the most part of the thirty-six day tour the weather was pleasant, and the scenery was beautiful. On their way home they visited the Bong Tso Lake, a large sacred lake in the mountains west of Bamutang.

All along the way they found the people really open to the Gospel, and in each village people begged them to come and establish a station in their area. At first it seemed that Yengin would be the best place, but the American Consul would not approve it due to the constant tribal feuds around there. Later, however, the Consul did give permission to establish a station at Atuntze, several days' travel to the south..

At that time it seemed that the best use of missionary personnel was to have Dr. Wohrley take care of medical work, Mr. Emerson to do educational work and Russell to continue with the evangelism. That left four missionary families and one single lady to carry on the evangelistic work around Batang.

61

Russell and I felt very strongly about establishing new out-posts. One day when Russell and I were talking about this, he said, "You know, I sat by Dr. Shelton when he was dying, and at that time I prayed, and made a vow to God that I would carry on Dr. Shelton's work, so that he would not have died in vain. I really believe it is God's will that the outreach should be extended. Let's really pray that it will be possible to open a new outpost, and that God will use us in opening it."

And we <u>did</u> pray that way.

6
Journey to Inner Tibet

Ever since coming to Batang we had eagerly awaited an opportunity to go across into Tibet. Now, in May of 1925, that opportunity came. The Morse family received an invitation to spend a month or so as guests of one of the wealthiest families in all Tibet. One member of that family, an attractive young man about twenty-four years old named Buh Ra-Ga, had come to Batang earlier to be treated for opium addiction. His family lived at Bangdat, just a short way from Gartok, the capital of Mar Kham Province.

Buh Ra-Ga's father had died a few months before and he, being the eldest son, was left with a great responsibility. That was probably the reason for seeking a cure from the opium habit. As is common in such cures, he was quite nervous, so it was important to keep him busy, and his mind distracted from thoughts about his addiction. Russell always tried to be friendly and helpful to everyone, and spent quite a lot of time getting acquainted with this man. He was able to help him in numerous small ways, and we often invited him to our house. He enjoyed Eugene and Robert, both of whom spoke Tibetan fluently. Russell took Buh Ra-Ga on short hunting trips and found him to be an excellent marksman. We enjoyed his company and he said, "Now, I want to enjoy your company for a while at Bangdat."

Subsequently, this young Tibetan merchant and his younger brother, Buh Dor-Jeh, offered to make all political arrangements and, as a token of their friendship for us, to let their home be our headquarters during our stay in Tibet.

A combination of unusual difficulties delayed the start of this trip until the fall of 1925. Dr. Hardy, Mr. Peterson, and our two Tibetan evangelists had gone to Yachow and Chengtu, expecting to be gone three months. Instead, it was nearly six months before they returned. While they were away, Russell was doing the evangelistic work of Lee Gway Gwang and Tu-de-bao as well as his own evangelistic work at the hospital, church, Sunday School and outlying districts. Had he left before their return, there would have been no one to carry on those duties.

Also, the Shang Chen Tibetans were causing quite a disturbance. They, along with the Dru-wa-su Tibetans had been fighting with the Ra Nah lama's Tibetans, but were not able to win a decisive victory. They sent a message to the Chinese garrison at Batang, asking to borrow their cannons and machine guns in order to win, and threatening to take the guns by force if the Chinese would not help. The Chinese played for time until they could obtain reinforcements and mobilize three or four hundred fighting men from the Tibetan tribes just north and west of Batang who hated the Shang Chen because of their cruelties. We were warned that the Shang Chen might attack at any time, and the place might be besieged for several weeks. Although the mission houses were whitewashed and easily identified, the two houses situated among the Tibetans would be in danger of having their water supply shut off, as this was frequently done during a siege. The Jop-o-ding compound had their own water supply, so we were advised to prepare to move over there on short notice with as much of our goods as possible. It would not have been wise to leave on a long trip under those conditions.

However, the most serious reason for delaying our departure was Eugene's critical illness with dysentery the first weeks in July. The oriental germs seemed more virulent than those in

64

America, and did not readily respond to treatment. For two or three days, we almost despaired of his life, but with Dr. Wohrley's medication and our fervent prayers, he finally recovered, although he was quite weak for some time.

✟

On September 21, 1925, after a delay of four months, we set out on our venture into "the closed land" of Tibet. Russell had made arrangements to have our baggage taken on pack animals as far as the Yangtze River. All our neighbors came out to see us off, and even traveled with us a considerable distance from town. It was drizzling rain when we left, but that did not quench our spirits, for we believed that this was God's time for us to go on that long-anticipated and prepared-for trip. The motto with which we left Kunming for Batang nearly four years before was still good for this trip: "Trust in God and go forward".

Eugene, now four and one-half years old, and Robert, two and one-half, rode in the saddles in front of us. They were in the best of spirits, talking about everything along the road. It rained during the first two days, but we had saddle slickers that covered everything.

Dinner that first day was at a headman's house at Tea Tree Mountain village where we were treated with the warm hospitality which is characteristic of well-bred Tibetans. We had planned to stay overnight in a temple at Leh, but found that three very suspicious-looking men had already moved in. Ah Trin, our teacher, said we would probably be robbed during the night if we stayed there. It was even feared they might be spies for a band of robbers. Therefore we stayed at the headman's house. None of the Leh people had guns, but Russell hired two of them to go ahead early the next morning and check out the place about an hour's ride to the south, where the robbers usually ambushed and robbed people.

The Chinese said they would be unable to provide an escort for us that day, so the headman sent six young men to inspect and clear the road for us. However, the Chinese did send an escort of five soldiers just as we were ready to leave. The three evil-looking Tibetans were seen coming from the temple and going into the mountains, but not in the direction they had previously said they were going.

That night (our second), we camped near Drubalong, and slept almost as soundly as if we had been at home. Our little three-in-one tent was quite comfortable and didn't leak a bit. It had two berths, upper and lower, each wide enough for two people if necessary, and an extra cot. Our Tibetan companions didn't sleep so well, getting up several times to scout around for signs of robbers.

The next morning, I asked Ah Trin what kind of a night he'd had, and if he had seen any robbers. He said, "There certainly were robbers around, but they did not bother us."

I asked, "How did that happen? Did some of our Tibetan friends stand guard?"

With a shy smile he answered, "No, but a very excellent watchman helped me through the night."

I then asked, "Don't you know who it was?"

He replied, "No, I don't. In the morning he was gone."

I immediately thought of Hebrews 1:14: "...God's ministering spirits (angels) sent forth to minister for them who shall be heirs of salvation."

An interesting footnote to this experience is the fact that on our return journey, some of the local residents of the area quietly approached some of our helpers and questioned them.

"Who were the guards around your camp when you went through here before?" they asked.

"We had no guards except ourselves," was the reply.

"But we saw them! They were very big and tall, all dressed in white. The bandits had planned to attack and rob your party, but when they saw those big guards they were frightened, and didn't dare bother you."

When we were told about this, we felt it was further confirmation of God's care and protection.

✝

On the afternoon of the third day, we arrived at the ferry on the Yangtze River, where a "skin" boat was waiting to take us across. Usually wooden ferry boats were used to cross the river, but the rebellious Ra Nah lama tribe had captured and burned them all. These skin boats were made of yak hide stretched over a springy framework of tough boughs about the thickness of a man's thumb. The summer rainy season had been unusually late, causing high water on the Yangtze and its tributaries. Those boats looked mighty frail, but were really not as frightening as we had anticipated. It required four trips to take across our family and our five Tibetans, plus six horse loads of baggage and the saddles from our four riding horses. We sent the muleteer and his ten animals back to Batang. We enjoyed a most restful evening and night, and the next morning had an appetizing breakfast of fried potatoes, bacon, eggs, rice, and milk.

On the fourth day, Tsong Jang, one of the head traders under the Bangdat merchants, arrived at our camp with pack animals and riding horses. He came across the Hyeh Chu, a small tributary to the Yangtze, which was higher than usual because of the rains. We had sent Narjeh Tsering, our next door neighbor in Batang, to help, but he wasn't needed so he came back early with a plump pheasant.

Later in the day, while we were traveling, our lead mule mistook the path and went out on a very steep cliff. That confused the rest of the animals and one lost its balance and went rolling over and over to the stream bed below. Luckily, the tough little mule escaped with only a few scratches and the pack was in waterproof canvas, so there was no real damage.

September 25 and 26 (the fifth and sixth days) we traveled on toward Bong Tso Lake. This was the sacred lake in the mountains west of Bamutang, visited by Russell and the others on their thirty-six day preaching trip.

67

Along the way, near Dega-ding, we saw a woman about forty-five years old making a pilgrimage to the sacred Kawa Gabo mountains, prostrating herself all the way. She wore a kind of leather sandal on her hands and knees to protect them from the stony road. She truly was praying without ceasing, doing the best she knew how, and we thought, "What a pity that her devotion is so misguided." Our hearts were burdened as we realized her bondage to the powers of darkness, and we prayed that she would come to know the One who could truly set her free.

The trip was long, but pleasant, and took us through woods of evergreen, pine and fir interspersed with smooth and gently rolling stretches of park-like meadows from which not more than half of the flowers had gone. As we approached the pass, before reaching Bong Tso, cold breezes swept down upon us, and we put on our overcoats plus our raincoats. The climb up the mountain to the pass was gradual and not at all difficult.

We came to the far-reaching Bong Tso Lake just as the sun was setting, the last rays of which reflected from the clouds above, touching them with various shades of gold and yellow. The ground was wet and cold where we camped that night, as was the whole countryside. The children were tired, and crying from the cold and hunger. We put them to bed to get them warm and to keep their feet dry. By the time a hasty supper of fried eggs and warmed-up potatoes was prepared, they were fast asleep.

What a relief it was to be across the Yangtze River into territory governed by Tibet, away from the constant fighting, robbing, burning, and looting which had become a way of life in Yunnan and Szechuan provinces. Discipline under the Tibetan military commanders was very strict and punishment of offenders was terribly severe.

The younger of our two Tibetan merchant friends came down to greet us and escort us to Bangdat, according to Tibetan custom. Shortly after leaving the lake, we went through a storm of something, neither snow nor hail — more like sleet — which continued for an hour. We were relieved to get to the warm valley below the snow line, and the grasslands dotted everywhere with flowers. In the distance, we could see the tremendous range of snow mountains, sharp and white, marking the divide between the Mekong and Salween rivers.

✟

In caves among the nearby cliffs were cells of hermit lamas, only one of which was now occupied by a man about fifty years old. He had not left his cave for over three years. The entrance was sealed, with only a small opening through which food and other necessities could be handed to him by other lamas.

Around Bong Tso Lake, we saw scores of antelope and also a great herd of deer of a variety about as large as a mule. They lived mostly on one of the islands out in the lake, crossing over on the ice in winter. Going from Bong Tso to Bangdat, we also saw a great many holes of marmots, a hibernating animal about the size of a fox terrier dog. Some Tibetans say that during hibernation, the marmots are meditating upon the doctrines of the Goddess of Mercy; therefore, they are considered sacred. Others say their flesh is better than pork, so they are eaten freely outside the Lhasa government territory. There is a lama-imposed law against killing game in Tibet, but most of the people do not observe it. For instance, when our host came to meet us, he brought a fat antelope that had been shot about an hour before.

As we neared Bangdat, we were surprised to find such a fertile valley with many houses and fields, livestock grazing, and people reaping barley. Surely this was some of the most beautiful and awesome scenery in the whole world!

Although the house of the two Bangdat brothers was probably the largest in Mar Kham province, it was not very impressive from the outside, The great family mansion had been burned by the Chinese during the war about ten years before. Three huge and ferocious dogs, almost as large as lions, were chained outside the main entrance. The two creatures most

69

feared by Tibetans were snakes and dogs. Ne-ne-la, the young wife of the two brothers, met us at the main entrance and took us to our rooms. As explained before, the practice of polyandry was common in parts of Tibet.

We were surprised at the elegance, convenience, and cleanliness of our quarters. There was a great bay window about six feet square on the south side. Another window on the east side was about two and a half by three feet with thirty glass panes of various sizes arranged in a pleasing design. These two windows made the room very light and highlighted the decorations on the walls, ceiling, and sideboards. The walls and ceiling were all hand decorated with varicolored designs, such as flowers, religious symbols, and mythical creatures. The workmanship was very good, especially considering the materials available to the workmen, and their lack of artistic training.

The room was furnished with three sideboards, which also had varicolored decorations, two folding chairs imported from China, a large mirror in a gilded frame, two stands and two low tables. In front of each window was placed a low couch, padded with musk deer hair cushions and covered with beautiful rugs. Everything considered, our quarters would have compared favorably with many American summer resorts. This elegance was especially impressive to us because, in the five years we had been on the mission field, up to that point we had seen only incredibly poor and unsanitary Tibetan homes. We were so thankful that our Heavenly Father had made it possible for our family to have this vacation.

✟

Buh Ra-Ga had gone to Hlandee on important business. Besides being a son in a wealthy family, that young man was a civil official over a large part of the territory in which he lived. The family was also in charge of all trading operations for the Dalai Lama.

A day or two after our arrival, Russell went with the younger brother, Buh Dor-Jeh, to see a servant who had been attacked by a thief three weeks earlier. The servant had killed the thief in self-defense, but received many serious stab wounds in the process. Knowing the unsanitary condition of most Tibetans, Russell was surprised to find all of the wounds almost healed. The left arm was about half cut off at the shoulder and even that was healing remarkably well, although he had had no medical attention. After Russell had cleaned and dressed the wounds, he and Buh Dor-Jeh started back to Bangdat.

On the way back, they saw Buh Ra-Ga and a number of his horsemen descending the opposite slope on their return from Hlandee. Upon seeing Russell and Buh Dor-Jeh, they gave the Tibetan war-whoop, ran their horses across the valley and dashed through the brook to meet them. Although it had been nearly six months since Russell and Buh Ra-Ga had parted in Batang, his greeting was most cordial. He said his trip to Hlandee had been most successful and arrangements had been made for us to visit the Mar Kham military commander-in-chief there. However, he told us, the general was in the midst of preparations to move his headquarters to Dra-ya, nearly six days' journey from Bangdat, so he could not entertain as well as he would like.

Buh-Ra-Ga also said he was sending a messenger to Gartok, civil capital of Mar Kham Province, that evening and would ask permission for us to visit there, if we so desired. Of course, we were delighted with the prospect of seeing more of that interesting country and its people. Russell felt honored to be the first white man invited to this "forbidden land" in five years. I was one of the very few white women ever to have traveled in it. Also, I doubt if any other white children had been so privileged, except for Dr. Shelton's two daughters.

One afternoon, our host and hostess dressed Russell and me up in all the finery of a Tibetan lady and gentleman of Lhasa. A great amount of time was spent combing my hair into the proper style. My costume was very elaborate. The charm box alone, of pure gold set with rare turquoises, was valued at

71

2000 rupees by our host. I suppose the whole outfit would have been worth around 5000 rupees ($1000 U.S. at that time) as there were many gems set in pure gold.

One night, we stayed up until 10:00 p.m. while the Tibetans sang and danced to entertain us. They repeatedly asked us to sing and dance according to the American custom, but we could only respond with a few songs, which they seemed to appreciate.

✟

On October 1, Russell took a horseback trip with Tsong Jang and Norjeh Tsering to the top of the pass west of Bangdat and across the pasture land on the mountainside to the northwest. Concerning the trip he later wrote:

"We saw only five of the black tents of the shepherd people as most of them have moved into houses in the valleys. Our own sojourn in tents will have to be limited, too, as there was quite a heavy frost last night. Saw four large flocks of the Tibetan wild turkeys, but the dogs chased them so I had no hope of getting pictures. We later came onto a grassy place where a large herd of yak and dri (female yak for milking) were grazing. While I was focusing my camera to take a picture of a baby yak and its mother, I heard a great rushing sound, like a stampede. Turning around, I saw a dozen or more of the yak rushing toward me with their sharp horns tossing threateningly. Believe me, I was scared! They ran away when I threw a stone and shouted at them. Actually, they had been chasing our dog which had run to me for protection.

"Descending from the mountain we saw a Tibetan graveyard, the first I had seen. The Tibetans around Batang consigned their dead to the rivers, but the streams here were too small. The corpses are burned and the ashes placed inside a circle of stones, like a 'mani' pile, bearing the 'mani' prayer inscriptions. 'Mani' flags were put up. There were also several 'sakang', the little houses filled with images and idols."

During the day, we received a favorable reply about visiting Gartok. The Tigi, civil governor of this province, said it would be at least five days before he could receive us. He had received some smallpox vaccine from Lhasa and asked if Russell could administer it. The letter was personal, not official, which was proper as our vacation in Eastern Tibet was not a matter of state. The Tibetan officials were very cautious about anything involving them diplomatically. We sent an answer the next day before leaving to visit the military commander at Hlandee.

About 9:30, the evening of October 1, we heard a hubbub in the house outside our quarters. Russell rushed out to investigate, and found one man running around with a pine torch, thrusting it into the different rooms while a lama was throwing handfuls of barley around and chanting. One of the servants of Bangdat Tsong (the family name) had died three days before and this ceremony was to send his spirit out of the house to a more desirable abode. Apparently those folks didn't want the spirits of their dead friends lingering around. We wished they had known from the Bible that human spirits do not linger, but only unclean spirits which have dwelt in that person's body before he died. After the person dies, the unclean spirit goes out looking for a new "host" body in which to reside, but sometimes masquerades as the spirit of the dead person.

Russell and Eugene
with a rich
Tibetan merchant,
Buh-ra-gah, of the
Bangdat family

On our trip to inner Tibet we traveled on horseback, with the children riding in front of us. Although it was only October, we encountered snow, especially on some of the mountain passes.

Our Tibetan friends dressed us in the clothing of rich Tibetan noble families.

We met the governor, or "tigi", of eastern Tibet,
who wanted his picture taken with Russell.

We had a tent in which we stayed while traveling.
This picture was partially posed, in that the man at the side of the tent
was only pretending to churn Tibetan tea.
The man with his arm on the tent, holding a gun, is Buh-ra-gah.

7
Journey Into Inner Tibet (continued)

Just before noon on October 2, we left about half of our baggage at Bangdat and set out for Hlandee. It was about a three hour trip, but the climb was gradual and easy as we traveled through some more lovely scenery, probably the most beautiful in Eastern Tibet. Buh Ra-Ga was with us and undoubtedly did a great deal in smoothing the way. He seemed to have real influence with all classes, from the general down to the humblest peasant.

When we reached a point only about a mile up the valley from Hlandee, Buh Ra-Ga suggested we stop and rest while he and a messenger went ahead to notify the Dapon (General) of our approach so he would be duly prepared to meet us. After about twenty minutes we went ahead at a leisurely pace. About a half mile from Hlandee we met one of the Dapon's lieutenants, who told us that everything was ready for us. We found our tents pitched at one of the most pleasant spots in the valley, on a smooth natural lawn beside the Hlandee River, which was only a brook there. The stream was full of a small variety of trout, which had a string of black spots down each side.

The Dapon's servants came out to lead our horses across the stream and to help us alight. Four lieutenants waited on us with all the politeness and efficiency that could be wished for. The food was appetizing and the waiters kept urging us to eat more. Fortunately, we had learned to relish Tibetan food.

That night was very cold, and when we got up the next morning the ground was white with frost. Thanks to the Dapon, we had been provided with a fire pan which, when filled with coals from the cooking fire, made the cold more endurable. He had arranged for our every need while there, including meals, firewood, etc.

The Dapon and family, together with a number of officers and soldiers, visited us from 11:00 a.m. until after 2:00 p.m. He treated us with kindness and honor, as his equal, so our visit with him and his wife was more pleasant than we had anticipated. We knew he was greatly feared by all the common people, and had a reputation for severity and ill temper. It was plain to see that all his subordinates approached him in fear and trembling. The Tibetan army discipline seemed much superior to what we had seen among the Chinese.

During our conversation he inquired especially about Mrs. Shelton and her daughters, Doris and Dorothy. He said that Dr. Shelton was one of the best men he had ever known, and one of the best friends he had ever had. He seemed pleased to hear that the two girls cared enough about Tibet to plan to return there as missionaries.

For the first time we had a little difficulty with the language. The common people seemed to understand our Batang dialect even in this part of Tibet. The high officials, however, all spoke the Lhasa colloquial which differs a bit from even the standard written Tibetan of the books.

That evening we sat in our cold tent trying to be entertained by Tibetans dancing and singing around a bonfire. We almost wished we could dance so we could keep warm. Two of the Dapon's six bagpipers from the days of British rule, and a clog dancer also came to entertain us. Quite a number of the nearby country people came and joined in too.

The next day, while the Dapon was in the midst of preparations for moving to Dra-ya, his wife and son came to visit the boys and me. According to their custom, we had brought gifts

77

to them when we came to Hlandee. Now, also according to custom, the Dapon sent parting gifts to us, consisting of two bags of barley, about two pounds of butter, a leopard skin and a small piece of silk. They also gave our Tibetan helpers twelve silver rupees. The wife and son stayed several hours, and we had a most enjoyable visit. Russell took several pictures of the mother and son with Eugene, Robert, and me. He had already taken several of the general and his son and some of the soldiers. The Tibetans prized pictures very highly, because they were not common in that part of the country.

☩

We had been allowed to bring only a small amount of medicine with us from Batang, — what was considered enough for our own party. Although Russell had told no one he could treat sick people, they came anyway. As a follower of Christ, who "went about doing good", he tried to help them as much as possible.

Soon after we arrived in Hlandee a poor fellow, about forty years old, came with a combination of rather common ailments and knocked his head on the ground in front of Russell (despite his protests). It seemed impossible to refuse him, so Russell gave him what he thought was needed. The next morning the man came back again with a happy look on his face, bringing six big pomegranates. He said he was a poor man and couldn't buy medicine, but wanted Russell to please give him some more before he left. Of course, he did. Then they talked quite awhile about Jesus, and this seemed very wonderful to the man. What Jesus did for us seems wonderful to us, too.

Many others came to Russell, also. Some of them he could help with our simple remedies, but others he could not help. There was one who appeared to have a severe case of tonsilitis, from which the poison had spread over his entire body. Another man had such severe abdominal pains he couldn't straighten up, and had to walk with a cane. He apparently had appendicitis. Russell attempted to persuade these men to try to make the trip to the hospital at Batang.

We returned to Bangdat through a little snow storm on the afternoon of October 5. It was so nice to get back into our nice and convenient rooms. We spent the next few days resting, reading, and doing some packing for our hoped-for trip to Gartok. Russell developed some of the pictures he had taken.

Our hosts tried to have something special for our entertainment each day. The Bangdat family put up tents in a beautiful valley, not far from their home, where we were served "boudzas". This was made of chopped meat, pototoes, and onions wrapped in a thin dough with the edges pinched together all around and then steamed. We also had buttered tea.

✝

On October 8 all of us, including the Bangdat brothers and their wife, took a three-hour horeseback ride to the south. We climbed up a woodland road, then around the brow of a mountain to the head of a little valley. There we visited the caves of the lama hermitage. The mountain side was dotted with many hut-like entrances to the dugouts where the lamas lived.

It was all so simple and unpretentious we knew immediately that these recluses were really living out their vow of poverty. These woodland lamas were a great contrast to the sleek, haughty priests of Batang. These were of the Nyima or "red cap" sect, while the Batang lamas were of the Gelug-pa or "yellow cap" sect. There were usually about eighty lamas living there, but it was harvest time, and all except ten or twelve were away begging for grain.

The abbot, or "ken-bo" lived in a small three-room log cabin. It was clean but void of decorations except for several well-worn religious paintings, called "tankas", hanging on the wall near the idol shelf. Among his utensils he had a drinking bowl made from the top of a human skull. He also had a trumpet made from a human thigh bone. Despite this dreadful equipment, the abbot seemed very kind, humble, and straightforward. He and a few of his comrades entertained us with a long and quite melodious Buddhist chanting service in which drums, bells and a thigh bone trumpet were used. They had no objections to our taking pictures.

Russell and I had quite a friendly religious discussion with them. We asked them to tell us about their religion first, then we would tell them about ours. I told them about God, Sin, and Salvation. The abbot asked many questions about Christianity and seemed pleased with our answers. The lamas were very eager to accept the Gospel portions, written in Tibetan, which we had brought with us — almost grabbing them from our hands. They sat down beside the path and immediately started reading. Some said they had been told that the true Gospel would come from the west. We were the first white people and, of course, the first missionaries who had ever visited this hermitage.

On October 9 Russell spent several more hours developing the many pictures he had taken. He took a picture of Buh Ra-Ga all dressed up in the trappings of a great lama. Buh Ra-Ga enjoyed the make-believe, and laughed to think his picture would go to America to show our friends what a big lama looked like.

We had received no further word from the Civil Governor of Markham (the "Tigi") about visiting Gartok. Buh Ra-Ga thought we should try one more time, so we sent another letter by one of our Tibetan helpers, Ah kay. We told the governor we would be glad to visit Gartok amd administer the small-pox vaccine which he had received from Lhasa. However, if he wanted us to come, we would have to leave no later than the fifteenth, because we had important business awaiting us in Batang.

On October 10 the house was in a great bustle getting ready for the Dapon's stayover on his way to Dra-ya. It was off his main road but the Bangdat brothers were great friends of his, so they expected the Dapon to stay several days. Buh Dor-jeh and Russell rode out to meet him. He had only about fifty

80

men with him, as most of the soldiers had gone on to Ja Ga to await him. According to military custom his journey from Hlandee was heralded all the way by bagpipers, trumpeters, etc. His reception was elaborate. As he advanced to the main entrance between two files of armed horsemen, servants of the household burned pans full of evergreen twigs as a token of reverence and to make the air more fragrant. When he dismounted, four giant firecrackers were exploded near by and the Dapon's musicians struck up a tune from the housetop.

That night the house was crammed full of people. So many of the Dapon's followers came around to visit us that we finally had to close the large door of our apartment in order to have a little privacy. Some of them were quite polite, but others just stared as if they could never "get their eyes full" of the white people.

✞

Ah-Kay returned on the twelfth with a letter from the "Tigi" saying that he was eager for us to visit him there and that he would send a man on the thirteenth to prepare oola (transport) and to escort us. As we were preparing to leave, the Bangdat brothers presented Russell and me with lovely rings with turquoise settings. Upon our arrival, we had presented the Bangdat family with a hand-embroidered Chinese silk bedspread which had been brought up to us from Chengtu.

Finally on October 14, we left for Gartok. Our gifts for the Tigi were half a horse load of sugar cakes, a red silk Chinese shawl with hand-embroidered flowers, the same on both sides, two cans of Del Monte fruit and Russell's new Ingersoll watch. He had also developed some pictures to present to the Tigi.

Along the way we saw tremendous flocks of wild turkeys. It was quite a sight to see them running up the mountainside with the dogs in pursuit, soaring away across the valley when the dogs got too close. They can run very fast, do almost no flying, but glide very gracefully. Their calls are much like those of the American turkey. The breast meat is white like that of a

81

chicken but they are about four times as large. They are white with black tails and wings, and seem to be the most plentiful game bird in Eastern Tibet. We saw no other wild animals after leaving Bangdat but the Tibetans said there were great numbers of them back from the more traveled roads.

From the Do-ee La, a mountain pass between Bangdat and Pu-la, we had a magnificent view of the drainage basin of the Gartok River and the tremendous, massive range of snow-covered mountains across the Mekong, far above Yengin. We had wondered how people could live in a country of such high altitude and severe climate but we were now beginning to understand. The Creator had provided thickly forested mountains that they might not suffer so much from the cold. There were great grasslands providing pasture for large herds of yak, sheep, horses, etc. They had an abundance of meat and milk. Even the poorest had warm sheepskin garments. The black tents of the nomads, woven of yak hair, kept out rain and snow. Honey protected the faces of the women. Now we could see why this region was so well populated. The houses were usually larger and better than those around Batang. A few had been burned during the Chinese invasion, but there was not the constant fighting, looting, and burning which was so prevalent in Yunnan and Szechuan provinces. Under these conditions we felt it should be safe to send native evangelists to this wholly unworked field, even though foreign missionaries were not allowed to travel freely there.

About half a mile from Gartok two of the Tigi's deputies came rushing toward us as fast as their horses would go. We wondered, rather uneasily, what it was all about. As they came to us they brought their horses to a sudden stop, quickly slid off their saddles and ran to place "Katas" around our necks. The Kata is a scarf which prominent persons present to honored guests. These two were white, pure Chinese silk, about six feet long and two feet wide. The deputies escorted us to our quarters, going ahead to clear a way through the crowds gathered in the streets to watch us and our party pass by. A large crowd also stood around our quarters, not wanting to miss seeing the tiniest peculiarity of the white family and their retinue.

✚

Our quarters, though not as pretentious as at Bangdat, were quite comfortable. We were on the second floor of one of the largest houses in Gartok, and our Tibetan companions had nice rooms just below us on the first floor. The room was well lighted by two paper-covered windows, and contained one large table, one small table, a washstand, a long bench, a raised sleeping place, and a fire pan on a stand. The cooking was done in a nearby kitchen, called "ja kang" or tearoom. Our cook, Duje, accompanied us on the trip as it was customary to take one's own cook when traveling. We were just across the street from the Tigi's official residence.

A few minutes after our arrival we were visited by the Tigi's younger brother, Gna-o Lozong, who was also his treasurer. He was a young man about twenty-four years old with very pleasant manners. With him were several servants bringing a freshly butchered sheep, about a peck of flour, and fifty eggs. The sheep looked strange, having been skinned, with its head and feet still on and placed in a standing position by the servants. After a few minutes conversation with Russell, Gna-o Lozong left.

In a short while — before we even had time to clean up — a messenger came from the Tigi inviting us to come over and visit. The Tigi had only been in Markham about seven months. His fourteen year old son was with him but his wife was still in Lhasa. As with the Dapon at Hlandee, we experienced a little difficulty with the Lhasa colloquial language, but the Tigi was one of the most gracious, kindly, and considerate gentlemen we had ever met. The younger brother, with several servants, had waited at the gate to escort us to the reception room. There the Tigi greeted us warmly and without undue formality. Several kinds of dainty cakes were served with a tempting drink which resembled cocoa. Imagine our amazement to learn it was made with Lipton's tea with a large amount of cream and sugar!

That night there was a bed of coals in the firepan to keep us warm, so we rested well. The next morning we again went to the Tigi's place. He had received two vials of small-pox vaccine in a hollow bamboo case, and wanted Russell to vaccinate his household. Although Russell had never before vaccinated anyone, he knew how it was done and felt he could administer it as well as anyone else in town. At least, he had sterile cotton, gauze, alcohol, etc. With my help, he vaccinated the Tigi's son, brother, and five others. It took us two hours of careful work with the Tigi sitting through it all, an interested and sympathetic spectator. He offered to pay us for our labors and this gave us the opportunity to explain that our fellow Christians in America, in accordance with the life and spirit of Jesus Christ, had sent us into the Tibetan country to do such helpful work as this. He then asked us to please stay for dinner with him. Several different kinds of cakes, with "cocoa made from Lipton's tea" was first served. This was followed by the main course consisting of an excellently prepared "mien" — specially prepared noodles which are eaten with chopsticks, and four different kinds of side dishes. Even napkins were provided.

His Excellency had been out of Tibet only twice: a trip to Peking about twenty years previously, and his flight to India with the Dalai Lama when the British invaded Tibet. He must have observed some of the English dining manners while in India. He was also a very interesting conversationalist. He had been mayor of Lhasa for four years before coming to Markham Province and seemed to enjoy special favor with the supreme spiritual and temporal authorities of Tibet.

☦

It snowed that night and all the next day. Eugene and Robert were delighted as it had snowed only once in the nearly four years we had been in Batang. Because of the weather the Tigi let us stay "home". However, Russell did go out to visit three men who had been flogged for being drunk and fighting while looking after the Tigi's horses. The old father of two of them had come to beg Russell to doctor their wounds.

"We don't know what will become of us," he said, "because we have no one else to support us or help us, only our sons."

The older boy had been given one hundred fifty lashes, the younger boy fifty lashes and a kinsman one hundred.

Although the Chinese custom was to strike with a heavy paddle across the back of the upper leg, the Tibetans punished by whipping across the back of the knees while the culprit was lying prostrate. It was terrible punishment either way and the victims often died as a result of lack of after care, which resulted in infection and caused the bruised flesh to slough off. In severe cases, sometimes as much as a pound of flesh was lost.. Of those who recovered, a large number had to go limping through life with one or both legs crooked because they could not bear to straighten their legs while recovering from their wounds. Russell felt that the boy who received the one hundred fifty lashes would be one of those. All he could do for that poor boy was to dope his wounds with potassium permanganate solution to keep down infection, paint the surrounding area with iodine, plaster his wounds with healing ointments, then commit him to the merciful Father above who can even bring good out of evil. Russell sometimes felt so frustrated when confronted with serious illnesses or injuries and such a lack of medical supplies. It semed that schools in America should have courses in simple medicine and surgery for missionaries going to isolated parts of the world.

We were told that this Tigi was much less severe in his punishments than the former one had been. The dried human hands hanging in front of the Dzong (government building) had been cut off by order of that former official. Other forms of punishment might be to cut off the arms, legs, ears, noses, lips, and tongues, to pluck out eyes and break hands, besides the various forms of spanking and whipping. The taking of life was forbidden by the Buddist religion and by the decree of the Dalai Lama, but any other form of punishment could be administered. However, since this new Civil Governor had taken office, there had been only one other severe punishment.

✞

October 18, with all the country covered with a dazzling coat of snow, we put on our dark glasses for a ride out into the valley, with an escort to guide us. North of Gartok we saw a large lamasery which was only partially built. Because of a decree by the Dalai Lama that no one should cause stones and clay to "work" for three years, this lamasery had remained unfinished for almost that long. All of the buildings in Gartok, as well as elsewhere, were falling into disrepair because of that decree. Even the Tigi had taken quarters outside of the Dzong which were less commodious but far safer.

At 11:00 o'clock the Tigi sent a messenger to ask us to come and take pictures and then have dinner with him. The front yard had been entirely cleared of snow and we got some excellent pictures. We were shown over the residence, with its large and busy front yard. There were also three enormous Tibetan mastiffs as well as a long-tailed monkey and two spotted rabbits brought from the French Catholic priest's place in Yengin. Inside, the Tigi had a large collection of religious paintings, numerous cages of wild birds and five parrots on their perches.

We had expected to leave Gartok the next day but the Tigi insisted on our staying over to see his mounted militia on parade. He wanted us to take pictures to send to Lhasa as there had been no one to take any since Dr. Shelton's visit five years before. We counted sixty-two soldiers, all armed with Enfield rifles from India. There must have been no better in all the Orient than those Tibetans with their British military equipment and training.

We finally returned to Bangdat on October 20, a nice sunny day. There was a lot of snow on Do-ee La pass and the trip from there to Bangdat was rather cold. Eugene and Robert were all bundled up and hugged tight in front of us in the saddles, so they didn't seem to suffer, but my feet were frostbitten.

Soon after our arrival at Bangdat we met three Tibetans who had just arrived from Batang. They gave us the sad news that the buckwheat and millet crops were almost a total failure due to the very early and heavy frost. We knew this failure would take away half a year's food supply. Buh Ra-Ga had asked us to wait another day or two before leaving for Batang to give him time to find pack and riding horses for us. We took this opportunity to try to buy several thousand rupees worth of barley to help rescue the Batang folks from starvation. But the Bangdat people could not promise any.

On October 22 we were all packed and ready to go but Buh Ra-Ga said he had not been able to get all the horses together, saying, "Oh, please stay another day. What difference does just one day make, anyway?" These Orientals simply do not treasure their time as westerners do. Finally, on October 24 we started off to Batang. We were threatened with another delay because three of our mules had wandered off during the night, but we left anyway, accompanied by our Tibetan friends. We left Ah-Kay to bring us the remaining three loads.

Our Bangdat friends "saw us off" according to the most delightful Tibetan custom. They sent men ahead to a nice, park-like place along our road to build a fire and prepare cocoa brought from Lhasa. Here we stopped and had a farewell chat with Buh Ra-Ga, after which they bade us rise and placed white silk Katas upon our shoulders as a token of parting in friendship, and with best wishes.

Our first night on the way home was spent in a big house in upper Bamutang. The Bamutang people were very downhearted because the Ro-mee Tibetans had made a raid just a few days before and had driven off several thousand sheep, about a thousand yak, dri and zoh, along with several scores of horses and mules.

✝

October 25 we stayed in the headman's house in Kang-seh-ding, about a Sabbath Day's journey from where we stayed in Bamutang. Our host begged Russell to sell him a box of foreign matches. When Russell offered him a box of Chinese matches, he said, "No, I want to make gunpowder to protect my home and the Chinese matches won't do". They barricaded all their windows with stones as protection against attack from the Ra Nah Lama's renegades. They told us not to go outside of the house during the night as all the houses have guards, with orders to shoot any prowlers on sight.

The next night we camped in the "brush" on the south side of the Yangtze River about half way between Gonra and Drubalong. When the dogs suddenly began to bark, our Tibetans said that the thieves were probably prowling around. There were seven in our party, with as many guns, and they decided to issue a "manifesto" to any prowlers that might be around. One of our muleteers was a Tibetan from the badlands of Markham and he got up and "broadcast" a warning in language such as we had never heard before! All the guns were then fired off, and our "warriors" joined in the Tibetan war-whoop. Evidently that was effective for we experienced no disturbance during the night.

As we neared the end of this fantastic journey, more than ever we were convinced of the inexpressibly deep need of the Tibetan people for the Gospel. Even the hearts of some of the lamas of the Nyima sect were open to it. But we realized that Tibet was closed to direct missionary work because of the jealous fears of the priestly class which governed the land at that time. Short journeys into Tibet, of an unostentatiously evangelistic nature might be permitted once each year or two. However, we could see no hope of establishing mission stations there any time soon. Meanwhile, great numbers of Tibetans and tribespeople of Tibetan origin and religion were waiting to be evangelized in Chinese Tibet, and in the provinces of Szechuan and Yunnan. Great fields for missionary work, much more densely populated than Tibet, had been completely overlooked as a result of the sensational motto "On to Lhasa". We, too, were eager for the evangelization of the "hermit kingdom" but we could not forget that the Shepherd's love was just as great for those "other sheep".

On the evening of October 28, 1925, we arrived back in Batang. During this trip we had experienced much less in the way of physical difficulties and hardships than we had anticipated —in fact, a great deal less than we had been warned to expect. This was largely due to the kindness and help of the many friends the Lord had given us among the Tibetans. All things considered, we felt our trip into Tibet had been a successful one.

8
A Difficult Decision

When we arrived back in Batang, imagine our amazement upon learning that the Wohrley and Emerson families were preparing to leave. They had even given away or sold many of their possessions already. This news came as quite a shock to us, because we had planned for a long time to go together to a new mission post.

While we were away the Board had met and decided it would be too dangerous to start another outpost at either Yengin or Atuntze. They said it would be easier to protect all of the missionaries in one place. Needless to say, we were bitterly disappointed. We talked at length with Dr. Wohrley and Mr. Emerson, trying to persuade them to stay awhile longer, feeling sure our dream of a new station would soon be realized. However, they had already sent in their resignations and the mission had voted to accept them, so there was nothing any of us could do.

With heavy hearts, we resumed our regular missionary duties of evangelizing and teaching. Because of the unsettled conditions in that part of the country, itinerating was curtailed. I continued visiting and evangelizing among the women patients in the hospital and in their homes. I also had my work with the Sunday school class on Sunday morning and taught a women's Bible class on Sunday afternoons. I found out by accident that one of my women and her children were going without food in order for her to attend class. Each day that she worked, she was given enough food for her family, instead of money, but when she didn't work, there was no food. So she went without food in order to attend class each week! By December, 1925, attendance at the Tibetan Sunday school averaged around one hundred and seventy with the lowest at one hundred and forty-eight, and the highest at one hundred eighty-eight.

Russell sometimes brought some of his Tibetan friends home for dinner, and to talk about Jesus and the Bible. One evening, we invited sixteen Chinese Christian men for dinner and religious discussions and Russell was greatly pleased to hear one say to another, "He is so much like Dr. Shelton". Nothing could have pleased him more.

The day before Christmas, six hundred and forty-seven of the poor people of Batang were given a good dinner and a real good Gospel sermon by our chief evangelist. The crops had not been good and they had very little to eat. On Christmas day, a program was given in the large school room at the school building. There was singing by both natives and missionaries. One of the older missionary children told a Bible story in Tibetan. Then, the story of Joseph was dramatized by nineteen of our intermediate boys. The story of Jesus was retold by Lee Gway Gwang. He also gave a very good dramatization of The Prodigal Son to the audience of six or seven hundred people. He had a special talent for such things.

One day each week, Russell and one of the native evange-lists, along with some of the boys from his Sunday school class, went to two villages north of Batang, and another day to two villages south of Batang to preach about Jesus. The boys loved to go with him on his trips in the countryside. He wanted them to become accustomed to meeting crowds of people, and to singing and witnessing before them. He believed this was a good way to train and develop capable and effective native evangelists. He also arranged picnics, participated in boxing matches, and did many other things interesting to teenagers anywhere. His group of young people was modeled somewhat after the Christian Endeavor group he had led as a young man in his home church.

✞

In January of 1926, we were delighted to meet a Tibetan who was really interested in knowing about God. Russell first saw him at the mission clinic when our Tibetan evangelist, Tu-de-bao, was preaching to the Tibetan patients. He was listening very intently to what was said. Russell also noticed that he looked different in both dress and face from the others. He was about thirty-five years old and seemed well educated. After the service, Russell talked with him and found that this Tibetan had heard some religious teaching in China. In his hand he carried a spear-headed pilgrim staff with a prayer flag flying from the top of it. His home was about twenty-five days walk east of Batang. He said that, although he was a lama of the Nyi-ma sect, he had never lived in a lamasery because he did not approve of the irreligious and wicked practices of many of the monks in the lamaseries. One time at Tachienlu he had received some tracts and other Christian literature which were in the Tibetan language that he could read. Evidently, at that time his heart was not quite ready for the Gospel message, so he set out on a pilgrimage to Lhasa, the capital of Tibet. This pilgrimage was a difficult journey of nearly three months from his home.

He had a problem which weighed heavily on his heart. In his youth, he had killed a man. He decided to go to the noted Potala Temple in Lhasa to give a sacrifice that he might be forgiven, but even here he did not find the peace he longed for. He went to many noted Buddhist temples in India and stayed there several months. During that time, he became ill and had to go to a hospital, which was operated by a Christian mission. The short gospel messages he heard there every day helped him, but still he was not satisfied. Even so, he was not yet ready to turn away from Buddhism, and in a final effort to find peace, he made a pilgrimage around the great sacred snow mountain,

Kawa Gabo, across the Mekong River from Atuntze. Again he failed to find the peace he was seeking, but after all these long pilgrimages he was finally convinced that Buddhism was a false religion, which offered him no hope. Then he began to remember the Christian messages he had heard and the tracts he had been given. He decided to visit the missionaries in Batang and seek further information about Christianity. Upon his arrival he developed a headache and went to the mission hospital for medicine. That was when Russell first met him. After their many discussions, Russell commented that this man had a greater spiritual understanding than any Tibetan he had ever met.

In the days ahead, our Pilgrim Tibetan went with Russell on his weekly preaching trips to the surrounding villages near Batang and made remarkable progress in knowledge of the Bible. Russell and Tu-de-bao instructed him more fully in the Scriptures and found him a very apt pupil. He seemed to have a spiritual insight and intelligence, as well as power of character that was rarely found among those people. He came to our house to read the New Testament with us day after day. The most encouraging thing of all was the earnestness and ability with which he proclaimed the one God and His Son, Jesus Christ, among the Tibetans of Batang as he met them personally. He even learned the hymns and their tunes.

We prayed for him to be really and soundly converted, and to give his own life to Jesus. At last, the precious seed of the Gospel found fertile soil in his heart. He not only believed, but vowed to preach about the Truth of Christ thereafter. He witnessed on the streets of Batang with other Tibetans about this Truth.

He said that he could not have peace until he was baptized, as is taught in the New Testament; but first, he wanted to go home and explain this to his people. Then, before we realized it, he was gone and we never heard more of him. When he left, he was determined to return and help us in our mission work wherever we were. Because of his open expressions of his belief in Christ as his Saviour on the streets of Batang, we feared he might have been ambushed and lost his life on his long trip through the mountains to his home at Tachien-lu. But the Gospel seed had been planted, and we prayed for his safety and salvation.

✟

We realized, finally, that the opening of a new station by the Batang Mission was out of the question for years to come. We thought of those vast territories, densely populated, but with no opportunity to hear the Gospel. We gave months of prayerful thought to this matter, and considered the sacrifices which would be involved. We knew there would be no doctor at or anywhere near any new location we might choose. Then, too, I remembered the struggle I had in learning Tibetan when my health was poor, and in the light of my continuing frequent attacks of malaria, the thought of having to learn another new language was almost overwhelming. But in spite of these things, we decided that we could DO MORE for the Kingdom of God by resigning and going into new work elsewhere.

On January 20, 1926, we sent in our resignation. Dr. Osgood, the U.C.M.S. representative, asked us to reconsider, and we did so for almost three months. We finally realized, however, that we could not withdraw our resignation and AT THE SAME TIME keep our ideals of Christian service. We had come to this remote land to preach the Gospel and win souls for Christ, regardless of any dangers. We had God's promise of protection and were not afraid. WE KNEW WE MUST GO. On April 27, we sent a letter to Dr. Osgood reaffirming our resignation and asking that it be accepted. This was finally done.

We believed with all our hearts that the Lord led us to Batang, but we believed just as strongly that He was now leading us out into an extension of His Kingdom. We did not at all regret the nearly five years we had spent at Batang, for they were a preparation for the far greater usefulness which we hoped and expected to experience in this new field.

Our Tibetan and Chinese friends were so very good to us, and gave us meat, eggs, fruit, nuts, mien (noodles) etc. Three families invited us to dinner. A group of eight Chinese secretaries and other influential men invited us to a Chinese feast. The military commander, who resided in Batang, also invited us to another feast.

We received many gifts, including nine Tibetan rings, two of which were quite expensive, a string of corals, two strings of seed pearls and a silver string. Twenty-two Chinese men presented Russell and me with six scrolls beautifully written in gold. They were complimentary, telling of our purpose in coming to Batang, of our learning the language, and of our success in the work. Russell seemed to think more of those than he did of his diploma. The scrolls were brought to our house on trays, and upon arriving at our yard, they shot off fire crackers and then the men all came in and presented them to us. They were especially for Russell, but they included me, too. So far as we know, nothing like this had ever been done for any other foreigners.

We had tried to be good missionaries, and gave God the praise and glory for any success we had. Mr. Ogden said, with tears in his eyes, "I hope you will not give up Tibetan work. No one else has gotten the language any better than you folks have in the time you have been here." With all this kindness, and with our love for the Tibetans, it was really very hard to leave Batang.

So the precious days with our dear Tibetan Christians and friends drew to a close. How our hearts ached in leaving them. We had prayed for God's guidance and we believed that He wanted us to go and minister to those who were asking, — even BEGGING — us to teach them the Gospel. So, we felt we had to leave. We recalled that even the Apostle Paul did not stay and teach in one place for a long time, but preached a while and then left the believers in the hands of elders and went to new places. We, too, had found new places which needed to hear the Gospel.

A Difficult Decision

We succeeded in hiring riding horses and pack animals for our departure. The night before we left, all our Tibetan friends came and sang and danced all night according to Tibetan custom. It was their last time of fellowship, and their last chance to show their love and appreciation for us. The next day, September 27, 1926, when our food boxes and bedrolls were packed, we took leave of our house and our dear neighbors, all of whom were weeping.

With sad hearts, we crossed the little Batang River for the last time, and got on the main road. As we went around the curve of the mountain, we saw several tents pitched beside the road where the civil and the military officials, with other Chinese friends, were waiting to bid us goodby. As we approached, they began shooting off firecrackers, as is the Chinese custom. We stopped there a few minutes to bid them farewell. Next, there was a long line of missionaries, the native evangelists, teachers, orphans and school children. After that, we found our many Tibetan friends waiting along the way for several miles. Our neighbor and missionary friend, Marion H. Duncan, and our Tibetan teacher, Ah Trin, went with us to the top of the pass where Dr. Shelton was killed, about six miles out. Kam Ling, a good Tibetan friend, went with us all the way to Atuntze as our guide. Being familiar with the country, he was able to lead us over a better and shorter route. So ended the first stage of our missionary life.

9
A Trip to the Dentist

Since the American Consul had given permission to open a mission post at Atuntze, we planned to leave our baggage there with our cook, his wife, Duje, and their two daughters. We arrived in Atuntze October 10, 1926, after fourteen days of traveling, then spent three days finding a place to rent and getting everything settled.

Russell needed dental work done as soon as possible, but he did not want to leave the boys and me in a strange village. Some good missionary friends at Wei Hsi (way-shee), a ten-day trip by horse from Atuntze, had invited the children and me to stay there while Russell was gone. We decided that would be the best thing to do, so we took with us cots, bedding, cooking utensils, and other things we would need for light housekeeping. Our cook's wife, Duje, came along to assist me. Wood had to be gathered and cut, for cooking over an open fire, water carried, washing done by hand, etc., as modern conveniences were unknown in that part of the country. We left Atuntze October 14, and arrived in Wei Hsi on October 23. All of the missionaries seemed happy to welcome us.

One of the new missionary families was living in a large, new two-story building, which was partially unoccupied. They very graciously offered two large rooms for our use. One problem was that in that area there was a near-famine situation. There was no milk to be had, and that was hard on the children. We were able sometimes to get Tibetan butter, which had

97

quite a few yak hairs in it, and tasted like cheese. We were able to buy flour, cornmeal, rice, eggs, and occasionally some meat. However, in spite of difficulties, I was happy to be near Christian friends with whom I could have good fellowship. There was a nice yard where the boys could play. Sometimes I took them to a nearby grassy mountain to play while I studied and outlined some Bible work. And so the days passed!

Russell was anxious to make the trip to Kunming as quickly as possible so we could start our new mission station. He and Kam Ling, our guide from Batang, left Wei Hsi December 1, 1926, and made the hard, dangerous trip to Kunming in just twenty-eight days.

The Japanese dentist in Kunming gave Russell a general anesthetic, but, after one full hour was able to extract only five teeth. Two foreign missionaries who were medical doctors, advised him to go to the British endowed Matilda Hospital in Hong Kong at once. He was utterly heartsick to think of leaving his family for the long time it would take to go so far away, and of course such a trip involved a lot of expense. However, God greatly comforted him with His many promises.

He made arrangements at once to go on the little narrow-gauge French railway to Haiphong in Indo-China (now North Vietnam) and left January 2, 1927. This part of the trip took four days. From Haiphong, he took a small steamer and arrived in Hong Kong in three days. It is a long story, but God daily comforted him. "We must, through much tribulation, enter into the Kingdom of God."

The doctor in charge of Matilda Hospital was very good to Russell, and had him stay in the hospital all during the entire twenty-two days it took to finish having his dental work done and to get his new dentures. He left Hong Kong for Haiphong on January 31, 1927.

Russell made the trip from Hong Kong to Haiphong on board the small steamer, "Tonkin". On the ship, he met the Magistrate of Kunming and also a very friendly English-speaking Frenchman. This Frenchman was extremely helpful in getting Russell through French customs with almost no delay and at no cost. It was the Chinese New Year and customs were officially closed for several days, but with this man's help, Russell was able to get through the "red tape" and quickly leave Haiphong for Kunming.

✝

Kam Ling, Russell's traveling companion, was waiting when he arrived in Kunming. Together they went to find several pack animals; then, to buy food supplies and other necessities. Fortunately Russell already had changed his Hong Kong paper money into Yunnan silver money. After three weeks, he was finally able to start the long trip home on March 2. However before leaving Kunming he went to see the military official and obtained a travel pass which helped him through many potentially dangerous situations, especially during the first two weeks of his trip back to Wei Hsi. Russell wrote about that trip to friends in America::

"On leaving Kunming, I felt much like the Israelites leaving Egypt for the promised land. I felt a deep assurance that the time had come, although I didn't know just how a way would be opened through the Red Sea. Well, I stepped out and when we got to the "Red Sea", the way opened up.

"At Pi-che-gwan, about ten miles west of Kunming, I was held up for about an hour by soldiers of General L'ong who was the chief 'rebel' against Governor T'ang. I might have gotten into a lot of trouble here if the Lord hadn't given me victory in my heart, so that I could face everything in undisturbed serenity of mind and with manifest friendliness toward the soldiers. Having a special pass from General L'ong and being able to speak Chinese as well as Tibetan, helped me get through without having my boxes opened and many of my things confiscated.

"We arrived at Anning-cheo (pronounced Ah-ning-jeo) about two hours after dark on a cold, windy and moonless night where we slept upstairs over the stable. The muleteer had come in and announced that the local authorities were about to commandeer

*our pack animals to take things to the troops at Pi-che-gwan. I was
too tired and sleepy to get out of bed, so I told him to insist that we
had a special letter from General L'ong. Our horses were not com-
mandeered, so we went the next day to Lao-yao-gwan, near where
Dr. Shelton had been kidnapped. This place had been wholly
burned the year before by bandits. Upon our arrival, we noticed
quite a stir in the town and were none too happy to learn that a
band of about 200 robbers were camped about five miles away and
were expected to attack the town during the night. The military
commander assured me that we could take refuge in the "ying-
p'an" (fort), but I declined. However, I did sleep in all my clothes
except my boots, ready for any emergency. I must confess that I slept
fairly well; but some of the Tibetans with me lay awake. They told
me of hearing troops marching through the town during the night
going toward Kunming to take part in the revolution. Perhaps
that hindered the robbers from attacking the town.*

*"The next day, at Lu Fong, we heard that the next town, Shay-
tsi, had just been attacked and burned and that it might still be
occupied by the bandits. Here I faced the prospect of either being
delayed several days, going on half way to Shay-tsi and then having
to return to Lu-Fong, or just taking my chances on pressing on to
Shay-tsi with the "expeditionary forces" the next day. I wondered
whether I would ever see my beloved Gertrude and Eugene and
Robert again. But God gave me peace in my heart and I told the
military commander that I would try to go as far as his troops
could go. He said I could do so if I would pay him $35.00 Yunnan
paper money, (eqiv. to about U.S.$7.50).*

*"We started out the next morning with an escort of about 160
soldiers. About half way to Shay-tsi, a man came with the news
that there was a band of robbers ahead. This made me curious as I
have always heard so much about robbers in China, but have never
been an actual eyewitness to a fight between them and the soldiers.
I had been an "ear" witness several times at Batang. Well, the
escort rushed to the top of a ridge a few hundred yards ahead of the
caravan. There was a lot of shouting, above which several shots were
heard, and the soldiers did some skirmishing around. Since we
couldn't see anything we went into a hut and prepared a bit of
dinner.*

"After dinner, with the soldiers going on before, we plodded through the heat and dry dust to Shay-tsi and found only ten or twelve of the largest houses in the center of town had been burned. We learned that the other troops had come up, and that we could find a clean barn loft to sleep in. The streets were littered with wreckage, several of the townspeople had been killed, and a dozen or more had been taken off to be kept for ransom. Believe me, we were glad to get away from that district early next morning. Thank God for the delay of my departure from Kunming, for I can now see what I missed. He orders our "stops" as well as our steps, don't you think?"

✝

On March 29, 1927 a messenger came from Russell saying that he would be arriving the next day. We were all so thankful to God for bringing him back for we had prayed long for his safe return. God was so good to us all. The next morning, Eugene, Robert and I walked a long way to meet their Daddy. He had been gone for four months and we had missed him so much. But oh! when we saw how thin his face was, we almost cried. The removal of his teeth, and the long and strenuous journey, had taken their toll. He was extremely happy to be back home again with the family.

He told us about one upsetting experience he had on the way from Kunming to Wei Hsi. At one of his stops, he was very weary and quickly retired. His gums were still sore, so he removed his precious dentures and laid them on a small table beside his bed. When he reached to pick them up the next morning, to his dismay they were not there! and his heart sank within him. He looked every place in his little room, but couldn't find them anywhere. He called Kam Ling to help him search for them. They searched the room again and went through all of his things, but still no dentures! As a last resort, they moved out the simple bed, then carefully searched inch by inch along the crack, where the mud walls met the floor, and finally discovered a small rat hole. When Kam Ling dug down to the bottom, there were the dentures! Russell said that after all the misery he had endured, plus all the expense, and the strain of having to spend such a long and lonely time away from his family, he was ready to tear that place apart if he had to, in order to find his dentures. He was indeed happy and praised the Lord that he had found them. Although we have laughed about it many times since then, it was anything but funny at the time.

The children were so happy to have their daddy back home We were all anxious to hear all about his trip and the dangers he had encountered. He said, "There have been many roaring lions along the way, but as we came to them, we found them all chained. Not one of God's promises have failed". Duje, our cook, had prepared a nice dinner for that evening, and we truly had a "Day of Thanksgiving".

While Russell rested for about a week, we read the many letters from loved ones and dear friends, expressing their love and encouragement. They were surely helpful in the long journey into the hard field. We were still very happy in our decision to start a new station either at Atuntze, or some other place between Atuntze and Wei hsi, although the American Consul was trying to discourage us from going back to Atuntze. We were anxious to get started and do our very best for God so that we would have no regrets when our life's work was ended. We were both learning to walk day by day in faith, looking unto God.

✞

Yunnan Province, in which we were now located, was almost independent with a government all its own. The Governor was practically a military dictator, but was very friendly to Christian missionaries and other foreigners. Of course there was always the possibility of some other power taking over. Our work was to be in the northwestern part of Yunnan. The pure Chinese were in the minority, and work would be mostly among the various tribes who lived in the region. We decided to go as far as Yea Chi, a four-day journey toward Atuntze. We left April 15, but because of heavy rains, it took us eight days instead of four. We surveyed the territory around Yea Chi for a possible location for a new mission post.

Then on April 27 we received some shattering news. A special runner arrived from the missionaries at Wei Hsi bringing the following communique, dated April 4th, from the British Consulate at Kunming:

> In my previous notification I recommended that British subjects in the interior should be prepared to leave by the shortest route when it should become necessary for me to advise such a course. I regret to say that that time has now arrived. I have received telegraphic instructions from our ambassador in Peking — 'It is pointed out that a peaceful local situation and promises of protection by local authorities are NO justification for disregarding this intimation, and if people persist in staying up-country after receiving it, they do so at their own risk and incur a heavy responsibility.' I have, therefore, to request you to convey this information to the members of your mission, and I cannot too strongly urge them to withdraw at once by the safest route."

Russell hastened to forward this notification to Batang and to our French friends at Tse Drong (*Tsay Drong*). We had previously been notified that our American Consul had been called to Peking and had authorized the British Consul to see to American interests until his return to Kunming. He had also appointed executives of Standard Oil Company and the Y.M.C.A. as a committee to aid the British Consul.

As we were considering and praying about all of these conditions, we read in our "Daily Light": "As I was with Moses, so I will be with thee; I will not fail thee nor forsake thee. Be strong and of good courage". We decided we should proceed to Tse Drong, a Catholic center two and one half days' journey from Yea Chi. We crossed the Mekong River on a rope bridge and went to the Catholic Mission where Father Ouvrard lived. The children and I stayed there while Russell returned to Atuntze for possessions we had left there. These were all brought down to Tse Drong. where we could store them.

It was so hard to delay our hopes and dreams of starting a new mission station. But we were again comforted and encouraged by the words of Joshua 1:9: "...be strong and of good courage; be not afraid, neither be thou dismayed; for the Lord thy God is with thee whithersoever thou goest".

10
Our Jungle Journey Begins

On May 10, 1927, we were joined by two other missionary families, Mr. and Mrs. J. Clifford Morrison of Canada with their two babies, ages two years and thirteen months, and Mrs. Mary E. Lewer a widow with two small children ages six years and two years. These two families had left Wei Hsi about May 3rd, led by Mr. E. G. Barton, an English adventurer who happened to be in Wei Hsi at the time. The Morrisons were expecting their third child and Mrs. Morrison was quite ill for most of the hazardous journey.

After conferring with the other missionaries, Father Ouvrard, some of the Tibetans and Mr. Barton, who seemed to have some knowledge of the territory, we decided upon the almost unknown route from Tse Drong over the Himalayan Mountains to Fort Hertz (an English government outpost; formerly called Hkamti Long — later called Putao) in Upper Burma. Mr. Barton said he thought it should take no more than three weeks to reach Fort Hertz, where additional supplies could be obtained, and from there we could go on to the beginning of the Burma Railway at Myitkyina (pronounced Mitch-e-nah).

The course we chose would lead us through tangled subtropical jungles, over great snow-covered mountains, across swollen and often unbridged streams, and through a no-man's-land in which primitive tribespeople were a law unto themselves. But we had no alternative, as other routes were either closed or dangerously infested with bandits.

We began the arduous task of repacking for the long journey across the Salween River gorge, and two high mountain passes into Burma. Each pack had to be carefully weighed to be sure it was within the limits for carrier loads. The proper number of carriers had to be engaged through the native headman, Ganton, who went along as coolie boss. Ganton, a shrewd, seemingly frail, always cheerful old fellow, was a Nashi-Tibetan who spoke a number of languages, and he promised to go as far as possible — at least to the Salween Valley. He had been a guide and interpreter for Capt. F. Kingdon Ward, of the Royal Geographical Society of England, who was one of only two white men to have ever made the dangerous journey across Upper Burma — and that was in the dry season. The other was Prince Henry of Orleans, who had blazed the way thirty-four years earlier.

Carriers were recruited from the surrounding areas — a few Chinese, but mostly Tibetans. All the helpers were new to us except Ah-sam, who had been helping us for about two weeks. Sixty carriers started with us, with an extra man for every five, to carry their food, bedding and other essentials. We hoped we could hire others from villages along the way to replace any wanting to leave.

Large round bamboo baskets were prepared for each child to ride in, to be carried by specially sturdy and reliable Tibetans. Each had a seat in the center, and a bow across the top of the basket to hold an oiled sheet for protection from the rain. Light hwagans were made for the women, consisting of a bamboo woven chair swung between two poles held on the shoulders of the carriers.

There was some controversy over whether to take horses. It was settled by taking them, with some Tibetans to help with their care. We could not even imagine country through which we could not take horses.

✝

On May 23, 1927, after a cordial farewell to all of those who had been so kind to us, we set out. Had we known all that lay before us, our courage might have failed, for the misery of the constant monsoon rain storms, flooded streams, and muddy trails was truly beyond imagination. We had been having nice sunshiny weather for the last ten days, but a drizzle of rain began upon our departure and continued most of the day.

The Mekong River here flows at an altitude of about 6,000 feet, at least a thousand feet lower than the Yangtze which flows on the other side of the high range. Few had been privileged to climb the towering ranges separating the mightiest streams of China, if not of Asia. According to geologists, the whole region was once one vast, high plateau, now intersected and eroded by some of the longest rivers in the world. The Yangtze, the Mekong and the Salween all have their origin in the high plateau land of Tibet. They cut through 20,000-foot-high mountain ranges, flow parallel, north to south for some distance in western China, at one place within forty-eight miles of each other as the crow flies. As Captain Ward said, "It's not very far as the crow flies, but a long way if that crow had to walk". Yet, the mouths of these great rivers are separated by thousands of miles. The Yangtze, mightiest and longest of them all, flows parallel to the Mekong for many miles. After making a huge loop, it becomes part of a boundary for the provinces of Yunnan and Szechuan, and eventually enters the Pacific Ocean at Shanghai. The Mekong parallels the Salween for a great distance then forms the border of Burma, Thailand and Indo-China (that part now called Laos, in the area now known as the "Golden Triangle"), and enters the tropical South China Sea near Saigon, in Vietnam. The Salween, after flowing a long distance within Tibet, forms the border between Burma and Thailand, then empties into the Indian Ocean near Moulmein, Burma.

We three missionary women were the first white women ever to cross this indescribable region, and our children were the first white children to make this trip..

We traveled through a forest of pine, yew, maple, mountain ash, birch and some other huge trees we could not identify. As the chill of evening fell over the valley, we entered into the snow line with scattered patches of snow among the trees and rocks. Mr. Barton had gone ahead to check the condition of a "rest house" built by the Catholic Priest. We found him trying to overhaul the debris of what had at one time been a hut. It was hopeless, and as the drizzle of rain set in again, we found some firm ground on which to pitch our tents. Russell laid down sticks and stones as a protection from the muddy ground, piled our loads on this, and covered all with oiled sheeting.

Our carriers went away to find places to sleep — some in hollow trees, or under trees, some among the rock or roots of some of the larger trees. This was their custom for the balance of the trip.

There was rain, mixed with some snow, most of the night, which got into our tent and on our clothing. It was miserable putting this damp clothing on the children and ourselves. Dry firewood was very hard to find, either for drying clothes or for cooking breakfast. And it was still raining. This became our way of life, more or less, for the remainder of this miserable, agonizing trip which proved to be of 70 days' duration.

The carriers were late and it was noon before we broke camp, with a long and strenuous climb before us. The snow became deeper and the horses struggled through the drifts. The hwagans could not be carried in the snow so the women had to walk, with two guides helping them much of the time. We climbed up the snowy cliffs and waded through snow drifts up to our knees. The carriers with light loads went ahead to break a path through the snow for the heavier burdened ones, as well as for the horses and the rest of us.

The walls of the valley rose in sheer cliffs upon both sides. We were in constant danger from avalanches, and from time to time we could see and hear these great snow slides pouring over the precipices like great waterfalls.

About an hour before sunset, only a few hundred yards before the timber line ended, we came to a leaky hut. Mr. Barton and some of the Tibetans were scooping snow from the roof and low entrance. He said, "Come in and make yourselves at home". We did — much to our regret. The fire which he had kindled filled the hut with smoke and melted the snow on the roof. The dirt floor became muddier and muddier from the leaking roof, so we, the Morrisons, and Mrs. Lewer pitched our tents in the open, upon the snow, tying them between nearby trees. Pine branches on the floor of the tent formed a carpet over the snow. A log fire just outside of the tent warmed our feet somewhat, but it was imposssible to get really warm..

✝

We broke camp early the next morning in dreadful anticipation of what lay before us. Before nightfall, we must cross the great Si La pass, where the very high altitude brings on terrific cold. Viewed from our camp, there seemed no possible way up it. Yet, our Tibetan carriers said there would be a way. So we plodded on. Since the day before, we had been wearing our sunglasses to protect against snow-blindness. Some of the Tibetans had masks made of long, black yak hair, but others could only shield their faces with their arms.

Now we realized that there really were places where horses could not be taken. Their hoofs sank through the deep snow and they sank down and floundered about. Many men pulled and pushed, but, by noon, the horses were still less than a fourth of the way up to the pass. Mr. Morrison had succeeded in taking his little pony on, but the rest of the horses were left for the night in the care of some of the Tibetans in the shelter of a projecting rock.

From the Mekong, we had climbed about 10,000 feet to Si La pass, at an altitude of around 16,000 feet. From the top of the pass a breathtaking panorama was spread before us. Far below us on the west, lay the Ser-wa Lung-ba, the "Valley of Hail" which is narrow and extraordinarily deep. To the east, the crest of the Yangtze divide could be seen beyond the wooded valley by which we had ascended.

The climb to the pass had been difficult, but was as nothing when compared with the tortuous descent. It was very steep and covered with frozen snow from five to ten feet deep. We women had two guides each, one in front to chop out small "heel" holes, the other behind to hold our hand. One carrier slipped and went screaming down the slope at breakneck speed, rolling over and over. Suddenly his pack-load broke loose and shot on down the mountain and the poor Tibetan slowed down and came to a groaning halt in a pile of snow, after having rolled about a hundred yards. Russell examined him as soon as he could, and found he had no broken bones, but was just badly bruised. He arranged for him to be carried into camp, even if some loads had to be left on the mountain. This was only the first of many such falls.

✞

As evening fell, a bitterly cold wind blew up from the valley below. After what seemed like an eternity of suspense, we reached the snow covered, frozen Sewa River, which comes from an old glacier and flows directly into the Salween. We trudged several miles, on ice, down the valley to reach a "rest hut" of the Catholic priests. It was a dilapidated place just a little better than the one east of Si La. We divided off the one room for the three families and Mr. Barton. Because the altitude here was about 12,000 feet, we expected a very cold night, so we lighted fires in the room. It commenced to rain — an almost daily occurrence since this was the monsoon season. The roof leaked in places, and as the fire began melting the snow on the roof, new leaks sprung up. We spent a miserable night, holding umbrellas over the children and ourselves. All the bedding got wet, even though the cots were covered with oiled sheets. The next morning dawned clear, but it seemed a long time before the sunlight crept down the forested slope and reached the valley below.

What a sorry sight we were! Not one of us had escaped being fearfully red and swollen from sunburn and snowburn. The poor little children's tender faces suffered most, even though we had tried to protect them, for out of curiosity, they would expose themselves from time to time to see what was going on.

Ganton reported that all but about fifteen of the carriers were disabled by snow-blindness or other things, such as bruises from falls. His own eyes were so inflamed, he could hardly see. Russell went to see what he could do for them. They were scattered all through the woods, huddled up and shielding their eyes from the light. He put boric acid solution in their eyes, but could not imagine how they could possibly be well enough to go ahead the next day.

Ganton called the able-bodied carriers together and we promised them extra pay and the use of our sunglasses if they would go back and bring the pack-loads left at the top of the pass and various places on the mountainside. Also to bring the horses, if possible. They returned toward evening with the missing loads, but reported that the horses were gone and only the outfit for Mr. Morrison's pony was there to bring. Evidently, the Tibetans who had been left in charge of the horses had taken them back to Tse Drong which was just as well. We three women spent the day trying to dry clothing and bedding, whenever there was an hour or two that it wasn't raining.

Mr. Barton decided to go on ahead to the French Catholic compound at Bahang, where we expected to arrive the next day. Ganton warned him against it, but, when he could not dissuade him, instructed him as well as he could. At 4:00 P.M., Barton and his two Chinese coolies left.

✝

To our surprise, when morning arrived, all the Tibetans came to carry our loads. Five of them had slipped and taken that terrible fall down the slope from Si La Pass, but no one had broken any bones. We felt we had much for which to be thankful. Instead of following the Sewa to its junction with the Salween, we climbed the mountain west of it. The ascent was steep at first, but traveling became easier near the top. About noon, we reached the pass, which is called Nyi-ser Ri-go, meaning "top of the mountain of yellow bamboo". It was about 500 feet lower than Si La Pass. Most of the day we waded through snow up to our knees. The cold was almost unbearable.

As we looked beyond at those great, forbidding, snow-capped peaks between the Salween and upper Irrawaddy, across which we still must pass, we trembled and our hearts felt faint. We wondered if we would ever get home again — or if we might all die out there around some of those unknown passes. And what would happen to our children if we should die and they be left? We soon roused ourselves from such thoughts, though, and started on the final descent to Bahang. We were pleasantly surprised when we came out into a vastly different climate, where the air was balmy and the mountains about us were green. We could even see some fields on the mountainside. Then we saw on a knoll below us, the whitewashed buildings of Père André's Catholic Mission. As we drew close, we could distinguish Mr. Barton, and we were sure the long-bearded white man with him was Père André.

Soon we reached that haven of refuge, and were made to feel welcome. How wonderful it was to have a floor under our feet, a roof over our heads, a real fireplace and dry wood with which to cook, and even a place to wash and dry clothes. We had been so wet and so cold for five long, seemingly endless days! Eugene and Robert were so happy to get out of those baskets and go exploring around, while we arranged our pack-loads as they came in. They were fascinated by some white and yellow and black rabbits in a wire cage.

But there was more. We had scarcely gotten the boys bathed and dressed, when in came Père André to invite us to the evening meal. Such a meal! It was evident he had spared no effort, and surely he must have summoned all his knowledge of French cooking. He had used some local produce, but some other foods surely must have been imported from France. It was a lonely life he lived and visitors, — even non-Catholic Christian missionaries — were welcome. We experienced our first good night's rest since leaving Tse Drong. What a welcome breathing spell! We washed and dried clothing and bedding, dried and mended the wet and broken bamboo pack baskets. And we rested.

The mission station was built on a knoll 3,178 feet above the Salween, where the climate is never uncomfortably hot. Numerous native huts were scattered around over the countryside. Père André spoke Lutzu fluently and, of course, French, but could not understand English, Tibetan or Chinese. Therefore, Mr. Barton, with his knowledge of French was of considerable help as interpreter in making arrangements toward continuing our journey. We inquired about the road to Fort Hertz. Heartsick because of what we had already gone through, and awed by the terrific peaks yet before us, we wondered if we should stay here awaiting further developments in China, or if we should press on as speedily as possible. We were learning to sympathize with the children of Israel in their desire to return to the familiar places and things in Egypt! We decided to push on.

On Sunday, Père André sent us a leg of lamb, a cake and some delicious wild strawberries. Everything tasted so very good, especially after our diet of rice!

One of the great problems facing us here, and many times later, was that of engaging porters and interpreters. We were told we had no prospect of hiring carriers to go as far as Fort Hertz. We needed a Tibetan and a Chinese who could also speak Lutzu, Lisu, Nung and perhaps Kachin. Ganton more nearly filled that requirement than any other we had heard of and his insight and skill in dealing with the different native peoples was a wonder. But he was old and frail and had promised to go only as far as the Salween.

When we left Tse Drong, our Yunnan silver money, wrapped in packages of either $50 or $100 each, had been divided among various pack-loads. Russell now discovered one of the $100 parcels was missing. He thought it must have been lost during that awful descent from Si La Pass, when several carriers had fallen and their pack-loads had broken loose and went tumbling down the mountain. He discussed this with Ganton and they decided the man who was carrying the load was responsible and should go back to find it. Russell left it to Ganton, as coolie boss, to inform the carriers of their decision. A reward of $4.00 was offered to the finder. All payment was to be delayed until the money was found.

Sunday, May 29th was spent resting at Bahang. We certainly needed it. The Lutzu Catholics began to assemble early for mass and the courtyard was full by the time services began. They seemed to be a mild and friendly people. The priest shortened his religious service so he could have more time for visiting and conferring with Mr. Barton, the only one in our party who could speak French.

Monday, our third day in Bahang, was far from a day of rest. We needed to know how many fresh carriers could be recruited. Those who had obtained substitutes could be paid in full and excused to return home. Those who had not, were paid in part to assure their going on until we could find replacements. All of this had to be talked over between Ganton and Russell in Tibetan so the natives could understand and be sure their wages were not being "squeezed" by their coolie boss. Then Russell had to talk much of it over in English with other members of our party, and occasionally Mr. Barton had to confer with Père André in French. Our carrier finally returned with the missing $100 exactly as we had originally tied it up. He had also found two of Russell's books. Those honest people were surely worth being taught to become disciples of Christ the Savior.

Paying off the helpers was an arduous half day's work. They would accept nothing but Yunnan silver. Fortunately, Russell had exchanged all of his Hong Kong money for silver coins while in Kunming, but others had no silver money. Therefore Russell had to handle the "paying up", not only for our own men, but some for the Morrison's, others for Mrs. Lewer and several for Mr. Barton. Then there were some which we all shared.

Père André and Mr. Barton arranged for the head-man (Ko-ruh) of the Catholic village of Pon Dam to recruit twenty carriers and to meet us at the town of Sukin. He had made the journey to Fort Hertz once before and knew something of the languages to be spoken and difficulties which might be encountered en route.

11
Jungle Journey (continued)

On Tuesday, May 31, 1927, we were able to make an early start from Bahang. Père André gave us rabbits, a sheep, dry beans, etc., to augment our dwindling food supply. He was such a kind person and we were very grateful.

We descended 1600 ft. to the Doyon River, went down the valley for about five hours, then crossed the river on a bamboo bridge built by the priests. We passed numerous villages along the Doyon, which was a swift, broad river. We climbed over a high spur separating the Doyon from the Salween and came to the village of Pon Dam. Descending almost to the Salween, we saw a fertile little plain on the border of the river, dotted with a score or more Lutzu houses. The Catholic priest was building a new mission house which became the southernmost Catholic center in that region. We stayed that night on the unfinished second floor of that building.

✝

Now we were confronted with a new kind of obstacle. The Salween was in flood stage and there was no bridge. Investigation showed four dug-out canoes made from logs. The two larger ones were about twenty-five feet long, but only eighteen to twenty inches wide. We wanted to send our loads across that evening, but the Lutzus emphatically refused. They promised to try the next morning if there was no more rain that night. It did not rain and we were up at dawn carrying our loads to the river.

The morning was beautiful, but when we saw the long, slender boats and the mad, racing waters of the Salween, our hearts beat faster with trepidation at the thought of crossing that raging torrent. What mishap would befall us? We prayed that God would guide and steady the rowers of the boats. Those ferries were always made where there were two backwaters almost opposite each other. The boat was rowed and pulled up one backwater and into the shelter of a promontory beyond which the water rushed outward toward the middle of the stream. The boat was carefully guided into the swift stream from the top of the backwater, and then the fight was on. Carried rapidly downstream, the shouting and grunting rowers exerted prodigious efforts to get the boat into the backwater on the other side. With our hearts in our mouth we sat tensely still while water from the paddles splashed over us and the river came within three or four inches of the top of the boat. After midstream was passed we began to feel the upstream pull of the opposite backwater. Our hearts were filled with great thankfulness as we entered that haven and set foot on the opposite shore. It took many trips to get our entire party and all of our loads and carriers to the other side, but the crossing was made without mishap. Mr. Morrison's pony swam the river.

After crossing the river we discovered that one of our aluminum canteens was missing. This was serious since we would soon enter the fever-ridden jungles of Upper Burma where we would need boiled water, and our remaining canteen would not hold enough water for our children. We realized that we had no recourse but to trust in God and go forward.

✠

Some of the Lutzu carriers recruited from Pon Dam were young women. The way they carried their loads, — supporting them with a strap around the forehead, or with a kind of wooden yoke fitted over the shoulders, — was a new sight to us. They walked along with their hands free to twist hemp fiber into thread for cloth. One end of the fiber was held between

117

the teeth, while they used their hands to split, twist and join the small strips together. From time to time they would take a new supply from a cloth bag in which their food was also carried. We learned that the hemp thread was used there for many things beside cloth, such as rope, and strings for their crossbows. When the girls were not so occupied they simply clasped their hands behind their heads to better balance themselves, and pattered on in their bare feet. The clothing of both men and women was made from either hemp or cotton, very drab and uninteresting. One distinctive item of wear was their leggings, which were strips of hemp cloth wrapped around their legs as a protective measure against insect bites.

We climbed high above the Salween around one ridge after another. The weather was nice and our hearts were light. The Tibetans sang in their high melodious fashion, and their voices echoed and re-echoed across the valley. They could be heard a mile away. There was a romantic air about it which would haunt us for a long, long time.

At dusk we arrived at a small Lisu village and pitched our tents beside the river. We sent Ah-Sam to the village to try to buy meat or vegetables but he returned empty-handed. This was the time of the year when it was most difficult to obtain food as the new crop was not ready to harvest and most of the last year's reserve had been eaten. Soon the people of that region would be going to the forests to dig roots for their food. We wondered if we would be learning to do that, too. Ah-Sam said it would take constant vigilance to replenish our food supplies from there on. Strange to say, these people kept no milk cows, so we would have to depend entirely upon our canned milk for the six children.

It rained during the night and on into the next morning. Our carriers had spent a miserable night in the Lisu huts because they were infested with fleas. The climate was becoming quite semi-tropical and we saw several great clumps of gigantic bamboo trees. The mountainside across the river seemed steep and rocky, thinly forested with pines in the lower regions. Higher up were more level places where the Lisu had built their villages. While we were at Wei Hsi we had become acquainted with some of the Lisu people who lived mostly in the outlying districts. We liked them very much.

As we approached Sukin, the country appeared to be more populated. There was a lovely valley several hours journey north of Sukin, full of rice fields. As we stopped for our noon meal, the people swarmed about us in friendly, but shy curiosity. The whole valley south of Pon Dam had never heard the Gospel. Russell said, "I wish I could speak Lisu. Who knows but that God will call us to this region as part of our work when next we return to the Tibetan borderland. I feel that I could come to love these Lisu people and give my life to living among them for Christ's sake". How prophetic! We could not know — nor even imagine — that in twenty years that whole area would be a well-taught and very prominent part of our mission field.

Leaving the Lisu community, we traveled one of the most difficult and dangerous paths of the journey. Mr. Morrison sent his pony around on a long detour that brought him to Sukin three or four hours after our own arrival. It wasn't long before we all began to wish WE had taken that detour! Our path lay along a jungle covered cliff directly above the swirling waters of the Salween River. Digging into crevices of the rocks with our toes while holding with our hands to overhanging vines or projecting rocks, or roots of trees, we made our way across the precarious precipice cautiously, carefully with bated breath. Reaching a more broad and level place formed by a dip in the spur, we paused a while to rest. From there, the precipitous decent was so steep the heavier loads had to be let down by ropes tied together. Mrs. Lewer and I stood at the foot of the precipice as the carriers started down with our children on their backs. We closed our eyes, held hands, and prayed. Sometimes a foot-hold on that sheer cliff was no larger than a spool. Just a little slip and one would be cut to pieces on sharp rocks or fall into the rushing river. Our precious children had learned to be as still as mice, clinging around their carrier's necks. How we admired those men. Do you wonder that we were learning to love them?

Emerging from the tortuous jungle-covered cliff path, we followed a safer route through tiny cultivated fields to a large stream flowing into the Salween. Over that stream was an excellent wooden bridge, evidently built by the Chinese. We crossed a large, fan-shaped, terraced rice field, just beyond which was the sprawling Chinese village of Sukin with about a hundred families, including many Lisu Gold, washed by primitive methods from sand, was one of the exports from that region. A year or so before, we had heard from some travelers that to the south of Sukin, salt was so prized it could be exchanged for an equal weight of gold.

We arrived in Sukin June 2, and stayed there three days while Russell paid off some of the coolies and hired others. We stayed at the home of a prosperous Chinese merchant and many people were very kind to us. We left there on June 6, which was a dismal, rainy day. Not long after leaving, Mr. Morrison's valiant little pony finally died of exhaustion. As we left Sukin, we had to cross several small, rain-swollen streams, where the carriers took the women across on their backs. We slept that night in a Chinese-style house at Heh-wa-di, the last Lisu village before crossing the border into Burma.

✝

Our passage over the Salween-Irrawaddy divide was even more difficult than crossing the Mekong-Salween pass. For four days we suffered indescribably, struggling through deep snows and being drenched by heavy rains. For eight days we traveled without seeing even the smallest sign of human habitation. We waded through snow going over a 12,000-foot pass, then slogged through mud almost to our knees and waded through water up to our hips. The coolies had to clear a path in the jungle for us to walk, and camp sites had to be cleared by cutting down trees and underbrush. Only the children in their oilcloth-covered baskets escaped being drenched by the constant monsoon rains, and even they got wet at times. Our feet were always wet and our shoes rotted off. Fortunately, Russell had bought some extra shoes for himself while in Hong Kong and I had some extra ones, too.

At one place along the way, we made camp on the mountainside under an overhanging cliff. The coolies were becoming increasingly frustrated by the rain, because it froze on their backs in the higher altitudes. In the heavy rain the next morning, they refused to pick up their loads, and some of us who understood the language heard them talking about running away and returning home. They were very concerned about their food supply, and were afraid they would not have enough for the trip home. What would we do if they abandoned us there? None of us knew how to get out of that jungle. Several of us stood together and earnestly prayed. Oh! how we prayed! Like a miracle, in about half an hour, the sun came out. The coolies picked up their packs and led us on out to the Tulong River, the headwaters of the Irrawaddy.

We arrived at the Tulong River on June 15, crossed on a rope bridge and soon came to Tu-Long (now called Mon-di), the first village after crossing the border into Burma. We were privileged to stay in a house the first two days we were there. (Mon-Di later became a center of our mission work in that area.) We paid off the porters, thankful that they had stayed with us that far, and hired new ones. Since Mrs. Morrison was ill the whole trip, I helped all I could with her children, especially feeding and washing,the baby, and trying to dry diapers, in addition to taking care of my own two boys.

✝

We left Mon-Di on June 18, climbed up another steep mountain, and crossed several swift tributaries to the Irrawaddy.

121

Sometimes we went on shaky bamboo bridges, sometimes on swinging bridges and sometimes we were carried across.

During this part of the journey we encountered many ingenious methods of crossing streams. Besides the rope bridge and the swinging bamboo bridge, we saw a kind which used three large, strong, bamboo hoops hanging from a rattan cable stretched across the river — especially on the rivers that did not have high banks. Two boards were passed through the hoops and the passenger must lie prone while being pulled across by means of a rattan rope. Because the main suspension cable had to be pieced together to make it long enough to span the river, there were numerous knots. This made it necessary to give the rope a hard jerk whenever the hoops hit a knot.

At one river we came to a bridge of this kind, and while waiting to cross, the carriers — including the ones who were carrying our children's baskets — had set down their loads on the very narrow path. Suddenly I heard a scream and turned around to see Eugene's basket tumbling down the steep bank toward the raging stream below. I was terrified, and felt so helpless as I saw his basket falling. I cried out, "Oh God, save him!" Eugene was only six years old, but somehow he managed to grab hold of a small branch and stop his fall, just at the edge of the raging torrent. One of the carriers scrambled down and rescued him and even retrieved the basket. Later, when it was my turn to cross the rain-swollen, raging stream, I had to lie flat on my back on the board, holding Eugene tightly, with both arms, so that I was unable to hold on to the board. I was truly frightened, for I could feel each bump or knot in the rattan cable, and felt sure the whole thing would be pulled out from under us! Each child had to be accompanied by an adult.

Another type of bridge was made with two bamboo poles, each about the size of a man's arm, which were laced together and laid across a stream. One mis-step meant that you were gone. It made no difference which method was used — they were all frightening. We usually sat down on the other side and wondered how we got there. We often had to wait from half a day to all day while a bridge was either being repaired, or rigged up from whatever materials were available.

✟

While traveling down a valley the next day, we became aware of a roaring sound, then felt a light mist which became heavier as we went along. About two miles farther down the valley we came to one of the most picturesque and amazing scenes of the entire journey. Here we beheld a great waterfall which fell from a height of about two hundred feet, pouring over the edge of a cliff into the swirling pool below, which emptied into the raging main Taron River . The flashing drops and iridescent spray amid the green foliage on either side looked like diamonds shining against green velvet.

The only way to get across the river, to continue our journey, was to wade through the swollen river, passing behind the falls. We didn't know whether we could make it or not, but had to try, for we couldn't turn back. There was a terrific wind and suction caused by the force of the waterfall, accompanied by a heavy spray. We attempted to shield ourselves from the wind and spray with three parasols, but the force of the wind turned them inside out and tore them to tatters. We were drenched through and through. As we waded into the swirling water below and behind the falls, the native guide who was assisting me became frightened, let go of my hand and plunged ahead into the current to make his own way across. Russell grabbed me in time to keep me from being carried downstream by the swift current, and swept on into the main river. He then helped me the rest of the way to the bank. The children, in their baskets covered with oil sheeting, were the only ones who didn't get wet. How thankful I was that the men carrying them were sure-footed and brave. After that ordeal, we spent the night in the jungle beside the waterfall.

At one point the Tulong carriers we were now using became more and more disgruntled with Mr. Barton's handling

123

of them, for he often whacked them with his cane so they would move faster. He would say, "The discipline is good for the troops", but the "troops" rebelled. One of our interpreters came to Russell one day and told him the men were going to kill Mr. Barton as soon as they found him alone. They had put down their loads and refused to go on.

We discussed this new crisis with the other missionaries and Ganton. Our solution was to promise that Mr. Barton would go on ahead of the rest of us, if they would promise not to kill him. The next problem was to convince Mr. Barton that the situation was serious. He just didn't believe it. After much persuasion, however, he finally agreed to take his own two Chinese coolies and go on ahead. We were now close enough to Ft. Hertz that we felt that he would have no trouble getting out. We heard later that he was successful.

✟

We continued on through the jungle, in spite of the fact it rained some every day, and we crossed many rain-swollen streams over all kinds of bridges. After crossing the big N'Mai River at Pangnamdin, we enjoyed the luxury of staying at night in bamboo huts with thatched roofs, built for government inspectors and/or tax collectors. It was such a relief not to have to pitch our tents in the mud.

We had overcome many obstacles such as jagged rocks, slippery surfaces, crumbling cliffs, creepers that tripped us, and worm-eaten tree trunks from which insects swarmed. We had climbed almost vertical ladders made by driving wooden stakes into the face of overhanging bluffs, and crossed frightening bridges, but now we encountered another kind of misery: Leeches! Miserable, crawling, clinging creatures, the leeches were everywhere. They dropped from bushes, they crawled on the ground, and fastened themselves onto the legs of any travelers. Even Russell, in puttees, was not spared from them. Although their puncture was not painful, it often caused a wound which spread and became infected. One bit four-year old Robert in the eye and it became terribly bloodshot. We were worried about what that might do, but the natives said, "Don't worry, it will clear up in about two weeks." And it did. As if that weren't enough, we also encountered the small, blood-blister flies which did their part to increase our discomforts. They caused small blood blisters to appear wherever they bit, and the bites itched terribly. As we descended farther toward the plains, we were attacked by hordes of virulent mosquitoes, and clouds of tiny sand flies.. By the time we reached Ft. Hertz, both Mr. and Mrs. Morrison were ill with malarial fever. That trip had been especially hard on Mrs. Morrison.

✟

On July 7, we were more than happy to see the great grassy Ft. Hertz plain, with a clear, quiet river, and no jungle. We slept that night beside the smooth river. It was there that our friend and guide, Ganton, left us to go back home. I don't know what we would have done without his help. We were so thankful he had come that far with us. At this point, it was decided that since there were not enough canoes to take all the missionaries on to Ft. Hertz at one time, the Lewer and Morrison families would go ahead. Our family stayed behind, and that night we stayed in the house of a kind, hospitable Shan family who took pity on us and prepared a good meal of fresh corn, squash, rice and other delicious things. What a change from our recent starvation diet!

The next morning our caravan overseer arranged for us and the children to be taken by dugout canoe to the landing place closest to Ft. Hertz, while the carriers walked. It was an exciting trip in the narrow 18″ to 20″ canoes. We had to sit quietly in order not to "rock the boat". Water splashed by the paddles, a leak in our canoe, and occasional rain showers kept us all rather wet, but when the sun shone it was warm. Eugene and Robert soon fell asleep with their heads in my lap. Russell and the oarsman had to keep bailing out the water all the way. After going several miles we met another canoe coming downstream, bringing an official from Ft. Hertz to greet us. He even brought some wonderful treats for the children, such as crackers and jam, which we had not had for so long. The children soon woke up and how they did enjoy those "goodies"!

In the middle of the afternoon, we landed as close as possible to Ft. Hertz. I wrung the water out of the boys' sweaters and put them right back on them, then they rode the rest of the way in their baskets on the backs of our carriers. A horse was provided for me to ride those three hours but Russell had to walk the entire distance, mostly through flooded rice paddies and small streams, on his sore, ulcerated feet. Looking down from my horse, I saw what I first thought were small snakes wriggling through the water. Later, I learned they were 6" long "elephant" leeches! I was told that if they were not removed, they could kill a person in one night by sucking so much blood.

Ft. Hertz at last! We finally arrived July 9, 1927, forty-eight days after leaving Tse Drong. While there we stayed in some unoccupied barracks on a hill. What a welcome change it was to be in actual buildings for at least a few days before leaving on the last 218 miles to the railway. And what a contrast it was to the leaky tents and bamboo leaf huts which had been our shelters along the jungle trail.

Ft. Hertz was a disappointment, and not at all what we had expected. Although it was called a British outpost, there was not a single Western person in the place, but only Asians, whose language we didn't know. However, there were several small shops where we could buy some much-needed clothing and food, for which we were very grateful. We were able to sell some clothes we could do without, and thus got money for immediate use in buying food.

We had no Burmese money and, to our dismay, our Yunnan silver was not acceptable there. Russell immediately telegraphed the Hong Kong and Shanghai Bank for the transfer to Rangoon of our bank accounts, in Indian Rupees. He also wrote and telegraphed the American Consul for assistance in expediting the transfer of our funds, or aiding us in obtaining credit while in Ft. Hertz. He also asked the American Consul to send word of our safe arrival to our home address in America. We later heard that family and friends were greatly worried about us, thinking we were lost somewhere in the mountains. Meanwhile, we washed clothing and bedding.

We repacked our remaining few things which were worth taking on. We had already discarded along the way many things which had molded and were unfit for use. We also rested for a while. Then Eugene became ill with malarial fever, and I worried about him. There had been so many mosquitoes in the jungle. With some quinine and much prayer, he was greatly improved by the time we had to leave.

After a two-week wait, we received our money and prepared to depart. We had had a very welcome time of rest and recuperation in Ft. Hertz, and Eugene had recovered from his malaria. However, we still had twenty-one days of travel ahead of us before we reached Myitkyina. It was difficult to obtain carriers, but the Ft. Hertz official, Lahpai Yao, a Kachin Baptist Christian originally from the Baptist Mission School at Myitkyina, was of great assistance. He hired coolies to carry our loads, two men to carry our boys in their baskets, and one horse which Russell and I took turns in riding.

✟

We left Ft. Hertz for Myitkyina on July 26, following the British-built administrative horse road, with government "dak", or rest bungalows at intervals easily reached in one day of travel.. It rained often but not as hard as before. Both Mr. & Mrs Morrison became so ill they had to be carried all the way from Ft. Hertz to Myitkyina on makeshift litters. One day, when we were unable to hire enough carriers, our coolie boss arranged for two elephants to carry our loads. Eugene and Robert watched intently as the elephants were being unloaded that evening. When the driver asked if they would like to ride, they both said , "Yes, Yes!" So, with our permission, they rode around the enclosure under the driver's supervision.

On August 15, 1927, a few hours before we expected to arrive at Myitkyina, we saw coming down the road something that looked like a car. As it drew near, we saw it WAS a car. Our boys had never seen one and it had been six years since Russell and I had. Some dear people had come to meet us and give us a ride those last miles of our seventy-day journey. I was overcome with the kindness of those precious Christians and the tender care of our wonderful God who walked with us all the way. We remembered again the precious promise He had given us when we were trying to decide about that dreadful trip across the Himalayas. Surely He had fulfilled His promise — "As I was with Moses, so I will be with thee; I will not fail thee, nor forsake thee. Be strong and of a good courage; for the Lord thy God is with thee whithersoever thou goest".(Joshua 1:5-9)

We were delighted when we were invited to stay at the Baptist Mission Home where Rev. and Mrs. George J. Geis were working. They supervised a grade school, a high school and a Bible school. We were told the students had been praying for our party since they had heard we were coming on that jungle trip. We enjoyed staying there and getting acquainted with the Geis family and the students. We were so tired after the long, hard, wet trip, we were urged to rest for almost ten days before proceeding on to Rangoon.

✟

Early in the morning on August 26, we left Myitkyina on the small railway. It was a long, extremely hot trip, especially going through Mandalay. I am sure Kipling's "Road to Mandalay" was not the one we had just traversed. Arriving in Rangoon in the early evening of the next day, August 27, we were met by members of the Baptist Guest House.

Rangoon seemed very hot to us, but it was beautiful, and we were relieved and happy to be there. We were surprised to see people splashing water from hydrants over themselves to try to keep cool. We went down town to buy some decent clothes for the boys and ourselves. Eugene and Robert looked so nice in their English style shirts and short pants. After a few days in Rangoon, on September 6, 1927 we boarded a steamer and began our journey to America.

On our way back to America we visited the pyramids in Egypt, and rode on camels. None of us thought that was very comfortable.

Soon after our return to the U.S. in 1927 we had a family picture taken. Eugene, Gertrude, Robert, Russell.

12
First Furlough

The steamer on which we traveled was going to America by way of Europe. We stopped a day in Colombo, Ceylon (now known as Sri Lanka) and enjoyed seeing the sights. From there we sailed on to Aden in Arabia, Massawa in Abyssinia (now Ethiopia) and on up the Red Sea to Suez and Port Said. We arrived in Port Said on September 26, 1927, twenty days from the time we left Rangoon.

From Port Said we went by train to Cairo where we visited the Museum of Egyptian Antiquities. It was a vast and wonderful building stored with all the treasures of Egypt from about 3000 B.C., and we were fascinated. Most of the items that had been removed from the pyramids, temples, rock tombs, etc. were there, including the gorgeous findings from the tomb of King Tutankhamon (King Tut). One of the mummy cases from that tomb was made of 900 pounds of pure gold, most exquisitely engraved. We looked at Rameses II, the Pharaoh who so cruelly oppressed the Israelites, and also the other Pharaoh, during whose rule the "exodus" was made. One could spend many, many days at such a place and still not see everything.

The next day we rode on camels outside Cairo and went across the Nile River to see the pyramids and the Sphinx. The steps made from blocks of cut stone were too high for a child to climb, so I took care of the boys while Russell climbed to the top of the pyramid. Afterwards, I climbed half way up, to the entrance of the rooms where the caskets of the royalty had been kept. Many valuable ornaments and other articles had been left for the spirits of the departed to use. Among them, as I remember, were some beautiful jars for perfume and many kinds of basket ware.

☨

That night we took the train to Jerusalem, where we hired a Christian Arab and his car, to be our guide and provide transportation for the eight days we spent in the Holy Land. From Jerusalem we went about fifteen miles south to Bethlehem and visited the Church of The Nativity, owned by Greeks, Armenians and Catholics. This church was built over the spot where Christ was supposed to have been born, and the manger was in a cave underneath the altar. Outside the town was a beautiful hillside where, in olden times, shepherds had herded their sheep.

Returning to Jerusalem, we went to the Garden of Gethsemane and saw the centuries-old olive trees that were believed to have been there in the time of Christ. We then climbed to the top of the Mount of Olives and crossed over to Bethany, home of Mary and Martha, where their brother, Lazarus, had been resurrected.

From Bethany we went down to Jericho, then south to the Dead Sea. The two boys waded into the water and got so very sticky from the salt they had to be washed with fresh water before putting on their clothes. On the return trip, about half way between Jericho and Jerusalem, the guide stopped at a little village to show us where the Good Samaritan had aided the injured traveler. There were few roads, and those off the main highways were very rough and full of curves. To avoid them, we had to go back to Jerusalem before going on to Nazareth.

We passed through Bethel and Ramah, in Samaria, on the way to Jacob's well at Sychar, where Jesus asked the Samaritan woman for a drink of water. We looked down into the well by candlelight and were given a small bottle of water from the well. We also saw where Ahab's old palace was being excavated.

Going on to Nazareth, where Jesus spent his childhood, we wondered if He had time to play in the nearby fields, among the fig trees and mustard plants that he later used to illustrate His teachings. We saw the well where Mary and Joseph drew water. There seemed to be many more Christians in Nazareth than in any of the other places we visited. At Cana we felt we were back in Biblical times, seeing the women in their flowing robes, carrying the large earthen jars that were still being used for water.

We descended to the Sea of Galilee, and to Capernaum situated on its banks. We spent the night in the German Catholic hospice, "Tabgha", cooled by breezes from the sea. In the evening Russell fished in the sea, and caught three small fish which he was pleased to have cooked for our breakfast. We rented a small boat and sailed a while on the sea.

Our Arab guide continued with us, by car, through Tiberias and around the southern end of the Sea of Galilee to Gadara, where Jesus cast out the devils from the insane man and made him well again. The place was covered with thorn bushes which seem to be native to Palestine. Each thorn was about an inch long and I couldn't help but think of Christ's crown of thorns.

We then went on to Mt. Carmel and climbed to the monastery on top of it, and got a wonderful view of the Mediterranean Sea. Early the next morning, we sailed on a coastal freighter from Haifa, which lies at the foot of Mt. Carmel. We stopped a short while at Beirut, then went on to Tripoli. From Tripoli, we sailed on to the Island of Cyprus and, while our ship was anchored there for two days, we went ashore to see the people and the shops. I was especially impressed with the dainty, handmade lace. It was so beautiful.

☦

We continued our journey, passing the Island of Rhodes en route to Athens. While in Athens, of course we went to see and take pictures of the Acropolis and the Parthenon. Leaving Athens, we went to Corinth, sailed down the narrow canal and across the Ionian Sea to the Adriatic Sea, and landed at Venice, Italy, the city of unique canal streets. We took a ride in a gondola, then went to see the glass blowers making all kinds of beautiful glassware, for which they are famous. Going on by boat, we saw St. Mark's beautiful Cathedral where the many pigeons were being fed, mostly by tourists.

From Venice we traveled by train to Milan, where I had an exciting but somewhat frightening experience. In Milan there was a magnificent cathedral that I very much wanted to see. Our train stopped there only about an hour and there really was not time to go, but I took a chance anyway. Keeping an eye on my watch, I succeeded in getting to see some of the wonderful building. I even counted the number of steps around one of the immense columns. The ceiling with its lovely colored glass and the paintings all around were so unusual. But I could not tarry, so I hurried back to my waiting family and the train. The one thing for which I had not allowed time was the delay at the gate where my ticket was supposed to be shown. Then when I reached the gate I suddenly realized that Russell had my ticket so I could not show it. I could hear the conductor calling, "All aboard," and could see my two little sons waving their arms frantically toward me and calling, "Mama, Mama". The conductor saw me as I darted through the gate and ran as fast as I could toward my family on the train. That sympathetic conductor even stopped the slightly moving train to wait for me! My, what an experience! I surely thanked God and that good conductor for helping me get back, and hugged my dear ones, from whom I had almost been separated.

Next, the train took us to Lausanne, Switzerland where we stayed all night. We were privileged to see the beautiful Lake Lucerne, and to watch while cheese was being made. Going on to Paris, we enjoyed seeing the great Louvre art gallery and the wonderful Eiffel Tower, as well as many other interesting places.

Crossing the English Channel to London, we found accommodations in a clean rooming house, then visited all the usual tourist sights such as London Bridge, Buckingham Palace (the King's residence, where we saw the changing of the guard), Westminster Abbey (a beautiful cathedral), Big Ben, a beautiful park, and the Tower of London, where the largest diamond in the world is displayed on special occasions.

Crossing the Atlantic, we had bad weather all the way, and a rather rough crossing. We arrived in New York the first part of November and were delighted to find that Mother Morse had come all the way from Oklahoma to meet us. Mr. & Mrs. Charles Wiesenberg, of the Christian Witnesses to Israel organization, also met us and took us to their home and entertained us royally, as their own family, for about three days.

It was wonderful to be back in America, our very own native land, after that terribly hard 70-day trip from Tse Drong. The boys were so excited and happy. They had heard us talk about America but Robert had never been there and Eugene couldn't remember anything about it, since he was only four months old when we left. Now Eugene was six and a half and Robert was four and a half.

We stopped in Cincinnati, where we visited with Bro. Edwin Errett, of The Standard Publishing Company, and went to see the Cincinnati Bible Seminary which was just getting started. We didn't linger long, though, because we were so eager to see our families in Oklahoma, at Norman and Tulsa.

Our families were in good health and very happy to see us and our children, and the boys were just as happy to meet their grandparents, aunts, and uncles. Russell and I were so very, very tired we felt we just had to rest for a while, so for a few months we spent much time just visiting with our families, and accepted only occasional speaking engagements. By March of 1928, we were sufficiently recovered to accept more invitations, and to speak in many different states. Sometimes we went together, other times separately. The grandmothers were happy to take care of our sons when we both were away.

I spoke several times at West Side Christian Church in Springfield, Illinois, and they chose me to be their "living link" missionary. This relationship lasted, and they continued to be very faithful supporters all through the years of our missionary service.

While in Norman with my parents I enrolled Eugene and Robert in a summer course of Kindergarten and first grade work. This course was offered by the University of Oklahoma so students in their educational department could gain experience through practice teaching. Our boys had never been in school before but thoroughly enjoyed it.

Russell enrolled in a post-graduate summer course at Phillips University in Enid, Oklahoma, his Alma Mater, where he enjoyed meeting his former professors and many friends. While there he also met Ward S. Humphries who later became pastor of the Hollenbeck Heights Christian Church in Los Angeles. Because of this acquaintance, Mr. Humphries recommended Russell to his congregation and they chose him to be their "living link" missionary.

✝

We decided that we should move to Los Angeles when the summer courses were over, so Russell could enroll in the Bible Institute of Los Angeles Medical School for foreign missionaries. His goal was to better prepare himself for missionary work in an area where the nearest doctors were about a month's journey away by horseback. However, by the time the summer course was over, Russell still had several speaking engagements to fill and could not leave Oklahoma immediately. I went on out to Los Angeles in August in order to enroll the boys in school. Fortunately, I was able to rent a small house near the home of my brother, Frank G. Howe, who was an attorney. Their children were about the same age as ours and they all attended a nice public school just two blocks away. The cousins enjoyed getting acquainted and being together that year. Russell came out as soon as he could and entered the medical school. He was able to make up the work he had missed.

While we were in Los Angeles, a very important event occurred. Our third son, Russell LaVerne Morse was born January 4, 1929. He was a precious, loving baby. When I had sufficiently recovered, I helped Russell with his speaking commitments. While in school, he continued to accept week-end speaking dates in the Los Angeles area. When he finished the medical course, we concentrated more on visiting and speaking at the various churches in the area, until time to return to the mission field. Meanwhile, we watched the political situation in China very closely. When Chiang Kai Shek came to power, he took a strong stand against communism and sent Russians home, so we felt it would soon be fairly safe to return.

As we prepared to return, we had to purchase and pack enough supplies to last five years, including medicines, household supplies, groceries, and clothing. In buying clothes and shoes for the children we had to estimate their growth rate for those five years, for there would be no place to purchase more later if we miscalculated. We decided it was better to have more than we needed, rather than less. As it turned out, this preparation of supplies helped us survive the "depression years" of the 1930's.

Robert (left) and Eugene (right) had an opportunity to get acquainted with one of their cousins.

It was a treat for me to get to spend some time with my sister Helen (left) and my mother, Margaret Howe (center).

Russell's sisters, Eva (back left) and Louise (back, right) enjoyed having Eugene (front left) and Robert (front right) close enough to "spoil".

13
Return to China

We had to apply to the Chinese Embassy in Washington, D.C. for visas to return to China. After receiving them, we left the United States on August 9, 1929, following about the same route as our first trip to the mission field, going by way of Tokyo, Hong Kong, Haiphong, and then to Kunming in Yunnan Province. We traveled second-class this time, which cost us about $300 less than first class, and was still quite comfortable. There were several other missionaries traveling this way too.

When we arrived in Kunming, we found that eight or nine of the resident missionaries had come to the depot to meet us. Out where the forces of heathenism were so dominant, and Christians so few, it warmed our hearts to find them welcoming us. They invited us to stay with them while waiting for our trunks and boxes to arrive. Once they were in hand, we had to repack some things, to meet the size and weight requirements for the standard pack-mule load.

However, our greatest delight upon arrival in Kunming was to find Tu-de-bao and Della Fu waiting for us. Tu-de-bao was a Tibetan evangelist who had worked with us in Batang. After leaving Batang Mr. & Mrs. Fu had worked and studied temporarily at the Legation of Tibetan and Mongolian Affairs in Nanking, the then-capital of China. There had been an understanding that they would work with us when we returned to the mission field, and we knew they could be of inestimable help in many ways. So when they heard we were returning to China for Christian work, they came to join us, and accompanied us through Wei Hsi and on to our new mission base in Yea Chi.

Tu-de-bao was a good team worker. He preached well in both Tibetan and Chinese, was a fairly good artist on evangelistic posters, and could play the organ a little. Della, his wife, had an unusually good education for that part of the world. She could play the organ and sing, had quite a bit of experience as a teacher and, like her husband, spoke both Tibetan and Chinese fluently. Della could also write understandably in English. They both were consecrated, cultured, and capable. They had two fine sons when they came to us — John and James. A third son, Joseph, was born January 4, 1931, on LaVerne's second birthday.

Tu-de-bao wanted another name, so we gave him a new one. His Chinese name was Fu Chung Ruh, or C. R. Fu. Tu-de-bao was a boyhood nickname meaning "under protection of the Earth God". Since he had been a Christian for many years, and wanted to get rid of that old heathen name, we changed it to Clifford R. Fu, in honor of Russell's living link pastor and personal friend, Clifford L. Carey of Hollenbeck Heights Church of Christ in Los Angeles.

✝

We left Kunming by horse caravan, and arrived in Wei Hsi on January 26, 1930. The children and I rode in chairs and Russell rode a horse. It was a very cold trip in the winter season, since much of the road was at 6000 to 8000 ft. elevation, and we had to cross high mountain passes en route. Our baby, LaVerne, was ill while in Kunming but seemed to gain a little strength on the way to Wei Hsi. Russell and I felt that his powdered milk formula did not agree with him and decided that he would be better off with cow's milk. Tu-de-bao was instructed to buy one or two cows as soon as possible after arriving in Yea Chi, where we had definitely decided to establish our mission base.

While in America from November of 1927 to August, 1929, we had kept in touch with our former helper, Duje, and her family. With her husband and three small daughters she had moved from Atuntze to Tse Drong, where her husband and one daughter died. When we were within a half day's ride of Wei Hsi, what a pleasant surprise it was to see dear Duje and her two little girls waiting for us! They had traveled eight days just to meet us. We were truly happy to see them again.

While Russell went on ahead to Yea Chi to find a permanent house for the family, we found temporary quarters for the children and me in a "wing", or about half, of a dirty old Chinese house at Wei Hsi. That house was not only dirty, but extremely drafty, with the cold wind blowing in from all directions. We had no proper stove for heat, and LaVerne became ill with the flu. His illness became worse, and gradually developed into pneumonia. I cared for him day and night. Being in such a cold, drafty place, with the baby so sick, I became very discouraged and sometimes felt I could scarcely stand it any longer. I held LaVerne in my arms to keep him warm, and prayed to God for his recovery. I was very thankful to have Duje with me to care for Eugene and Robert, and also thankful that they remained healthy.

LaVerne's sickness became worse, and I began to despair of our baby's life, so I sent for Russell to come at once. However, by the time he arrived a few days later, the baby was slightly better and continued to improve until an epidemic of measles broke out. In his weakened condition he fell a victim to that also. For several weeks he was our chief concern, and several times was near death. But God answered our prayers and he began to recover slowly.

As soon as LaVerne was well enough to travel we went on to Yea Chi. Our supply of powdered milk was almost depleted and we were anxious to be where we could get fresh cow's milk for him. We arrived at Yea Chi on May 1, 1930 and again stayed in rented temporary living quarters. All Russell had been able to find was an old, very low, two-room barn which he had rented and started immediately to renovate and remodel. The tribal chief, or local "king" was not in favor of a mission post in his village at first. But we prayed much and at last he gave his permission.

Russell had hired what carpenters he could find to start work on the house, but they were very slow, and unskilled compared to the Chinese carpenters in Batang. Also, while he was away, all work had stopped. The barn was part of an apartment-like complex built around a courtyard, with living quarters on three sides and one side open. Our outside wall was also the wall of the garden of the "king's" eldest son and family. Our landlord, Wang San Ye and family, lived on the opposite side of the courtyard.

When Russell first went to Yea Chi, he had started a vegetable garden, and by late May we had some fresh vegetables. There was an old Chinese man who had worked for one of the missionaries in Batang and later for the French priest in Tse Drong. Russell hired him to be our gardener.

✟

From the very first our main emphasis was on preaching the Gospel. Before our home was finished enough to be used, we preached anywhere and everywhere we could — on street corners, at the city gate, under trees in the village, and in the homes of the people. I also started a Sunday School for the children of the village.

Later, after all repairs were finished on our home, we held church services in our living room, as well as daily morning prayer meetings with our helpers. The influence of the Gospel in that region began growing more rapidly than the workers on hand could care for it. We were surprised and also encouraged when one day, not very long after we started our mission work, a Christian Lisu man came from one of the villages near Wei Hsi saying, "The Lord told me you need me and for me to come and help you preach to the Lisu." His name was Swa-mi-pa, and he had been a Christian for several years. He had been

142

led to Christ by the missionaries at Wei Hsi who had evacuated with us over the mountains through Burma in 1927.

Swa-mi-pa proved to be a very capable and devoted helper for many years. He brought with him his son, Pu-shi, whom we gave the name of Daniel. Daniel was about the age of Eugene and Robert and he stayed in our home. In the evenings I taught him Bible along with our boys, and later he went to the local Christian Chinese school opened by our mission in Yea Chi.

To help in preaching to the Lisu, Mr. Fu and Russell recruited two young Christian Lisu men, Ge-zong and Matthew, from near Wei Hsi, to interpret for them on evangelistic trips to surrounding mountain villages. In the meantime, Mr. Fu studied the Lisu language, while Russell and I reviewed Tibetan and Chinese. We remembered more than we had expected after being gone for two years. We also started to study Lisu. I was amazed at how fast Eugene and Robert picked up the languages.

☦

The sick and afflicted began to come to Russell for treatment, and before long he was treating twenty to thirty people a day. They not only came from nearby, but even from villages two or three days' travel away. This prepared the way for our evangelists to preach in those villages. Russell received a call from a large Lisu village called Lo-to-lo, located about two hours' easy ride up into the mountains. There was a very sick man there, and Russell was able to give treatment that saved his life. Another time, out of desperation and as a last resort, he was called on a difficult confinement case, and saved the life of a mother of four children, whose husband was nearly blind. Because of non-delivery of the placenta, a dirty old straw sandal had been tied to the end of the cord, inviting the afterbirth to "walk out". Over twenty-four hours later, it had proved ineffective. With proper medical treatment, Russell secured the desired results less than a half hour after arrival. People were totally ignorant of even common hygiene procedures, and unsanitary conditions were appalling. Women were not considered important enough for skilled help at childbirth.

Still another time, from a village about three hours north of Yea Chi, where we had never visited, the headman came, begging Russell to go and heal his son. He had brought a horse for Russell and they borrowed another one from our landlord for Mr. Fu. In recounting the incident to friends in America, Russell wrote:

> *"It was like an old-fashioned circus day when we arrived at Dza-nyi, and there were many people to help us get settled. Then the sick began coming and we were busy until dark. We treated the headman's son and all others we had time for, then retired for a rather sleepless night with the usual FLEAS. Morning brought more sick visitors. One man had even crossed the Mekong River on a bamboo cable to beg medicine for a relative.*
>
> *"We always took some time for preaching simple facts with ample illustrations. We also allowed time for questions and answers, including the frequent interruptions and comments to each other.*
>
> *"When the last 'patient' had been cared for I called for the horses so we could return to Yea Chi — but only one could be found — the one I had borrowed. 'Please stay another day', they begged, and their appeal was so pathetic I could not be angry at their simple, harmless trickery. One person asked if I had medicine for goiter. The growth was monstrous, but I painted it with iodine to be obliging. That started a procession. It seemed almost every person in that room had a goiter either large or small."*

The son of one of the Lisu chiefs at a community called Sha-to-lo had badly burned his leg about two months earlier and there had been no progress made in healing. The chief came with one of his other sons and a horse for Russell to ride, so that he could go and treat his son. Again, Mr. Fu went with him and they stayed overnight. While there he also treated a little baby, pitifully burned and neglected. The chief spoke quite a bit of Tibetan so there was no trouble communicating.

When treating sick people, Russell always prayed for his own guidance, as well as for the patient, and explained that it was not the missionary, but God who did the healing. These cases, and others like them in other villages, opened the way to tell about the greatest Healer of all. That is why we believe it is very important for all missionaries to have some medical training.

Early in August, Mr. and Mrs. Fu (Tu-de-bao and Della) went to Atunze to meet his mother and their children whom they had left in Batang. They were gone two weeks and preached in all the towns and communities along the way.

☩

We received a letter from Mr. Eugene K. Tarn, a devout Christian, who had been the postmaster in Batang when we were there. He and his family were in Chengtu, Szechuan Province, but wanted to join us in our mission work. Mr. Tarn had an A.B. degree from West China Union University, and could make more money as a postmaster or in teaching, but he wanted to devote his life to the Lord. Before we could make the necessary arrangements and respond, we received word that they were leaving Chengtu on November 4, 1930, trusting that the way would be opened for them to come to Yea Chi. And it was.

Celebration of the Christmas season was previously unknown in that part of the country, but for our first Christmas at Yea Chi (1930) we put up Christmas decorations in our living room, and had a tree in one corner. All this made the bare board walls look more cheerful. We had services every night from December 23 until December 27, with good attendance each time.

Two days before Christmas we received fifty parcel post packages from home folks and friends in America. About fifteen packages were medicine. Most of the rest we passed on to others. I fixed little bags of treats for the Sunday school children, which contained walnuts, chestnuts, and oranges, and a couple of Chinese doughnuts. Then I gave about forty of them other presents. We also gave out presents to twenty of our mission co-workers, their families, and servants.

The time came when our living room was filled to overflowing, so we had to divide the people and have separate meetings. I supervised the women's services on Tuesday afternoon and the children's services on Thursday afternoon. With two regular Sunday services and daily morning prayer services, we had ELEVEN services each week in Yea Chi plus weekly services in four neighboring villages in the valley and four mountain villages.

As soon as we heard that the Tarn family had arrived in Kunming in early January, 1931, we began looking for a house for them. There was very little to choose from, but after about two weeks of searching, we rented a rather ramshackle six-room house with adjoining garden and obtained a two-year lease. Russell hired carpenters to begin renovating it at once. We retained one room for a school room and another small chapel, as attendance at our night services had overflowed our living-room "chapel". We often had as many as SEVENTY packed in like sardines. We had brought with us from America a kerosene pressure lantern, which we used for evening services. Because it was so bright, it evoked a lot of curiosity among the natives, and may have helped to boost attendance at the night services. Since there were no street lights, we escorted people to the center of town after the service, and from there they scattered to their homes.

✝

We made several preaching trips in and around Kang Pu, a village about fourteen miles south of Yea Chi. Large audiences gathered and many sick people came for treatment. Soon they began asking us to establish another station near there. The property we thought would be ideal belonged to a poverty-stricken former tribal chief and his two brothers, who lived above the town of Kang Pu. We finalized a lease, with witnesses, and then the excitement began. The "king" of Kang Pu commanded the three brothers not to lease their place to the foreigners. He said we would corrupt their religion so he could not live and rule there. Also it was bad luck for the foreign mission to be located ABOVE the town.

Mr. Fu and Russell made the four-day trip to Wei Hsi to have the lease registered and found that the magistrate had received a letter from the Kang Pu chief, charging the three brothers with a "secret attempt to sell public land to foreigners". Russell was told, confidentially, that a fat bribe had been sent to block our lease. For over a week they negotiated persistently. The three brothers were threatened with imprisonment, and their ownership of the land was questioned. Mr. Fu was called a "foreign slave". We had a Chinese friend there who was an influential politician and he was untiring in his efforts on our behalf. Help was also received from an unexpected source. The elder son of the Yea Chi chief happened to be in Wei Hsi on business and we were greatly surprised by his help with advice and personal influence. Not long after our arrival in Yea Chi Russell had cured him and his wife of a much dreaded disease, and he was now showing his appreciation.

When Russell and Mr. Fu returned to Yea Chi, it was with the twenty-year lease all stamped and in order, and a letter to the Kang Pu "king", notifying him of the approval of the lease and instructing him that we must be treated well.

✝

We were happy to have two more Lisu preachers join our evangelistic work. Like Swami-pa, they had been converted by the missionaries at Wei Hsi. They went with Mr. Fu to hold an evangelistic meeting in the mountains near our Kang Pu outstation. Mr. Fu returned in a week, leaving the others to continue preaching, with the word that two whole villages wanted to hear more of the Gospel. Some wanted to become Christians. We always made sure that they were well taught before baptism, for faith as well as repentance is a prerequisite. How could they have faith without knowing Christ, the

Bringer of the Gospel? We wanted to build congregations that were solid, regardless of whether the numerical increase was slow or fast.

The authority of the Kang Pu "king" extended over a wide area, including several of the Lisu villages where teaching had been done. He resented our efforts to break the fetters of drunkenness and illiteracy with which the tribes people were held in bondage. He deliberately kept them in ignorance, and supplied them with whiskey, while also taxing them heavily. So when the Lisu preachers returned, bringing two converts with them, the "king" decided to test their genuineness. The two new converts were arrested on a false charge and brought before the "king", who ordered a jug of wine to be placed before them.

"So, you have become Christians, have you?" he asked. They replied that they had truly done so.

"Drink all of that wine or take a beating", he then commanded.

They refused, so he had them beaten, then bound and led away to prison. Two delegates of the Wei Hsi magistrate "happened" to be in Kang Pu at that time, and secured their release. The interference with religious liberty was a violation of the Constitution of the Chinese Republic. We were glad that Generalissimo Chiang Kai Shek and his wife were both Christians and therefore sympathetic to missionaries, and that religious liberty was being upheld.

An interesting side-light, or sequel, to these events is the fact that afterward both these men were able to study in short-term Bible schools, and both became leaders in the Tobalo Lisu church which was established later.

Our house
in Yea Chi.

Some Tibetan and
Lisu non-Christian
residents
of Yea Chi.

Some newly
baptized
Christians in the
Mekong Valley.

Our family in 1935. Russell is standing behind, and in front, left to right Robert, me (Gertrude) holding our new little daughter Ruth Margaret, LaVerne, and Eugene.

14
Ups and Downs

In late January of 1931, LaVerne again became ill with the flu and was very sick with a raging fever. By using what medicine was available, holding and nursing him for about three weeks, always with much prayer, he began to slowly recover. Until that illness, he had been quite healthy since coming to Yea Chi. He was such a sweet and bright youngster. He could speak Tibetan and Chinese as well as English, and was quick to entertain guests by offering them a chair or a magazine to look at, even though he was only two years old.

On February 14, our Chinese gardener, Ma Chin Wen, passed away after a long siege of influenza, complicated by asthma. He had been baptized November 9, 1930, along with our son, Robert. His last words to those watching over him as he lay near death were, "Don't be afraid, don't be afraid". He was buried on a beautiful hillside overlooking the Mekong River, where he had been buried in baptism.

✞

In early March an epidemic of sickness, which we later believed was an extremely virulent type of influenza, struck our village. We later learned it had been rather widespread over many countries. About 100 people in Yea Chi died suddenly, usually ten to eighteen hours after becoming ill. Our landlord's servant girl died, the first in our court.

Just six days later, on March 11, our own beloved Tibetan cook, Duje, was stricken and succumbed to it, leaving her two precious little girls,** Anzie Ruth, aged eight, and Drema Esther, aged four. We pledged to her and to ourselves that if our own lives were spared, we would always take care of them. Just the day before Duje died, she had been singing, "When He cometh to make up His jewels". She and I had made cookies to take to our new evangelist, Mr. Tarn and his family, who had arrived just four days earlier. She had gotten our supper, cleaned the kitchen and played with LaVerne while I was getting him ready for bed. A few days before that, she had inspired us by leading our daily morning devotional service even though she felt she could not adequately express what was in her heart. She was a wonderful Christian! She had been with us ten years, helping in every household capacity. We all loved her and missed her cheery spirit so much. It seems I had depended on her for almost everything, and there was scarcely a thing done that I did not ask her about. She became ill about 10:00 o'clock at night and was gone by 10:00 the next morning. We were all stunned.

Since there were no mortuaries, the landlord was anxious to have her body taken away as soon as possible. There was no time to have a coffin made, but we were able to buy one, already made, from an old man. It was a Chinese custom for elderly people to have their coffins made and kept somewhere in their house. Because Duje was a servant, the landlord would not allow her coffin to be taken out the front door, which was the only door out of the court. We had to cut a hole in the mud wall, in the back, large enough to take the coffin through.

After Duje died, our landlord had his priests try to chase out the spirits. They painted their faces to look hideous, beat gongs and yelled, and went into every room except ours. They had a terrible time because they thought the spirits would not leave, especially Duje's. They said she loved her children and refused to leave them. They then took great iron chains and

---

**See note at end of chapter.*

152

beat the sides of our house. The noise went on and on until we finally cried to God for deliverance, and He answered immediately. The shaman priests suddenly quit their noise and headed out the front gate.

Seven-year-old Robert then became quite ill with a high fever, and was even delirious. It seemed to us his symptoms were similar to Duje's, and of course that alarmed us. We stayed with him constantly and gave him what medicine we could, and we PRAYED. Oh! how we prayed! In answer to our prayers he was soon better. These frightening experiences were almost beyond our endurance, and only our faith and the comfort of the Lord brought us through. We kept remembering and claiming His promise that He would not let us be tried beyond what we could bear.

Then another blow fell — on March 19 our landlord died, the third death in our housing complex alone. Panic reigned; our servants threatened to run away; and our landlord's wife said we must move. We felt we had to get away for a while, so we went to a quiet place in the mountains about ten miles south from Yea Chi, for four days. We had nice, clean quarters and blessed quiet. When we returned we were able to persuade the landlord's wife to let us stay, and we all went back to our work with renewed vigor.

On March 7, in the midst of all the sickness, Mr. and Mrs. Tarn, their three daughters and young son had arrived. They had been held up for twelve days by deep snow on a high pass near Wei Hsi, which is four days' travel by horse from Yea Chi. When Mr. Fu went to meet them and try to assist them, he found the Tarn's one-and-a-half-year-old son very ill, so ran all the way back to Yea Chi to get Russell. Russell gathered up some medicine and went back with Mr. Fu. But by the time they got there, the baby was better, and continued to recover.

We were glad that the Tarns had come to work with us. Mrs. Tarn was a tiny, refined Chinese lady who had been one of my best friends while in Batang. Mr. Tarn started working right away among the tribes people. We furnished the room we had reserved in his house with benches — short ones for seats, and tall ones for desks, — and our school was under way. Mr. Tarn was supervisor and teacher. Nine students started, but by the end of the year there were thirty-six. At first, some of the native students were taunted for surrendering to the "yang ren" (foreigner), and some were even beaten. After the first children were taught to be good and set a good example, others began to understand what Christian education was about, and our enrollment increased. The school room was also used for church services. We just moved the benches around, with the short ones in front and the tall ones behind.

In June, 1931, Russell and Mr. Fu went for a week of meetings at Kang Pu and the Lisu community westward across the Mekong where Mr. Fu and our two Lisu teachers had previously done quite a bit of work. Some of the converts in this area had been persecuted and beaten for becoming Christians.

When we first went to Yea Chi, Russell had hired a native named Drang Wen Da as our interpreter and handyman. He went with them on this trip and interpreted for four nights the messages from God's Word on Sin, Salvation, and the New Man. On the last day, at To-ba-lo, after they baptized the last Lisu convert, Mr. Drang stepped down into the cold water and told Mr. Fu, "Now I must submit to Christ, too".

Two weeks later, when Russell and Mr. Fu made a similar trip to some other Lisu villages, they found that the Christians were standing firm, and their influence had spread. Among those baptized was one man who had been a spirit priest before he accepted Christ. He confessed that he had tried to use his power to destroy our Christian influence, but discovered that God's power was much stronger than demon power. He said all the Christians were covered with a white light, and he had no power over us, so he chose to be a Christian. He later became one of our most steadfast workers.

✝

On July 13, 1931 our whole family left for ten days among the Lisu Christians. LaVerne and I had not been well, and Russell thought a change would do us good. A hwagan was rigged up for me to ride in as far as the Mekong River crossing while the others rode horses. LaVerne rode with Russell or was carried by one of our two Tibetan girls. The first night was spent at our outstation at Kang Pu. The next morning, we crossed the river in dugout canoes and walked the rest of the way to Tobalo.

Our stay in the Lisu country was a busy one. Russell preached every night and some during the day. He spent at least two hours daily in medical work. Russell, with one of our teachers, took a trip far up into the mountains to interview, and try to win over, a native headman who had been threatening the Christians. The headman was gone, so they proceeded on to the last house up the valley, beyond which there was nothing but forest and mountain crags. They found two houses of surprising size and primitive comfort in a good-sized clearing. There were several large grain bins filled with corn, buckwheat, beans and wheat. In those two houses lived the grandparents, parents, and a recently married son and his wife. They were strong, intelligent, straight-forward pioneers, and all had accepted Christ. Since it was getting late, they insisted that Russell and his helper spend the night there. Russell conducted church services to which the neighbors also came. He could not help comparing this family and their possessions with the non-Christians, who lived in hovels and drank their wine.

The high spot of our trip was the baptismal service on Friday morning. Each night, we had conducted an "after meeting", at which candidates for baptism were carefully taught, and Russell asked questions to make sure their faith and repentance were genuine. Eighteen Lisu were baptised, and one Tibetan girl, A-mo, who had worked in our family for several months.

When we started the return journey to Yea Chi, we found the river had risen about ten feet and was too turbulent to be crossed in boats. We followed a trail along the river for two days, and had to make detours up the mountainside in several places where the path was covered by rising water. At last we came to a bamboo cable, or rope "bridge" just west of Yea Chi, which was high-swung on the sides, but in the center sagged fearfully close to the floodwaters. The rest of the family had already experienced the rope bridge crossings, but this was LaVerne's first time. Although he was securely strapped to one of the men, he was frightened, and screamed all the way across.

On July 24th Mr. Fu and his family left for four months of evangelizing in and around Atuntze. The rest of us were busy also. Mr. Tarn was teaching in the school, preaching, and learning the Nashi dialect. I visited in the homes and continued with the women's and children's services. Russell preached in our village and the surrounding region. Our efforts were being directed into four sectors: Atuntze, Kang Pu, To-ba-lo and our base in Yea Chi, and surrounding areas. We had four languages to deal with — Tibetan, Chinese, Lisu and Nashi, and there were already converts from each group. Our Yea Chi Christian group which had begun in May, 1930 with SIX (the Fu family, ourselves and our Tibetan cook), had lost two by death, but by October, 1931 had increased to EIGHTEEN. Our work among the Lisu in the To-ba-lo region had begun in April, 1931, with nothing, and six months later we were building a church, and had baptized SIXTY-FOUR new believers there. We had lost one by death and had one backslider.

✝

When we were in Long Beach, California, on our way to China, in 1929, we had met Miss Erma Warnick, who had come out to be a missionary. She was in Kunming working as secretary to the American Consul while she studied the language. She had been of invaluable help to us in forwarding packages and handling some of our funds, changing them into

Yunnan silver for us. She had also helped the Tarn family the month they were there, and had planned to come and work with us as an independent missionary as soon as she had learned enough Chinese. She was a dedicated Christian and a wonderful person. Not long after our terrible epidemic in Yea Chi, we received word that Miss Warnick had died from small pox, even though she had been vaccinated.

Now in October, 1931 word came from the Consul that it would be necessary for Russell to come to Kunming to help settle her "estate", inasmuch as she had been preparing to send on to us a considerable amount of our mission money when she suddenly became ill. He left November 6 on that exhausting sixty-nine day trip, riding horseback day after day.

From Kunming, Russell brought back a new worker for our mission, Miss Shu Djen Yang, who had been highly recommended by the missionaries there. She was originally a convert of the Chinese Home Mission, later a student nurse at the C.M.S. Hospital, had fairly good Bible training, and was experienced in both teaching and preaching.

At Wei Hsi, Russell found another worker, Mr. Lo Tse Chuen. We were well acquainted with him as he had been baptized in Batang while we were there and had come out with us as far as Wei Hsi. Now he wanted to work with us. He also knew the Bible fairly well, and we knew him to be an earnest worker, so Russell accepted him.

For the last three weeks of Russell's return trip from Kunming, he had a cold and a very persistent cough. Within a week after arriving home, because of his worn-out, weakened condition he developed influenza, which turned into pneumonia. Within two days his temperature rose to 105 degrees. He coughed so hard he spit blood, and he could hardly breathe because of the pain in his chest. In those days we had no sulfa drugs or penicillin, but I did all I knew how to do, and prayed day and night. Mr. Tarn and the others helped all they could. Our little group all prayed, and God heard our prayers. Where there were no doctors, one learned to lean hard on God. How thankful we were to have Him hear us.

Mr. Fu also had the "flu", and pneumonia, about the same time, but apparently he was in better physical condition, and his case did not seem so severe. Then, as Russell began to slowly recover I, too, had the "flu" but did not have pneumonia. We were all so weak we had to slow down on our mission work for a while. Russell felt the need of some outdoor exercise, and started planting a garden, which was very much needed, as fresh vegetables were hard to buy.

I had been teaching Eugene and Robert from the Calvert School Correspondence course since returning to Yea Chi, and resumed teaching even though I had almost constant aching in my limbs. This was probably caused from the malaria I had in Batang rather than from my recent illness. Russell finally decided to use a quinine preparation that had to be given hypodermically, even though he hesitated to do so. I felt a little better after that.

The Tarn family had valiantly and capably carried on the mission work while the rest of us were going through the various stages of influenza, which seemed to strike that region every January, February and March.

**NOTE: As they grew up, both Anzie Ruth and Drema Esther (Duje's daughters) became part of the family. Both accepted Christ as Savior at an early age, and gradually took their places in helping with the mission work. When the family returned to the U.S. after World War II, . Esther (then age 19) accompanied them, while Anzie remained behind to serve as companion and translator for missionary co-worker Miss Dorothy Sterling, R.N. As Dorothy and Anzie were traveling through Burma in December, 1949, Anzie contracted typhus, and died in Putao (formerly Ft. Hertz). Drema Esther stayed with the Morses, going with the family to Burma in 1950, and remained with Gertrude and Russell Morse until her marriage to Jesse Yangmi on April 15, 1963. Both Jesse and Drema Esther continued working with the mission until it became necessary to leave Burma. After work was started in Thailand, they formed their own mission organization, but continued to work closely with the rest of the family. Since she passed away in October, 1997, Jesse continues in this work.

15
Visiting Lisu Villages

The Chinese New Year celebration began February 17, 1932, and continued for two weeks. Most people stopped work at this time, but the missionaries and their helpers worked harder than ever. We conducted twelve nights of evangelistic meeting in our little street chapel, besides continuing our usual daily morning prayer meetings. Mr. Tarn, Mr. Fu, Miss Yang and Russell took turns preaching. The attention of the people seemed much more respectful and earnest than at our preceding series about eight months before.

At the conclusion of those Yea Chi meetings, Mr. Fu and Drang Wen Da (the converted "handyman"), visited our converts in the To-ba-lo region, across the Mekong River from Kang Pu. Due to Russell's absence and then the many illnesses, they had been neglected for several months. Our Lisu teacher, Swa-mi-pa, had done much to hold them faithful, but the native New Year celebrations, with its heathen festivities of drinking, dancing and spirit worship by all of the non-Christian friends had been too tempting for several families of the new converts. However, when our preachers visited, they attended the meetings and were quite penitent.

On Easter Sunday (1932) we had ten baptisms in Yea Chi and many more in the villages of Kang Pu, To-ba-lo and Dra-tsi-lo (pronounced Dra-tzi-lo) where we had outstations. Also, our dear Swa-mi-pa was traveling over the mountains teaching hymns and the Bible. He always had such a beautiful smiling face. From somewhere he had acquired a small accordion, and I can see him now — walking down those paths, singing at the top of his voice, with his hair blowing in the wind.

Following our Easter services in Yea Chi, Mr. Fu and Drang Wen Da again went to To-ba-lo to commemorate Easter there. Nearly two hundred Lisu people came to that two-day Easter celebration, and Mr. Fu baptized fourteen.

On one of Mr. Tarn's trips, he met two men whom he had known in Batang. One was Mr. Lwei Chen Hwa, who had been the magistrate in Batang for several years, and the other was Wang Hwai San, who was Mr. Lwei's personal attendant and body guard, and an expert in kung fu. Mr. Tarn talked to them about Christ and Christianity and they decided to come to Yea Chi to assist Mr. Tarn with his school duties.

✝

In May, 1932, for the first time in history, our village was visited by a Provincial Inspector of Education. You cannot imagine how important that was to us, unless you remember that our Christian school was the only serious attempt at education in all those border regions, except for one in Wei Hsi, four days' travel to the south. Remember, too, that the Yea Chi chief had made frequent attempts to stop our work. We thought, "What if the chief should bribe the Inspector to use his strong influence to have our school closed?" Well, we prayed! for the school was vital to all of our work. If the people could not read, how could they study their Bibles?

What that Inspector did for us surpassed our fondest hopes:

1) He reprimanded the "king" for oppressing the people, keeping them in ignorance, making himself rich, yet not using any of his wealth for public education;

2) he addressed the students of our school, saying, "Amid the darkness of the local 'king's' oppression you have a ray of light, in that the American missionaries have come and established this school with its capable

teachers. Make the most of your opportunity, by studying hard and becoming good citizens of the Republic. As for believing in Christianity, you have your freedom either to believe or to disbelieve."

3) He assured us that in spite of our lack of proper rooms and equipment, our school was the best-managed and best-taught north of Likiang, a city of about 40,000 population about ten days to the southeast;

4) and he commended our work to the Provincial Department of Education, thus helping us to secure better recognition.

Our Lisu teacher, Swa-mi-pa, brought us the news that on May 20 he had baptized four new penitent believers at Wu-ba-lo village in the To-ba-lo valley, and on June 5 had baptized fourteen in the newly opened Dra-tsi-lo valley. He said the converts wanted to be baptized without delay, so he had not waited until they could be examined by Mr. Fu or Russell.

✝

On June 18, 1932 the Chinese magistrate of Wei Hsi (who governed all that district, including the tribal kings) sent two militiamen with an urgent request for Russell to come at once and try to save his son's life. He had been very sick, and all other help had failed. His sickness had followed a violent beating by the father, and his condition had been made worse by Chinese drugs. Russell stayed several days at the magistracy, where he could look after the boy day and night, but the quarters were so damp and ill-ventilated that Russell decided to bring him back to Yea Chi. He was on that case for over five weeks, but could not save the boy.

That summer there was much sickness in our neighborhood — diarrhea, influenza and a queer kind of epidemic cough, as well as the ever-present malaria. On August 12 we were shocked by the unexpected death of Yung Je, one of our Christian Tibetan girls from Batang.

Meanwhile, several urgent requests for medical aid had come from the military commander at Atuntze, six stages north along the border. Although that town was notoriously wild and sinful, it was one of the most important trade centers between China and Tibet, and had a definite place in our future mission plans.

Russell felt this was a fine opportunity for an evangelistic tour, and talked me into letting 11-year-old Eugene and 9-year-old Robert go along with him and Mr. Fu. They took turns at preaching in both Chinese and Tibetan, and their messages were well received. Mr. Fu and Russell returned exhausted, but felt the trip was well worth the effort. For them, it was a campaign, but for Eugene and Robert, it was a picnic. During that tour, twenty-two new villages heard the Gospel for the first time.

While Russell and Mr. Fu went to Atuntze, our other evangelists preached across the Mekong, making four trips from Kang Pu and Yea Chi. During this time I kept busy, also. I wrote about seventy-five letters to our "rope-holders", ministered to the sick, listened to problems and helped Mr. Tarn and any others who needed it. I also canned all of the wild fruit I could get.

We learned that another village, Ai-wa-lo, was open to the Gospel, so in November, 1932 Russell went there to teach for two weeks. Fifty people accepted Christ as their Saviour and were baptized. On his way back, he stopped at To-ba-lo, where twelve more wanted to be baptized, in spite of the Kang Pu chief's continued persecution and the beating of two Christians from there.

☦

In December, 1932 we held our first Bible School at To-ba-lo for the new Christians, and several more were baptized in that ice-cold water. A log cabin had been built there for the Bible School. Mr. Fu had stayed to supervise the building, as we wanted it to be ready for the Christmas meetings. Many Christians came from the surrounding new villages, including Dra-tsi-lo and Ai-wa-lo.

We had a great Christmas celebration in Yea Chi. Mr. Tarn and I decided to present two Bible plays along with the preaching services. One was "The Prodigal Son" and the other was "The Birth of Christ." Mr. Tarn played the part of the prodigal son so realistically that his little girls broke out weeping when they saw him as a ragged swineherd lamenting his misfortunes. Our own Anzie, Duje's daughter, played the part of Mary in the story of Christ's birth. The village people attended the services, and seeing the plays seemed to help them get a better understanding of the messages that had been preached to them.

As we looked back on the year of 1932, we found that 118 had obeyed the Lord in baptism. These, with two in 1930, and seventy-two in 1931, made a total of 192 already baptized into His church where formerly there had been no church and not even one believer. These numbers alone, however, fail to reflect the total influence upon the region where hundreds more had started thinking seriously about their relation to the True and Holy God. The Gospel had been preached in scores of villages where it had never been heard before.

16
Sickness, Sorrow, and Loss

In the midst of our many trials in that heathen land, the daily morning devotional services held in our home, with all our mission group meeting together, proved to be a joy, and the source of great encouragement and comfort for all of us. These times seemed to give us the spiritual strength we needed to face each day.

There was always much sickness in the Yea Chi area, and in the early spring LaVerne again had influenza. By mid-summer, oriental amoebic dysentery and related diseases raged throughout the Mekong Valley, with unsanitary conditions and the effects of an extended drought contributing to the spread of disease.

In June, 1933, Russell and Eugene went on a long, three-weeks' evangelistic trip to the Salween Valley, accompanied by Eh-dzeh-pa, who was to be the evangelist and teacher in that region. Russell said he had never seen people more heart-hungry and earnestly seeking the truth. Fifty-five new converts were baptized on the west side of the river one Sunday and seventy-four more were baptized on the east side the following Sunday. With the thirty-seven baptized earlier in the year that made a total of one hundred and sixty-six. These believers were in two distinct but co-operative congregations.

Five days after Russell returned home he became ill with the amoebic dysentery that was so prevalent. Profuse hemorrhages from the intestines were extremely debilitating, and within four days he was quite emaciated. While Russell was still sick, Della (Mrs. Fu) came down with it, and a few days later, I also became ill. Although Russell and I were too ill and weak to leave our beds we sent medicine over to Della.

In some ways my case seemed even more severe than Russell's. Because I seemed to suffer more on alternate days, Russell decided I had malarial dysentery and gave me a French medicine which had been recommended to him. It was two weeks before I was able to leave my bed, and nearly as long before Russell was able to walk.

Della's illness was complicated by pregnancy, and became progressively worse. Sadly, neither she nor the child survived. Mr. Fu had bought an acre of ground at Gu-la Village, about a half hour's walk from Yea Chi, and here he buried his wife. We encouraged him to lead the daily devotional time to help and comfort him in his grief. He worried about his three little boys and how they would be cared for during his evangelistic trips. It was heartbreaking to hear little Joseph crying for his mother. Before the epidemic ended, scores of children and many adults died from the disease and many more suffered from complications for a long time.

✞

Yea Chi was a wicked, heathen village. One evening one of Mr. Lwei's young servant girls went to the mill to grind some grain and was attacked and assaulted by a gang of ruffians. One of them also had previously insulted our young cook. When Mr. Lwei and Russell tried to have the culprits arrested, the local police just shrugged their shoulders in a "so what" attitude. Then Mr. Tarn went with Mr. Lwei to take the case to the magistrate in Wei Hsi. He ordered two policemen to go to Yea Chi and arrest the criminals, but they never arrived there. When Russell sent word to Wei Hsi that the guilty ones had not been arrested, the magistrate investigated and found that the Police Commissioner and his two men had been bribed, and the men had never left Wei Hsi. They were summarily dismissed and two more policemen were sent with positive orders to make the arrests. One of the attackers was the headman's son and a relative of the "king", so they had, of course, tried to cover up the whole affair. When their trial came up, the one who had insulted our cook was fined and the other nine were jailed. The Wei Hsi magistrate had been educated at a mission school and was not as corrupt as many of the officials. Also, Mr. Lwei had been a magistrate for several years and still was influential. We hoped conditions would now improve so the young women could go out on the road without fear.

Reports from our outstations were encouraging. Despite much sickness during the summer there were very few backsliders among the converts. Our workers were too few to visit the different congregations and hold services more than once or twice a month in each place, and yet each group faithfully met together each Lord's day to study the Bible and pray together.

✞

In the fall of 1933, while Russell was at home, I went to Tobalo, for ten days of teaching and rest, accompanied by our three sons, Daniel (Swa-mi-pa's son), Miss Yang, and our cook. Tobalo was not a real village, but a scattered community, so it was hard for some of the people to come at night. Even so, twenty-five to thirty new Christians attended the Bible teaching services held each evening. We were always happy to teach any and all who could come. The log cabin, with three adjoining rooms, was centrally located, and was used as their church and Bible school. On Sunday, I went to the village of Drat-si-lo to teach the Christians there.

We acquired a fine location in the Ai-wa-lo valley to build a chapel and school for the combined congregations at Wu-ba-di and Wa-shi-lo-gai. Foreigners could not buy land in China, so we bought it in the name of our faithful Lisu evangelist, Swa-mi-pa. He signed an agreement for us to use it as long as we needed to, then it would go to him as a reward for his services which had indeed been outstandingly worthwhile. We also negotiated to buy a similar site in the Drat-si-lo valley, midway between Ai-wa-lo and To-ba-lo, where a horse road to the Salween Valley had recently been opened.

While I was in Tobalo, Russell wrote from Yea Chi that the evil and cruel Shang Chen tribe of Tibetans had raided the town of Chung-tien and surrounding region, taking food and everything else they could. Some of them went on to Atuntze and said they would come to Yea Chi. The nondescript local militia, with their ancient guns, or crossbows and poisoned arrows, went to guard the one pass north of Yea Chi and two to the east. Many women and children, with their household goods, were sent across to the west side of the river. If the Shang Chen really invaded Yea Chi, the plan was that everyone would cross the Mekong and then cut the rope bridge. But the threatened raid did not materialize, and we felt sure that God turned aside the danger in answer to prayer.

We returned from Tobalo after ten days, feeling refreshed. Just five days later Miss Yang announced her engagement to Mr. Fu. We were happy for them, and glad that now there would be someone to look after the three children while he was gone.

✝

In the fall of 1933 Russell was planning a trip to the Salween Valley but before leaving he had a good meeting at Tobalo, with three services. Six new converts were baptized. Then while Russell went to the Salween, Mr. Fu and Drang-wen-da went to Ai-wa-lo and Dra-tsi-lo, where the Gospel message was spreading rapidly.

In October (1933), Russell left on a three-week trip to the Salween Valley, taking with him our younger son, Robert, along with our faithful Lisu pastor Swa-mi-pa, Li-Chi-Chang, the pastor/teacher at the Kang Pu outstation, Eh-dzeh-pa, the evangelist/teacher from the Salween Valley, and Ho-bei-ma, who acted as interpreter and carrier. The pass over which they had to travel was only open from mid-May to mid-December.

On the second day out from Tobalo, they were met by ten Christian men from the Salween Valley who had come to carry loads for Russell. They went down the south side of the ridge beyond the pass to the hamlet of Ngwa-dza-mieh where there were two Christian families. Nightly meetings were held there and negotiations were started to acquire a chapel site. The converts had stood up creditably since the June meeting, but there was a crying need for pastors and chapels. Preparations were also being made to build a new chapel at Pu-ge-leh (Silvermine Ridge).

From Bu-la-di village, across a very high ridge, came a delegation interested in becoming Christians, asking for books and a teacher. It was arranged that Swa-mi-pa and Eh-dzeh-pa were to go there soon.

On the way to Latsa village, they met Aduh Heh-a-kwa, who was one of those baptized at Tobalo just after Easter. He had returned to his native village of Meh-la in the Salween Valley and settled down there to witness for Christ. With the help of only one Lisu beginner's book and the power of the Holy Spirit, ten families in his village had turned to the Lord and were meeting together for worship each Lord's Day. He had come now for more books, and Russell said that giving those ten books to Aduh gave him more joy than any other time he had given out books

Those primitive tribespeople, who had never heard of Jesus Christ and whose language did not even have a word for love, began gradually to understand and accept the message of God's love, and salvation from sin through the Lord. Those who were converted showed their heathen neighbors what it meant to be a Christian. They learned to pray, to study God's Word in their own language, to sing hymns, and to gather together as congregations according to the New Testament. Poor as they were, they learned to give whatever they could to further the spreading of the Gospel through native preachers and evangelists. What a thrill to hear the strains of "What a Friend We Have In Jesus" echoing in the canyons and mountains where formerly only Satan reigned.

✝

While traveling through the valley, Russell preached and taught the Bible each night, and each day prayed for and treated the sick who came for treatment and medicine. Nine more converts were baptized. Mr. Li did well in helping with the Lisu work, and was an exceptionally good traveling companion. And, of course, it was always a pleasure to travel with good-natured ever-smiling Swa-mi-pa.

After Russell returned to Yea Chi, Mr. Fu and Miss Yang were married. The local people, Christians and non-Christians alike, were all curious to see what a Christian wedding was like. It was a big event and we all had to help. In keeping with Chinese custom, the bride was dressed in dark pink, and was carried in a closed chair to the church. They were united in marriage by our pastor, Mr. Tarn. Mr. Fu had built a house on his acre of land, and they went there to live.

Meanwhile, I was busy teaching my children so they would not be behind their age group when we returned to America. Two afternoons each week I had the women's meetings and children's Bible School, and kept up with mission correspondence the other afternoons. When I could find time, I attended to the sick and visited in the homes. In the evenings, I again taught our children, along with our two orphan girls (Duje's daughters) and Daniel. So I was very busy.

✝

Along with the joys of missionary work, there are many sorrows, and on December 3, 1933 came one of the most traumatic incidents we had yet experienced. Sometimes a "wolf" gets into the flock, and these Oriental "wolves" are indeed fierce.

For some time there had been a problem of jealousy among the workers, and Mr. Tarn seemed to be the object of most of it. It was true that he received a bit higher salary, because of his experience, training, and position as principal, but the others seemed to think that he was just getting preferential treatment. Also, Mr. Lwei had asked Mr. Tarn to give his daughter Wu-

Lan in marriage to Mr. Lwei's son. Mr. Tarn replied that it could only be by the choice of the girl. This was taken as a direct affront. Although we knew about these things, we never dreamed that the resentment was so deep that it would result in physical harm to the Tarn family.

Then one Sunday morning, while we were all at church, and Russell was away at one of the outstations, someone slipped in and put some poison into the chicken soup or stew which was being cooked specially for Mr. Tarn because he had been sick. Of course the whole Tarn family ate it, and all were poisoned and very sick. All recovered except our earnest Christian worker, Mr. Tarn, who lived for two days. He had been ill with flu, and his weakened system was unable to cope with the poison. I immediately sent for Russell, but we were unable to save Mr. Tarn. Almost his last words were to his students, "Memorize Romans 8:28": "And we know that all things work together for good to them that love God, to them who are the called according to His purpose."

We were overwhelmed with grief and could not help crying, "Why, why?" This kind, cultured and intelligent man had been included in all of our future mission plans. His influence and ministry had greatly strengthened the people of Yea Chi, giving them a new sense of the Gospel as lived by such a man. They began to realize the difference between the old ways and the Christian way as taught by our evangelists. Mr. Tarn's good example would live in the hearts and lives of his students and others who knew him. He was, indeed, a martyr to the cause of Christ. The school had to be temporarily closed until new arrangements could be made.

Mrs. Tarn, my best friend in that primitive mission field, was overcome with grief and felt so lost without him. She and her five children were a two months' caravan journey away from relatives. They had all been such loyal helpers. Mrs. Tarn, according to Chinese custom, wanted to take Mr. Tarn's body back to Chengdu for burial, since that was his home, and where his parents lived. However, when they arrived at Wei Hsi, the officials there would not give them permission to transport the body through their area, so they had to have the burial near Wei Hsi. The mission, along with some individual contributions, provided for their trip back to Chengdu, with enough extra to purchase a small home there. We were relieved that their loyal cook could accompany them.

Because of all this, Russell was so upset he could neither sleep nor work. We were both very weary already, and this additional blow had been almost too much. Then the Lord sent a "ministering angel" to bind up our broken hearts. Brother Heo, a Christian government school inspector came to Yea Chi, the first time such a man had ever been there. He was really a pastor in southern Yunnan Province but had obtained the position of inspector in order to help the school boys of Yunnan in a Christian way. He was a graduate of Nanking University who spoke good English, and was a convert of L. Chas. Beals, a long-time missionary to China (by that time retired). Brother Heo was such a comfort to us, and after his visit Russell was able to sleep much better. Also he stopped grieving so much. We thanked the Lord for sending Mr. Heo to help in our time of need. After a short stay in Yea Chi, Mr. Heo went on to Tobalo to visit our work there, and in a few days Russell and Robert joined him.

Although Russell was still weak, he resumed preaching at our outstations, as well as at home. Our evangelists, Mr. Fu, Swa-mi-pa, Drang Wen Da, and others continued to work faithfully in the five Lisu outstations in the Mekong and Salween Valleys. Mr. Li Chi Chang evangelized in the Kang Pu area.

171

17
Second Furlough

Because of our expanding mission field, it was becoming more and more urgent that we have additional help. For a year or more we had been earnestly asking our Advisory Council in America for help in getting more missionaries to assist us. Under consideration was a young missionary couple, Dr. and Mrs. Norton Bare, who had arrived at the Batang mission just before we left in 1926. The great depression in the U.S. and consequent loss of income had caused problems for the U.C.M.S., and then after some of their buildings were burned in an attack by Tibetan marauders, they had closed down and sent their missionaries home in 1932. Dr. and Mrs. Bare had visited us in Yea Chi on their way back to America and we were favorably impressed by them. They had been in Batang long enough to learn Chinese and Tibetan, and we could certainly use a doctor, so we thought they would be just what we needed. We were also interested in Vernon and Mona Newland who were anxious to become missionaries in China. They, too, seemed well qualified and arrangements were made for them to join us. Now, with our health so depleted from overwork and tragedies, we desperately needed a furlough, and we urged our Advisory Council to do all that was possible to speed up the departure of the Bares and the Newlands.

The Gospel was spreading from the Mekong and Salween Valleys in China, across the next mountain range, which formed the China-Burma border, into the Irrawaddy Valley in northernmost Burma, to a place called La-ta-go. Through the efforts of our native Lisu evangelists, churches began to spread through the sub-tropical jungles of northern Burma. Here both the Lisu and Rawang tribes made a primitive living by clearing patches of the jungle on steep mountainsides, where they planted meager crops of rice, corn and millet. Sometimes they had to use their crossbows with poisoned arrows against wild animals to protect their crops, and to provide meat.. Before they became Christians, they often used them against each other, as well.

In the fall of 1934, in anticipation of the arrival of Dr. Bare and his family, we began packing most of our possessions to be put in storage. Eugene and I did most of the packing while Russell was away. Our fourth child was due in February, and we were anxious to start on our trip home as soon as possible. Because of the uncertainty of caravan traveling we wanted to allow six weeks for the journey to Kunming.

We were very happy when the Bares arrived in November, 1934, and immediately began explaining the work and introducing them to our evangelists. They decided to stay in Kang Pu instead of Yea Chi, leaving any available housing for the Newlands, who arrived a little later. We arranged for our two orphan girls, Anzie and Drema, to stay with the Bares until we returned.

✝

At last we were on our way! Because I was between six and seven months into pregnancy, I rode in a hwagan, which is much like a hammock chair and suspended on two long bamboo poles, with a good back and a foot rest, while Russell and the boys rode horses. We went through Wei Hsi, Tali-fu (pronounced Dali-fu) and other small cities without mishap until we arrived at the last regular "horse inn" before the walled city of Tsu Hsiung. Eugene and Robert, who understood Chinese well, were in the courtyard watching the caravan men unload our baggage. The men of the household were talking

173

strangely, saying "they" were going to take the big boy with his father, but not the smaller ones. The boys immediately came and told Russell what they had heard and he, remembering other things he had heard along the way, began to be alarmed.

I was always tired and not feeling well by the end of the day's travel, so as soon as we had eaten supper and the cots were put up, I went to bed. Late that night Russell heard loud talking downstairs, so he slipped quietly into a hayloft where he could see and hear a group of men sitting around and drinking in the landlord's room. They were drunk and talking rather loudly in Chinese. Russell listened long enough to learn that they planned to kidnap him and Eugene the next morning as we went around the base of a high mountain, and hold them for a large ransom.

He came back from the hayloft to our room, white and trembling and, as always, we took our troubles to the Lord. With His help, Russell began to formulate a plan. We had two trustworthy Tibetan helpers with us and we had an American missionary friend, Miss Cornelia Morgan, who lived at the Bethel Mission in Tsu Hsiung, about a half day's journey away, where there was a large magistracy. He wrote a note to Miss Morgan, telling of our predicament, then contacted our Tibetans without being noticed and told them of the kidnap plans.

The next morning Russell told me to stay in bed that day, and told the caravan leader that I was too ill to travel. He told them we would have to stay there until I felt better, but he would pay them for the lay-over time. Since I had been ill most of the trip, that aroused no suspicions. Meanwhile, our Tibetans had slipped away early that morning with the note hidden in one of their boots and delivered it to our friend. She then notified the magistrate, who did not question the information, because there had been a great deal of trouble at that particular spot — the same place where Dr. Shelton was kidnapped in 1920, and where many robberies had occurred.

The magistrate lined up fifty soldiers (who were opium smokers) and chose eight of the best, with their "best" (least rusty!) guns, and sent them to protect us. They arrived at sundown, and our messengers, who had come most of the way with the soldiers, slipped quietly in after dark. The amazement on the faces of that band of men was a sight to behold. Our Tibetans told us of hearing the landlord, who turned out to be the leader of the group, say "Now we can't carry out our plans, since the soldiers are here". Then he questioned each one, trying to find out who had told of their plan. They all denied it, and he said, "Well, surely one of you did".

After we arrived in America and I was telling my mother of this experience, she remembered that at about that time she was awakened in the night with the terrible feeling that something was wrong. She woke my sister and said, "Helen, get up. Gertrude is in trouble and we must pray for her". On checking back, we found it was the very day that we were so earnestly praying for a solution to our dilemma. The Holy Spirit had awakened my mother, thousands of miles away, so she could add her prayers to ours. And God answered them.

✝

After seven more traveling days we reached Kunming and stayed at the China Inland Mission with dear Bro. H. A. C. Allen and his wife, who were always so kind and helpful when we passed through. After about five days, seeing that Russell was exceedingly nervous from our past experiences, they both advised us to go on to Hong Kong, where we would be entirely separated from the mainland of China, in a place where Russell could really relax. Also, because of my condition, they advised us to take along a Christian nurse whom they found for us. The Allens made all of the necessary arrangements for us. We appreciated so very much all their kindness and helpfulness.

We proceeded by rail to Haiphong in what is now northern Vietnam, where we boarded a small, very crowded boat for Hong Kong. Because there had been trouble with pirates on the South China Sea, all foreigners were locked in the first class accommodations, away from the second class, which included our native nurse. There was only one cabin available, so the boys slept in the officers' lounge. The boys were excited about the possibility of an attack by the pirates, but that did not occur, for which we were thankful. Russell and I felt we had had enough excitement for one trip. We could obtain permission for our nurse to come to us, if needed, but someone had to be there to unlock and relock the door.

In seven days we were safely in Hong Kong. We stayed at a mission home for a few days, then Russell had a boil on his hand which became infected. He had red streaks going up his arm that looked like blood poisoning, so went to the hospital for treatment. The doctor examined him and said he had never seen any living person with such low blood pressure. That was why he had been so weak for such a long time. He was kept in the hospital for over a week. When the time came for our baby to be born, I had to go alone, but I knew Russell was somewhere in one of those many big buildings.

✟

On February 25, 1935, our little daughter Ruth Margaret Morse was born. After riding six weeks in a hwagan, escaping from robbers on land, and pirates on the sea, our baby daughter was finally in my arms! She was a beautiful, blue-eyed, dark-haired smiling baby. Russell was soon able to come and see our long-looked-for little girl, and the boys rejoiced that at last they had a little sister.

Three weeks later the doctor gave permission for us to sail for America. We obtained tourist class cabins on one of the "President" line ships, and had a very nice trip home. We stopped in Japan, where we visited with our missionary friends, the Cunninghams. They talked to us very urgently about joining them in the work in Japan, begging us to give up the work in China, and come take over the work in Japan when they retired. But we told them God had given us the work in Lisuland and we couldn't give that up. Even at the time we were there, in 1935, Japan was working to build up and strengthen their military forces, and having frequent military and naval maneuvers. It was only a few years later that there was war between Japan and the United States. However, at that time we had no inkling of such a thing, and we enjoyed our ten days of visiting there, before proceeding on to the States. We arrived in Seattle in April, and spent a few days there visiting with Russell's sister, Mrs. Louise Whitham, before going on to Oklahoma.

I was still weak and didn't seem to be recuperating properly, so we went to the Mayo Clinic in Rochester, Minnesota to try to find the cause. We were told it was too soon after the birth of my child to make a proper diagnosis. Then both Eugene and Robert had infected tonsils so we took them to a Christian hospital in St. Louis to have them removed. We finally arrived in Tulsa where we visited with Russell's parents and two sisters, then went on to Oklahoma City where my mother and my school teacher sister lived. They owned a duplex there and we moved into the unoccupied side of it. Our three boys needed to be in school and that duplex was conveniently located for school children. LaVerne was six years old, and in the fall of 1935 entered public school for the first time in his life. Eugene and Robert attended a fine junior high school, where they enrolled in ninth grade.. Their grades were among the highest in their class, and they were especially complimented on their excellent English, which made me very proud. There was even a write-up in the paper about them. They both liked music, and were delighted to find they could enroll in any instrumental course they wished. Robert chose to study trumpet, and Eugene decided to try learning to play the violin.

Russell accepted many speaking invitations, often taking with him his mother, Mrs. Ruth Morse, who always enjoyed the fellowship. Russell's dear mother had very much wanted and prayed for a son to dedicate to the Lord's work. He had been interested in mission work since he was a youngster, and had been quite active in young people's work. Mother Morse's prayers were answered. She became our forwarding agent while we were in the mission field, and made an inestimable contribution to our work. She labored faithfully, not only for the mission work, but also in her local church. She was truly zealous for the cause of Christ.

18
Asia Again

In the summer of 1936, after the school term had ended, we took our children to the MINN-IA-DAK Christian Service Camp at Worthington, Minnesota. We later attended the Lake James School of Missions, where we met Miss Isabel Maxey and her family. Her father was a minister in Ohio, where she had helped him in his ministry. She now made her decision to join us in our mission work. Knowing her strong Christian family background strengthened our belief and assurance that she would be a dedicated worker. Her brother, Mark, later became a missionary to Japan. After leaving Lake James we went to Cedar Lake Christian Camp and enjoyed a wonderful fellowship there. During Russell's travels he visited Johnson Bible College in Tennessee, where he met Harold Taylor, who was seriously interested in missionary work and he, too, decided to join us in our work.

It had been our intention to leave for China by the end of 1936 so, in the fall, we began buying clothing in graduated sizes for the children, and collecting other supplies we would need to take back with us. Eugene, now 15, and Robert, 13, had both made the decision to finish high school through the American School correspondence course from Chicago. They considered the mission field as their home and felt they were needed there. I began teaching them even before we left the United States.

We left for California the first part of December, 1936 to board the ship for the beginning of our return journey to Yea

Chi, but a severe shipping strike held up our departure until February, 1937. While we were waiting for the strike to end I received word that my mother was quite ill with pneumonia, so I returned to Oklahoma City to be with her until she began to recover. During the eighteen months we had stayed in Oklahoma City, I had learned that my mother prayed for me all day long when I was away on the mission field. One day the postman had asked me, "Are you the missionary your mother has been praying for?" Although she did recover from that illness, it was the last time I saw my precious mother, as she passed away while we were in China.

Russell took advantage of our delay to purchase what medicines he thought he would need, along with a few other supplies. The strike was finally settled, and on February 16, 1937 we were finally able to leave. Our many Christian friends from the churches in Los Angeles and Long Beach escorted us to the boat and sang hymns until the ship was about to leave. Then we all sang "God Be With You Till We Meet Again." It was both a happy and a sad farewell. We sailed on the "Taiyo Maru", a Japanese steamer, which proved to be quite pleasant and comfortable. Our two new missionaries, Isabel Maxey and Harold Taylor, were happy to be with our family, actually on the way to Lisuland in West China. Our furlough had been a bit longer than usual, first because of the weakened health of Russell and myself due to the strenuous and exhausting circumstances of the previous term, and then delay due to the long shipping strike.

✝

We arrived in Hong Kong after making short stops at Honolulu, Tokyo, and Kobe. My health had not improved, and Russell decided I should go to the Matilda Hospital to get a checkup. As I walked in the door of the doctor's office, the doctor pointed at me and said, "That young lady must not go home". When I protested that I had a two-year old baby daughter, he said that others could take care of her. He insisted that I stay in the hospital for an immediate examination. They found that my red blood count was seriously low, and it was dangerous for me to be up. I remained in the hospital for two weeks of rest, and Isabel and the boys took care of Ruth Margaret. The doctor wanted me to stay longer, but we convinced him that Russell could give me the necessary shots, so he finally consented, after giving detailed instructions about the treatment. When I returned to my family Ruth said happily, "Mama sick, NO! Mama stay with me".

Although I was still quite weak we sailed for Haiphong as soon as we could. We all decided to try always to thank God for everything, good or bad, along the journey. We did not have to pay customs on our hand baggage at Haiphong, only on our freight. When we had finished with customs, we proceeded on that same narrow gauge railway we had traveled before, and arrived in Kunming on April 21, 1937.

We hoped to be ready to leave for Yea Chi within two weeks, but as usual in the Orient, it took much longer than we had anticipated. As soon as our freight arrived, we started repacking it for the caravan animals, but the heavy rains started, causing more delay. Our cook, Hlanzone, had married while we were away, and she and her husband, Chang Hsin Hsien, arrived from Yea Chi to help us on the road. How wonderful it was to have them with us! and to hear all the news from Yea Chi.

Isabel decided to stay in Kunming to study Chinese and wait for a friend who was to join her. Robert had broken a tooth while we were in Honolulu and needed work done on it while we were there. While waiting for travel arrangements to be completed, both Eugene and Robert worked on their correspondence course and did well. In between times, Eugene helped quite a lot on repacking our baggage into the right size boxes for carrying on horse back.

☩

We finally left Kunming on June 26. We traveled on two busses, as this mode of travel had been recommended to us, but both vehicles were ancient, and before long they began having trouble, so we did not arrive at our destination until dark. We tried again the next day but the bus still had trouble, so we decided to hire ponies. On July 8 we finally arrived in Tali-fu, where the China Inland Mission welcomed us to their mission home. We were so thankful for their wonderful Christian hospitality and, of course, for the nice English food and good beds. We enjoyed visiting with those dear people.

We left Tali-fu as soon as we could arrange for transportation. As I was not yet equal to riding a horse a chair was provided for me. About an hour after we left, I was stricken with bacillary dysentery which made me so weak I could not stand and could hardly sit. By the time Russell caught up with me I was barely conscious. The pain was terrible, almost like cholera. He gave me some medicine which helped get me through the day. That evening he continued the treatment and after several days I was better and able to travel, for which we were thankful.

We arrived in Yea Chi about a month after leaving Kunming. Dr. Bare and his family had gone on to Atuntze, leaving Mr. and Mrs. Newland in charge of the work. We found the Newlands busily packing to leave for Atuntze, also, but were happy to meet them and hear of their experiences. We were extremely glad to see our evangelists and old friends in Yea Chi and to find they were still carrying on the work.

It was much too crowded for us all to stay with the Newlands, especially while they were trying to pack, so Russell, Harold, Eugene and Robert went to our outstation at Kang Pu. It was awfully hard to find suitable food there, and the first day Harold became ill with a strange sickness. He could use his hands, but could not stand up. Our cook's husband, Chang Hsin Hsien, also became ill with the same sickness. Russell brought them both back to Yea Chi, but neither he nor Mr. Newland had ever seen anything like it, nor could they find anything about it in the medical books. Russell treated them the best he could, and they both gradually began to recover.

While Harold was confined to his room, he helped me a great deal by teaching LaVerne his Calvert School lessons, and sometimes writing letters for us. The Newlands finally were able to leave for Atuntze on August 27.

All of the main evangelists came to Yea Chi from the outlying congregations to welcome us back and to confer about the work. They all reported an unusual amount of sickness in the Mekong Valley and said it was much worse among the Salween Valley villages. In some places it was so bad that families fled into the mountains. This sickness severely tested the faith of the new believers. As non-Christians they would have called for their spirit priests (sometimes called shamans) in such cases. A few who were not thoroughly grounded in the faith DID call the spirit priests, but later came back and confessed their sin.

✞

Russell was eager to get into the field again, and as soon as he had taken care of the most important things in Yea Chi he made a trip to Tobalo and taught there for a week. That autumn of 1937 he also went on across the very high pass to visit the more than fifteen congregations in the Salween Valley. A representative of each of nine of the churches in that area came to escort him from Tobalo over the pass. It took a day and a half to climb over the pass to the nearest church. Horses could not climb that mountain. From all he could see and hear, the Christians and evangelists had been faithful to Christ. How we did praise God for that! Christians and evangelists were going deeper and deeper into the jungles and mountains to preach. They had even established three small churches on the Burma side of the border, about two to three weeks' travel from Yea Chi, as the Lisu there were also hungry for the Gospel.

While Russell was away I kept busy writing letters for the mission, supervising Sunday School, visiting in the homes, caring for the many sick people who came for medicine and other help, speaking at some of the services or helping our pastor, Lee Chao Shen. He had been converted while in our

Sunday School several years before, had served the church faithfully and had married one of our Christian girls. Now they had two nice little boys. As always, we held daily morning worship services for our workers and ourselves.

At that time we had about fourteen Lisu preachers who were earnest and faithful. They were not paid a salary, but we gave them salt, tea, and once a year a small bolt of blue cloth, which was enough to make a shirt, coat and a pair of trousers. For the Lisu, tea with salt in it was a real luxury, and in exchange for either tea or salt, the Lisu would willingly give food. We also gave each preacher several copies of question-and-answer Bible primers in the Lisu language, which could either be traded for food or sold for a small amount of money, but only to those who seemed genuinely interested in becoming Christians. We found it was always best to ask for something in return, because then the books became much more important to them.

After settling our family in the adobe house vacated by the Newlands, we decided to have the loose tiles on the roof cemented on to help prevent leaks in the rainy season and to keep out the winter winds. We also had three windows put in the mud walls. For storage space, we fixed up a rough attic, which we laughingly called our RATtic because of the rats running around up there.

✝

That Christmas season of 1937 was a happy one for all of us, both at Tobalo and Yea Chi. The Lisu Christians of the Mekong Valley decided to have a united Christmas celebration at Tobalo. It was really a "convention", lasting from Friday night to Sunday night. Russell, Eugene, Robert, and Harold (who had to be carried in a hwagan), all went on Wednesday, December 22, to help with preparations for accomodating so many people. On Friday the Lisu began arriving from Yea Chi, Kang Pu, Drat-si-lo, Wa-shi-lo-gai, Ba-loh and other places. About three hundred were in attendance. One old brother from our northernmost Mekong congregation walked FOUR days to be there.

I had not planned to go, but Russell sent word for me to come if possible, so I made arrangements for the cows, chickens, geese, pigs, etc. to be cared for. With me on the twenty-mile trip were Hlanzone (our cook), Drema Esther (our younger orphan girl who had returned to us from Atuntze), LaVerne, and Ruth. We had one hwagan in which we took turns riding, except Ruth, who was carried on the back of one of the men. When we arrived in Tobalo just at dark on Christmas Eve, a long line of Christians stood waiting to shake hands and welcome us.

There were preaching services that night, of course. After the service, most of the three hundred Christians gathered around bonfires, which provided light as well as warmth, and sang hymns. I don't think they slept much that night. The next day, the 25th, we had two long services. On Sunday morning we all had communion together as we knelt in prayer. At meal-time, everyone ate together and had a time of fellowship. The mission furnished the meat, the Christians from other villages furnished the rice and other food, and the Tobalo Christians did the cooking for the two meals a day. Sunday evening was the farewell service. I'm sure everyone felt that they had had a spiritual feast.

We returned to Yea Chi on Monday, and on Tuesday evening began our revival meetings which continued until the next Monday. We had some fine sermons, and the attention was unusually good.

In February, 1937 we started back to Asia with two new recruits, Isabel Maxey and Harold Taylor. L-R: Isabel Maxey, Robert, Russell holding Ruth Margaret, me, Eugene, LaVerne, Harold Taylor.

A rope bridge crossing across the river.

An alternative to the rope bridge, when the river isn't too high.

A Lisu congregation in the Salween Valley.

Another Lisu congregation in the Salween Valley.

19
Trials and Travel

In 1938 we began hearing reports about the Sino-Japanese war developments which were quite disturbing. The capital was moved to Chungking in Szechuan Province. The remote province of Yunnan suddenly became very important in China's defense system. Under pressure from the provincial government, using forced labor, work was being carried on day and night on a motor road from Tali-fu (pronounced Da-LEE-foo) to the Burma border, later known as the Burma Road. It became famous during World War II as a major supply route, and was the scene of many fierce battles between the Japanese and the Allied Forces.

Robert had to return to Kunming for further dental work and Lee Chao Shen and Daniel accompanied him. They made that entire strenuous trip in thirteen days. Before the motor road was built, it would have taken a month. Now the bus service from Tali-fu to Kunming reduced to only two days what formerly took thirteen days. Isabel Maxey was still in Kunming and we hoped the boys might accompany her back to Yea Chi.

When Harold Taylor had become ill with that strange illness which made him unable to walk, Eugene had taken over caring for him, taking his meals to him, running errands, etc. Gradually Harold's condition had improved to the point where he could walk around some in the house and yard, but he still was not strong enough for the rough trails. However, he was anxious to help with anything he could do, and was a willing worker. His illness was later diagnosed as a form of polio.

✝

It is hard for most people to visualize the problems that beset missionaries in that primitive land. Consider one not-too-unusual example. One Sunday when our pastor and evangelist, Lee Chao Shen, was eating dinner with his family and guests, an out-of-town tax collector came to his house to collect the equivalent of $4.00 in taxes. There was no money in the house, so the official said he was going to shoot him. When he said that, Lee Chao Shen's wife and guests jumped in front of him and begged, "Don't do that". A local official gradually pushed the tax collector out of the house.

The evangelist's relatives came running to our house to get the money but when they returned, the official had gone on to the next house. Lee Chao Shen took the money to the local official to give to the tax collector but the collector refused it, saying, "He will have to bring it in person so he can be punished". Punishment was usually a beating and a fine of $100 or so. Occasionally the offender was hung. This man had been cruel to several others in town, kicking and slapping one man, and most of the villagers were angry. We heard later that, in one village, he had killed one man and caused two others to jump in the river and drown.

The local official brought the money back to Lee Chao Shen, who was now at our home, but he refused to accept it. The local official was afraid to disobey the out-of-town official so he threw the money on the floor and left. We would not let Lee Chao Shen take the money to the collector, as we felt he had done no wrong and should not suffer. We also advised him not to return to his home for a while but to stay with some of his many relatives who lived all around us. Russell was away that evening so Eugene, our cook and I went to take the money to the collector. He was busy, fining a crowd of opium smokers, so I returned home to put Ruth to bed. While I was doing that, Eugene again offered the money, but again it was refused.

189

The next morning the local official, nervous and still afraid, came and begged me to go with him, with the money, because he had stood up for the evangelist. We all prayed before leaving. I explained the circumstances, and presented the money to the Yea Chi "king", but he didn't dare take it. Just then the tax collector came, and again I offered the money to him, but he just shrugged his shoulders and very impolitely said he couldn't take it. I told him the local official had thrown the money on my floor, it was not mine, and I would throw it down on their floor. Furthermore, I told him I was an American lady, accustomed to being treated in a polite manner, and if he were a gentleman he would not act that way. I also said that I would report the matter to Kunming — and a lot more. A large crowd of townspeople had gathered, and highly complimented me for my courage in speaking my mind. Threatening to report the incident to Kunming made the local officials take notice immediately. I got only as far as the door when they asked me, very politely, to come back to try to settle the matter. They said they would ask the collector to take the money if I wouldn't report it. I agreed to speak to him if he would act like a gentleman. We talked for a long time and finally the collector told the local official to take the money, called the matter finished, and bowed me out. We heard later that he ran away, probably with thousands of dollars. So passed another crisis.

✞

In the early summer of 1938 Russell made an extended trip to the Salween Valley, and while there wrote:

"Last Friday afternoon, June 24, I had the surprise of the year when, just about an hour after my arrival from the south, two young men — H.A. Howard and P. S. Chaplin, from the 60th British Rifles — arrived from the north. They had come over part of our 1927 trail from Forth Hertz (Putao) to Sukin in the upper Salween Valley. Both were emaciated, rain-soaked, lousy and suffering from poisonous ulcers on both legs caused by leeches and other insects. Chaplin was so crippled he had to be carried in a hwagan. I promptly gave each a shot of iron and other needed medicine. I

also shared the best of my food supplies. They were plenty glad to stay overnight.

"They were lieutenants in the Royal Army stationed at Maymyo, Burma. They were fishing in the Irrawaddy on their vacation and had lost their way. From Fort Hertz they had tried to go east, then south around "the Triangle", a specially savage and practically unadministered part of Upper Burma, where there are no proper roads. They said their meeting with and treatment by our Christians all along the way this side of the Salween-N'mai divide, beginning at Hei-wa-di, was one of the best demonstrations of Christian missionary work they could imagine.

"At every village our Christians came to shake hands, give food and shelter, and at night these two 'refugees' sang with them in English those hymns that they recognized. In all the books they found our name and address, so had planned to come first to Yea Chi. But the Chinese magistrate at Sukin treated them as suspicious characters because they had no passports, and insisted on sending them directly to Kunming. Just before leaving, Chaplin insisted on giving me and 'our boys' one complete outfit for mahseer (a kind of tarpon) fishing."

Russell's five-week tour of the churches in the Salween Valley was very successful and heartening. At the Pugeleh chapel in West China, on a ridge above the Salween River, on one Lord's Day the attendance at communion was two hundred thirty-eight (238), with no special drive. That was the largest single congregation he had seen, up to that time, on the Tibetan Border. Seventeen villages were represented in that "central Salween" congregation. From Pugeleh he went to Sidodi where we had baptized our first converts in that region, in 1934. Although no chapel had been built there yet, there were fifty-seven Christians and five visitors at that meeting. Going on to Yeh-gu where our faithful Christian co-worker, Adeh Heh-a-kwa, had started a church with ten families and one Lisu primer, Russell found there were now one hundred and ten converts and fifty candidates for baptism. They had built a bamboo and thatch chapel before we even got around to visiting them. This was always our goal — to teach the native Christians to go forward on their own, without depending on help from "foreigners". Adeh was still the pastor and one of the leading workers in the Salween Valley. As always, after services, Russell prayed for and treated the many sick who came to him for help.

✝

Russell always liked to grow things and had developed an experimental and demonstration garden which he hoped would supply some of the elements missing from our diet, the lack of which sapped the strength of all of us. Also, he hoped it would contribute to better living for the two thousand or so Lisu who had become Christians since 1929. In the Mekong Valley, grape vines planted in 1934 were now beginning to bear fruit, as well as some of the fruit trees. We had several varieties of plums, apples, apricots, peaches, cherries, and figs. During 1938 Russell planted two hundred new grape vines and one hundred fig trees from cuttings, and a number of new fruit trees from buds and grafts. He was beginning to experiment with oranges and lemons also. There were trees and gardens planted at all of our stations.

In the Salween Valley at that time it was impossible to get any milk products or wheat products, and vegetables were either few or non-existent. Very little fruit was available except native rough-skinned, bitter tangerines and scrawny wild peaches, and they were hardly fit to eat. Russell said, "The Lord helping me, year after year, as we labor to build up the churches in the spiritual things of Christ, we shall seek to improve their conditions in these material things, also." That is why for several years he made the introduction of vegetables and fruits a side-line — sort of a modern-day Johnny Appleseed.

✝

In June we started preparing a room for Isabel Maxey. Robert, and his two companions, having completed their medical treatment and purchase of supplies in Kunming; planned to bring her with them when they returned. While they were gone, Harold (Taylor) helped me paper the ceiling and everything looked quite nice when we had finished. Isabel arrived August 10, 1938, together with Robert, and his two companions/co-workers, Daniel (Pu-shi), and Lee Chao Shen. We were all so glad to see them and to have Isabel with us at last. She proved to be a good and dedicated worker, and an excellent addition to our mission staff.

☩

In August Tibetans attacked Atuntze and burned several houses. The Newlands were held captive in their home for about twenty-four hours. They were unharmed, but the attackers killed the official who had hanged one of their leaders. Mr. Newland wrote asking if his wife and children could come to Yea Chi where it seemed safer. Of course we asked them to come, especially as Mrs. Newland was expecting a child in September. She and her two children arrived the latter part of August, while Mr. Newland stayed to care for the wounded in Atuntze. Their baby son was born September 6th, with Russell, Isabel and myself assisting. Mr. Newland arrived four days later, and as soon as Mona was able, they went to Kang Pu for three months to study Tibetan, then went home on furlough.

☩

In the fall of 1938, even though Russell was not strong, he wanted very much to visit the large new Christian community in the N'Mai Valley of Northeast Burma where already there were three or four little bamboo churches. He took seventeen-year old Eugene, and a number of Lisu helpers to carry primers, food, bedding, medicine and other necessary items. Several days before they could hope to arrive at their destination, when they had almost reached the snow line below the mountain pass into Burma, the weather suddenly turned to cold rain, sleet, wind, and even snow.. Russell began to feel weak and feverish, and they decided to return home.

With the help of Eugene and others, he managed to make the two-day descent to the Salween River at Ma-ji. But when

193

they crossed the bamboo rope bridge, Russell was so weak that someone had to slide down the other side to pull him up the incline. Eugene found some bamboo for poles, and made a hwagan for his father who was then carried two long days' journey, to Pugeleh. Russell's fever continued to rise, and Eugene cared for him carefully and tenderly. Following Russell's instructions, Eugene even gave him injections. Our Christian Lisu friends carried him for two days over the pass to Tobalo, and others brought him the rest of the way home to Yea Chi.

Eugene was very relieved to finally get his father home, and the rest of us were very disturbed to see him so sick and weak. We studied Russell's medical books for symptoms such as he had, and decided it must be typhoid fever. My previous nursing experience with high fever when he had pneumonia helped me now in knowing what to do. During that time I was so glad to have Isabel as a companion to help me.

Two or three days after Russell was brought home, Dr. Bare passed through Yea Chi, and stayed a day or two. What a blessing it was that he came just when we needed him so much! He examined Russell and confirmed our diagnosis of typhoid fever. He gave us helpful advice and some medicines he had with him. Mr. Newland came from Kang Pu with some additional medicine. We nursed Russell week after week until he finally began to convalesce, and we fervently thanked God.

✝

When it was time for our regular Christmas conference at Tobalo, Russell was still weak but felt he should go, so he rode horseback as far as Kang Pu, then walked on to Tobalo. Eugene, Robert, Harold, and our Yea Chi Chinese evangelist went with him. Lee Chao Shen preached and Russell showed pictures, including "Life of Christ", etc.

Lee Chao Shen had started building a home in Yea Chi, and Isabel asked that a second floor be added for her living quarters, with extra space for storage. This was gladly done, and she moved in sometime early in 1939. One day, the heavy trap door of the store-room fell on her upper arm, tearing a large piece of flesh loose. Before she fainted she sent for Russell who, fortunately, was home at the time. By the time he arrived she had lost quite a lot of blood, but he cleaned the wound and sewed back the almost-severed piece of flesh, all without anesthetic. The wound healed nicely, with no sign of infection.

A missionary's life in those primitive and isolated regions "where China, Tibet, and Burma meet" was far from simple. We had to do for ourselves so many things for which city dwellers could call a specialist. We had to be doctor, gardener, shoe repair man, barber, photographer, teacher of one's own children, and much, much more. There was no electricity, and we had no modern roads. On the paths over which we traveled, even a bicycle could not be used.

✝

Early in 1939 Harold Taylor met Ada Sayer, a young single missionary lady, and after several months of corresponding, they decided to marry. After their marriage they left us, and established their own new mission in Tali-fu, a much less primitive field than our area. We had grown to love Harold, and were sorry to see him leave, but wished the two of them happiness and success in their life together.

As World War II progressed, repeated levies of men, money, grain, and transport animals affected even our isolated mission field area. Trade declined, and any remaining silver disappeared into hiding. Paper money was introduced, but it soon was worth only about one tenth of its face value.

By June, 1939 Russell felt well enough to make another expedition westward across the great divide among the Salween Valley Christians. He took 16-year-old Robert with him on that trip and became convinced that Robert would make an excellent missionary, along with Eugene. We had already decided that our own family would be our best source of assistance in our missionary work. Russell and Robert were away from home for a month, visiting scattered congregations one by one. Carriers from each village carried their loads on to the next village, then after a night's rest and a good meal returned to their homes. In one village, however, the loads were all packed up and ready for the day's travel, but no carriers came. In a letter home, Robert — who was then sixteen years old — described the situation:

> *"We got up early this morning and had prayer with the carriers from Yeh-gu before they left for home. We had an early breakfast, and had the loads all packed up, but the carriers didn't come. We found out the reason from the pastor. Everybody was slowly starving, and there were few people able to carry, so they didn't come. This is the first time, I think, that we've come down to the hard tacks of the starvation among the Lisu. It seems there is just nothing to eat, since rice is the only grain available, but at such high prices that no one can afford it. Therefore quite a few of them have gone to other places in search of food.*
>
> *"Eh-dzi-ma, wife of evangelist Eh-dzi pa, came down from her place up in the mountains to say hello to us, and present us with a chicken. On request of Eh-dzi-pa we had sent her a 'tong' (7 cakes) of tea by A-duh. She is quite an interesting woman, and was quite cheerful, and laughing. I found A-duh taking a big handful of potatoes — his own food — to give to her, and by questioning I learned that he had found on his visit to her that she also was slowly starving, living daily on <u>only</u> warm water with a little salt. We were so shocked, especially when she was so cheerful and laughing, that we gave her another 'tong' of tea and some potatoes."*

Russell and Robert were delighted to find that even in a year filled with war, conscription, bitter taxation, desperate famine, and a scarcity of Christian literature, the Lord had shepherded and kept and steadied those scattered congregations.

☦

In the fall of 1939, Russell and Eugene made another trip to the Salween for a month of visiting and preaching. In November, I began going occasionally to teach the Lisu in outlying congregations. Early in December I made a 12-day trip through those Mekong Lisuland mountains. I preached fourteen times, and climbed steep and narrow trails over high, cold passes.

While preaching in Chinese at Tobalo, the local elder who interpreted into Lisu for me broke down and cried when I said, "When Christians sin it is as if they cause blood to flow afresh from the Saviour's wounds." He began confessing various sins that the Holy Spirit had shown him, and to pray for cleansing and overcoming power. He had a vision in which he saw some people he had known, who were now dead, climbing up a mountain. Some went on up into a bright light, but others went down. He even told their names. He said those going up had earnestly tried not to sin, and those going down had been known to be sinful. Also, he was warned about the harmful effects on the body from smoking tobacco and drinking liquor.

As he told of his vision, others began to realize that God could see and know all. Many in that meeting were so convicted that they, too, began confessing their sins and wept out prayers for forgiveness. That meeting lasted all night and into the next morning, Sunday, until time for the services to start at 10:00 a.m. At the communion service, the emblems of our Lord's broken body and blood became much more meaningful to them than ever before. Thus was started a spiritual revival that spread like wildfire throughout the Mekong Valley.

Meanwhile, Eugene, Robert, and Daniel, together with some other Lisu friends, had gone over the pass to the Salween Valley for the Christmas convention there, and when they returned they told of having almost the same unique spiritual experiences. Eugene was asked to preach for the Sunday morning service — his first time to preach a full sermon in Lisu. When he was only about half-way through, he was interrupted, as people began to stand up, weeping and crying out for God's mercy, and confessing their sins. Before it was over, almost the entire congregation had confessed their sins, and asked for prayer on their behalf. Eugene never did finish his sermon! A few months before Russell had sent an APPEAL FOR EARNEST PRAYER to our Christian friends in America, and we were sure this was an answer to those prayers.

20
The Lord Giveth...
and Taketh Away

Because of feuding with the Yea Chi "king" and lamas at the lamasery just outside of Yea Chi, the Tibetans north of Atuntze were threatening to attack at any time. Early in 1940 we decided to move to Tobalo, across the Mekong River. At the same time, Isabel Maxey moved to our station at Kang Pu. It would not have been safe for her to remain alone in Yea Chi, because it was such a sinful place. In Tobalo, we had built a simple two-story house beside a rushing mountain stream where we could look out of our windows at almost vertical fern- and tree-covered mountainsides. The boys fixed a swimming pool in the stream, and there was a nice place for picnics beside it. Our house had the usual mud walls, but when curtains were hung and pictures were on the walls it looked nice. Some of the natives said, "It looks like Heaven".

Russell had already started an orchard at Tobalo and we had "tastes" of seven different kinds of fruit: apricots, plums, peaches, apples, prunes, grapes, and strawberries. I canned over fifty quarts of fruit besides making grape jelly and butter. There were two large walnut trees in the back yard, providing excellent shade. The nuts were "hard as a rock" so were not good to eat, but the oil from them was used for cooking instead of lard.

✝

By this time we were trying to care for over two thousand Christians in thirty congregations scattered through the Mekong, Salween and Upper Burma valleys bordering Inner

Tibet. These valleys were separated by great mountain divides, with passes which were closed by snow four to five months each year. The diagnosis and medical treatment of many hundreds of sick each month was taking more and more of Russell's time, and becoming almost a full-time job.

After the snows melted in the spring, and the pass was open, we began hearing of two or three false teachers in the Salween Valley. In June, 1940 Eugene and I went over there to teach. We took along LaVerne and Ruth Margaret, who rode horses most of the way. We found that these false teachers had done a lot of damage with their wrong statements during the three months the pass was closed. Eight of the preachers who had "stood firm in the faith" offered to go with us to meet them. We visited each village in which they lived and met them, one at a time. For every false statement they presented, the Lord undertook for us in a mighty way and we were able to turn immediately to the correct passage in the Bible to refute their wrong teaching. In spite of these false teachers, there was a great spiritual awakening and cleansing and growth among all the churches, and this was very encouraging to us.

In July, after our return from the Salween, Mrs. Lewer and her two daughters came for a visit. She had returned to her mission post in Wei Hsi after coming out with us over the Himalayas in 1927. Isabel came over from Kang Pu so we had a nice little group of Americans in our Tobalo home. We had a large bedroom which could accomodate six, so our four visitors, Ruth, and I slept in the "ladies' dormitory" while Russell and the three boys slept on cots in one of the rooms adjoining the chapel.

Mr. and Mrs. Bolton, also missionaries from Wei Hsi, came for an eight-day visit in August. We studied the Bible together while they were there. Mr. Bolton helped Eugene repair our radio so we could get the news. What terrible, terrible news it was, too! all about the war. Eugene went with the Boltons to Wei Hsi to get some mechanical parts, because they were preparing to move to Tali-fu where Mr. Bolton was to take charge of the American Primary School.

✝

On September 11, 1940 Russell and Robert left, intending to go to Kunming because they both needed dental work, and Robert needed glasses. They visited missionary friends along the way, and stopped in Tali with Harold Taylor and his wife. After hearing the latest war news, they decided it would not be safe to continue on to Kunming, because the Japanese bombing there had become so intense. However, in Tali, there was a refugee dentist from Canton who did a very good job of taking care of Russell's and Robert's dental work.

Even Tali did not escape the Japanese bombing, though, and there was no defense against it. The city was full of refugees, especially from Kunming. Whenever a bomb alert was sounded everyone ran to the fields to try to hide. Of course, the civilians suffered most, and even many of those who jumped into the lake were mercilessly strafed.

Because of the Japanese war, the Central China University, along with a theological seminary, had moved from Wu Han to Hsi Cheo, fifteen miles north of Tali. Robert had always been extremely interested in the Chinese language and wanted to enroll in the university. Classes in English were also offered and the school was sometimes called "Yale University in China" because credits from there were accepted at Yale University in America.

Russell went with Robert to visit the school and, after conferring with the president, decided to enroll him at once. It was now the first part of November and Robert had missed about six weeks of work but he felt sure he could make it up during the Christmas vacation. Although we would miss him, we were happy he could further his education. Robert studied there for the next two years, and was in the upper third of his classes even though most of them were conducted in Chinese.

✝

One day in mid-October, 1940 a messenger came from the Washilo-gai church, one day's hard walk from us, to ask me to come and help their elders to exhort one of their Christian families not to sell their daughter in marriage to a non-Christian man. That practice had been declared wrong by Russell and the elders and all had decided to follow the words in II Corinthians 6:14, "Be ye not unequally yoked together with unbelievers...". The church did not want to disfellowship this family but would have felt compelled to do so if such a transaction was completed.

I hated to leave LaVerne, now eleven years old, and Ruth Margaret, now five, for the three days necessary for such a trip. However, since there was no trouble in that area at the time and our Tibetan woman helper, Ah-mo, and our 17-year-old adopted daughter, Anzie, were both very reliable, I finally agreed to leave the next day, promising to return on Monday.

It was a very hard one-day trip along the steep mountains, across several high ridges, but the messenger boy and a companion escorted me and we arrived at Wa-shi-lo-gai in the evening. Our dear evangelist, Swami-pa, and his son Daniel, who had lived in our home for several years, and another school boy, A-hke-fu-yen, all lived in that village, so I did not feel like a stranger.

After exhorting the straying family and obtaining their promise not to make a wrong step, we had prayer and a church service. We were all happily united again by God's gracious help. The next day, Sunday, we had several good Bible studies and worship services.

It began to rain Sunday afternoon, continuing through the night and on into the next morning. On Monday morning as I prepared to leave, the Christians begged me not to travel that day. They feared for me to travel along the mountains in the continuing rain because of rocks rolling down the steep slopes or landslides covering the path, but I told them I dared not leave my children longer. After we all prayed I started out with A-hke-fu-yeh escorting me, and reached home Monday evening without mishap. The children were anxiously awaiting me and we were all very happy to see each other. When I removed my wet tennis shoes, which I had worn to prevent slipping on the path, I found that one instep was so painful I could not stand on it. I couldn't sleep that night, and had to stay off of it most of the next day.

✞

It continued to rain, and the To-ba-lo River began flooding and overflowing its banks into our garden and yard. Thus began a most frightening and staggering experience for the younger children and me. On the evening of October 22 we had our usual evening devotions and worship. We continued to remind our Heavenly Father that as Moses had told the Hebrew people to sprinkle the blood of their sacrificial lamb on their door post to protect them from the death angel, so we were trusting Him to keep us safe, under the blood of Jesus Christ, "our lamb", even as Rev. 12:11 teaches: "...and they overcame him (Satan) by the blood of the lamb, and by the word of their testimony, and they loved not their lives unto the death."

About midnight I awakened from a disturbing and unusual dream in which I was again reminded of the verse in Revelation, especially the part "—and the word of their testimony—". I had followed the first part of it but not the second part. In my dream I said, "Praise the Lord", and was immediately comforted.

I awoke to the sound of boulders and logs knocking against each other just outside my bedroom window, and realized that the situation had become serious. Quickly lighting a lantern, I called Anzie and LaVerne to go with me to see what had happened. As we walked along the garden path I almost stepped off into the swift river which had already cut off about a fifth of our yard. The rushing torrent had destroyed the dam Russell had helped build on a branch of the river, and it was now rushing down its old bed and tearing away at our yard. The water was clear up to our house on that side, and we were now completely surrounded by the two branches of the flooding river. I felt this explained the dream I had — Satan was trying to destroy us but God had warned me and brought that scripture to my mind. Returning to the house, we called Ah-mo to join us in prayer. We not only trusted God to protect us, but praised Him the rest of the night.

On the porch, Anzie and LaVerne found some weeds commonly used for pig food, and they began stuffing them into the small holes appearing in the northwest corner of the adobe wall, which was the one being bombarded the hardest. I prayed to God to save that corner, for I felt if it held, the whole house would be saved, but if it gave way all would be lost.

At dawn A-hke-fu-yeh came running to say that the smaller branch of the river had gone down, and the villagers on the mountain had placed a large log across it so we could cross over. While quickly dressing Ruth, who had slept through it all, I looked out of the window and saw a great wall of water coming down the main channel toward the house. At that time I could not imagine where it came from, but did not have time to investigate. I later learned it was caused by a field sliding down the mountain into the river, increasing the torrential flow and turning the river directly toward our house.

Ah-mo took Ruth across the log to safety while I hurriedly grabbed up a change of clothes for the children and two small blankets. As I stepped down into the muddy yard and saw it was still raining I remembered the rain covers I had left at the door when I returned from Wa-shi-lo-gai and turned back to get them. As I did so the Christians on the shore began shouting and LaVerne, who had stayed with me, screamed, "Mama, don't go back", so I went on across with him. We had barely gotten across when we heard the roar of the water and the house falling behind us. Anzie was praising the Lord so loudly I could hear her over the noise of the flood. Our precious God loved us so much he had saved the house until a way of escape could be prepared — literally a path through the water!

I shall never forget that day — October 23, 1940. We stood on the bank of the river watching the devastation. Parts of our house, most of our possessions, the church, and several log cabins went swirling down in that terrible, roaring, boiling water. We could see water cascading down the mountainside across the river where we had never seen water before. It seemed to us that the whole world was being destroyed. The only thing standing was the northwest corner of the house which I had prayed for so fervently through the night! I wondered — both then and later — if the whole house might have been saved had I prayed for all of it as earnestly as I did for that corner. In retrospect we believe God in His wisdom acted in our best interests, but in those trying hours we found events hard to understand.

We finally went on up the mountain and sat by the fire in the home of one of our Christian friends, with not even a comb or toothbrush, and practically no bedding. Where would we sleep? The Lisu people didn't have beds for themselves, let alone beds for guests. That night we slept on straw mats using our two small blankets for covering.

As soon as Isabel Maxey heard about the flood she hurried from Kang Pu, crossing the Mekong River which was also flooding. She had heard that Ruth had been washed down the river and drowned. Evidently someone had seen her large doll and thought it was Ruth. Needless to say, Isabel was happy to find Ruth alive and well. She very generously insisted that we come and stay with her at the outpost in Kang Pu until we decided what to do next.

Isabel wrote to Russell and Robert, who were still in Talifu, to tell them about the flood, our narrow escape, and the loss of our home and supplies.

"There is only one way to begin such a letter as this must be and that is to say: 'Praise God from Whom all blessings flow.' But

for His mercy and grace I might now have to say that Gertrude and the children were gone, rather than just to say that Tobalo — house, chapel, garden and orchard — is gone; washed down the Mekong River, and that by just a hair's breadth, a miraculous provision of God's, they escaped going too. I know you are now gratefully thanking God for this and girding your heart to hear the details. These I shall try to tell you in sequence as they came to me. But first, let me tell you, no man ever had a lovelier, braver and more saintly wife or no son a more devoted, consecrated mother than you have. A lesser woman would never have met the situaion so wisely and trustingly. She is a spiritual pillar."

Isabel told of the events described above, and continued with the account of our escape from danger.

"Gertrude carried Ruth downstairs and stepped out the back door onto a piece of ground which was suddenly bared for them by the Lord's hand. They all stepped out with a little basket full of clothes she thought somebody could carry. She didn't really think the house was going, and started back after a piece of canvas, as it was still raining, but LaVerne began crying then and begging her not to go back. Well, she didn't, for as she turned around to LaVerne, the house gave way and she didn't even see it go. When she looked again, every bit of the house was gone but the grain room and the little store room over it. Everything in the kitchen, living room, bedroom, boxroom and entry is gone — not a spoon or a toothbrush or a bar of soap left. Yet, the grain and lots of the canned food is saved and the suitcases and trunks in the grain room with your furlough clothes are here. Not one tablet of medicine is left, but the cows and pigs and chickens are all still here."

✝

Eugene was on a trip to the Salween Valley, but as soon as he heard about the flood, he came home as quickly as he could. By that time the water had receded, and we went to look over what remained of our possessions. We were astonished to find a mysterious, unexplainable build-up of logs, rocks, and clay, which formed a wall about seven feet high, extending around that northwest corner, with a space of about eight inches between it and the outside wall of what was left of our house.

What a wonderful prayer-answering God we have! I had prayed for that second protecting wall. Furthermore, when Robert returned to that area almost nine years later, that one corner of the house, for which I had prayed so hard, was still standing, a monument to God's power and ability to answer prayer.

The upstairs part of the corner had been used as a pantry and storeroom, where canned goods, and some other things were kept, and there we found a few new enameled bowls. Good! we could use those for dishes. A clean, old-fashioned rug was in one corner, and we could use that to sleep on. The large pressure cooker I used for canning was all right. The shelves which held the canned fruit were still fastened to the corner, but the partition which had held the other end had pulled away, and much of the fruit was lost, but we recovered about fifty quarts, still intact. One large tin of sugar and one of lard were saved.

In the lower part were the grain bins, with our small steamer trunks on top of them. The trunks contained a few clothes, most of which the children had outgrown, but some would be usable. We were especially thankful for the grain, as that had been a famine year, and we had been sharing it with the babies of the Christian families as they could not eat the coarse jungle food which was a necessary part of their parents' diet when food was scarce. We decided to build a small lean-to granary on the mountain side to hold the grain until we could make other arrangements.

We accepted our dear Isabel's invitation to put our pitifully few things with hers and stay for a while in Kang Pu. We were thankful that we had left two heavy comforters there that could now be used as mattresses. Isabel and I worked for many days making a change of clothing for Ruth, LaVerne and me. Contrary to his usual practice, Eugene had taken almost all his clothing with him when he went to the Salween Valley on a 1-month trip, so he was well supplied. Several people, mostly our Christian friends, came bringing various things they had found along the river banks after the flood. We mended everything of possible use. Also, we sent an urgent letter to Russell at Tali, asking him to bring what clothing and supplies he could.

21
Move Over the Mountain

When word of the flood reached our families and friends in America, most of them urged us to return to the U.S. at once. None of them could imagine how we could continue on without our supplies, especially since China was at war with Japan and it was very difficult to get things locally. We had heard that many of the missionaries in China were returning home because of the Japanese threat. We had been praying and seeking God's will as to what He would have us to do, even before the flood. Then, while we were in Kang Pu, about nineteen Christians, including several preachers and elders, had come over from the Salween Valley to beg us not to return to America right away.

"Don't leave us," they begged. "Come to our valley to live, and teach us the Bible, the way you did for the people in the Mekong Valley."

"Yes!" said one man. "We will build a house for you to live in," he added, as he turned to the others, seeking confirmation.

"Of course we will!" they agreed. "And we'll even share our food with you, so you don't ever need to worry about not having food to eat."

Because of the great spiritual hunger of the people in the Salween, we couldn't bear the thought of leaving them at this time. Their spiritual needs took precedence over our personal needs. After much prayer, God gave a verse to Eugene, which he shared with me: *"Seek ye first the kingdom of God and His*

righteousness, and all these things shall be added unto you."
(Matt. 6:33) We felt this promise was the answer to our
prayers, and accordingly we decided to stay with our dear Lisu
people. We promised them that we would come over to the
Salween Valley and teach them. Both Eugene and I were in
agreement, and at peace about this decision to move on over to
the Salween. We were extremely happy that Isabel also decided
to make the move with us.

This decision to move into the Salween valley was confirmed by Russell, as he wrote to his mother:

"Mother, dear, rejoice that your children, as soldiers of Jesus
Christ, are privileged to share 'the fellowship of His sufferings.' We
know that out of this seemingly greatest disaster of our lives our
Father will work His loving will for all concerned. He sees how
unwilling we are to leave all the 2000 Christians and the many
villages yet to be evangelized. He even allowed the flood at Tobalo
to destroy our mission compound, home, and our most valuable
supplies. We cannot ask to know His plan for us; we must be con-
tent simply to know that He still loves us and is over-ruling. But we
feel that we cannot leave until the Tibetan Lisuland Churches of
Christ have been re-confirmed in The Faith, for a terrific blow
such as has fallen upon us is an awful shake-up to them, too. We
have received so many years of mercies from the Lord, now let us
'count our blessings'. We will 'hold the fort' a while longer."

We worked hard to get our few things ready in order to get
across the pass before the snows closed it for the winter. About
the middle of December a number of the Christians from the
Salween Valley came to help us move. There were not enough
carriers to take the grain so that had to be left for later. We did
take our two valuable milk cows and one baby calf, which had
been kept in a barn on the mountainside, safe from the flood.
We spent the first night part-way up the mountain. Eugene
fixed up a canvas roof for shelter, and there was frost both
inside and out. We melted snow for water. At four o'clock the
next morning we were ready for the trail again. As we neared

the pass, the snow became too deep for either Ruth or the calf to walk.

Eugene said he could carry Ruth for a while. By this time she was crying from the cold. It was so cold going over the pass that her feet had almost frozen. I rubbed them briskly with snow, and then Eugene was able to carry her on his back, holding her feet in the pockets of his heavy, warm overcoat until we came to the stopping place.

One of the Lisu men agreed to carry the calf. We were coming to the really steep part of the trail, and someone needed to drive the other two cows, while someone else was needed to carry Ruth. Finally LaVerne, (who was 12 years old) said he could lead the cows — although he had to lead them down the steepest places. That freed the man who had been driving them, and he carried Ruth. Meanwhile, because of the deep snow, extreme cold and the high altitude, Isabel nearly fainted, so Eugene had to help her over the last part of the pass.

If you have ever climbed up a mountain and then gone right back down, you will have some idea how tired we were. We had to go down, and down, and down from the divide to get to Pugeleh. After a while we came to a little knoll where some of the carriers were resting, and in reply to our question of how much farther we had to go, they pointed to another knoll away down below us. It was still a long way, and we needed to get there before dark. Finally, just at dusk we descended the last steep part. Men held lanterns and helped us over the worst places.

☦

When the Salween Christians learned we were going to move over to their valley, members of twenty congregations had decided to go to Pugeleh and be ready for their December convention by the time we arrived. So on the last part of the descent, we could see long lines of people with pine torches coming up the mountain, and soon we began to meet small groups of Christians who had come up the steep mountain to meet us.

As we approached Pugeleh, a solid line of Lisu Christians was waiting along the road, just outside of the village, to shake our hands and welcome us. They were jubilant that we were now going to live among them. None of them had ever seen Isabel, and few had seen LaVerne, Ruth, or me. Such a heart-warming welcome made all of our past hardships seem well worthwhile.

An old abandoned two-story adobe fort close to the church had been prepared for us to live in until a bamboo house could be built. It had gun holes all around the walls, and was very breezy inside. An open fire in the middle of the floor provided some heat, and the gun holes provided an outlet for the smoke. We had matting on the floor, but no chairs or other furniture. But in spite of physical hardships, we were happy to be there, because we knew we were wanted, and needed in the Lord's work.

According to Lisu custom the church was decorated for the convention. Just outside the door was an arch covered with greenery, through which one walked before entering the church. We had wonderful fellowship during the three-day convention, Friday through Sunday, but we missed Russell and Robert.

☩

Russell had been heartsick upon receiving word of the flood, but had started at once trying to gather supplies necessary to partially replace those that had been destroyed. In those war times it was difficult to replace anything. Other missionaries from Tali, Likiang, and elsewhere were very kind and shared generously of their goods, especially bedding and clothing, even though they also had difficulty in getting new supplies.. We could not begin to express our appreciation of what their help meant to us. Robert even sent back his bedding, since he was to continue his studies there in Hsi Cheo, and would be staying with Dr. Paul V. Taylor, dean of the college. Also, Russell was able to obtain a number of Lisu New Testaments which were greatly needed. As soon as supplies were collected and packed, Russell started for home, anxious to get back as quickly as possible and cross over into the Salween Valley before the heavy snows closed the passes for the winter.

The day after the convention closed, Eugene had left with thirty carriers to go to Tobalo to get our grain and the rest of Isabel's supplies. We prayed that Russell would arrive there before Eugene left. Each day there were heavy clouds, and it looked as if the heavy snow might come. Each day Eugene and the Christians prayed, and the clouds dissipated and the snow did not come. This went on day by day for almost two weeks, with the heavy winter snows delayed in answer to prayer. Finally about January 15, Eugene received word that Russell was coming, and went to meet him at Dra-tsi-lo, but had to wait several days before he actually arrived. At last Russell arrived, and he and Eugene came on together as quickly as carriers could be arranged. People were hesitant to make the trip over the mountains into the Salween valley for fear the snows would come and they could not get back home for several months.. Russell and Eugene arrived at Pugeleh in the afternoon, and the carriers wouldn't even wait overnight, but started right back, spending one night on the way and arriving home the next day.. The very next day after the carriers got home a big snow came, and closed the pass.

What a joyful reunion we had with Russell! We all had a good prayer meeting, and thanked God for His mercy in keeping the pass open until our men-folk and all the supplies got across, and the carriers had returned safely to Tobalo. Once the snows came, the pass was closed for about four months.

As soon as possible after Russell and Eugene returned, work was started on our bamboo house. Due to Eugene's building skills and leadership it was soon completed. From the hillside where it was built, we had a wonderful view overlooking a beautiful valley, snow-covered mountains, and the deep canyon of the Salween River below us.

As we were moving into that new home we began to understand God's wisdom in allowing our home in Tobalo to be destroyed. Had it been saved, we would no doubt have remained in the Mekong Valley instead of moving over the pass to be nearer to those thousands of people who were so eager to study the Bible. Soon representatives came to us from as far away as the most distant congregation in the Akyang Valley in Upper Burma, and from Champutong on the Tibetan border, asking us to locate at their villages. However, we had purposely chosen Pugeleh because of its central location. In the months before the pass was opened, Russell, Eugene, Isabel and I held many short-term Bible schools in the villages, and many people came to us to be taught. It was so rewarding to be able to teach these people who were so eager and hungry for the Word of God. In the joy of ministering to them, physical hardships were scarcely noticed.

✝

All of our books, the correspondence course lessons for the children, stationery supplies, and even pencils had been lost in the flood. We decided the best thing to do for LaVerne and Ruth would be to send them to Bolton's school for missionary children at Tali, two weeks travel away. Mr. Bolton had begged us to send LaVerne when they first went from Wei Hsi to take charge of the school.

Eugene needed dental work, and I needed to buy supplies and material to make both children school clothes, so it was agreed that we should be the ones to take them. We took Drema Esther to stay and look after Ruth, who was barely six years old. Also, it was time for Isabel's furlough so that was an excellent opportunity for her to go. She traveled with us to Tali, went on to Kunming by bus, flew to Hong Kong and then on to America. She had become so much a part of our family we knew we would miss her very much.

We left Pugeleh in late April, 1941 and reached Tali in May. I spent many days sewing and getting the children "settled in" as this would be their first time away from me and the family. We went over to Hsi Cheo to see Robert and to get the name of his dentist for Eugene. After the ordeals of the past several months, I was badly in need of a rest, and this I was able to have while Eugene was having his dental work done. During Robert's summer break from school, he and Eugene made a 6-week trip to Kunming. There they attended a Christian summer camp with a group of Chinese young people. They had an opportunity to make some friends and have Christian fellowship with young people their own age. Remember that this was during World War II, so it was not surprising that while in Kunming, they also experienced five days of bombing by Japanese planes. Residents of Kunming had to flee out on the big lake outside of town, and hide on islands. It was a memorable experience for them.

After Eugene got back, we bought our supplies and hired pack animals to take them as far as the Mekong River. The animals could not cross the river, nor could they negotiate the narrow paths and steep mountains on the other side, so after crossing the river by boat, Eugene arranged for carriers to take our supplies the rest of the way. We arrived back in Pugeleh in September after a long, hard journey. Both of my heels were bleeding after the steep descent from the pass down to Pugeleh.

We had arranged for Daniel (Pu-shi) to come over from Wa-shi-lo-gai to stay with Russell while we were away, and to accompany him on his preaching and teaching trips. Ah-mo, our Tibetan helper, came from To-ba-lo to help Anzie, who had become a very good cook. With a Lisu boy to take care of the cows and the milking, Russell fared very well, but they were all lonely and he said, "Don't ever go off like that again".

We received word that Bolton's school vacation started in October and arranged for a missionary from Likiang to pick up our children when he went after his own. Russell met them at Likiang and brought them home. The school later had to close because of the danger from Japanese bombing.

Meanwhile, after the Easter convention, Russell had sent fourteen of our preachers 10 days' travel south down the

Salween Valley to Lu-da, where the China Inland Mission people were holding a three-month Bible school for the Lisu. We were proud of the reports they sent back concerning our group. It was good to know they would be that much more prepared to "shepherd the flock" when we had to go on furlough.

It was in December that we heard the shocking news that Japan had attacked Pearl Harbor, thus bringing the United States into the war. We could scarcely believe it, nor could we foresee the effects this would have on other parts of the world, including the part where we were.

✝

In the spring of 1942, Drema Esther and I went to Ma-di and Go-da, just one day's travel south of Pugeleh, to teach and then stayed on for the Southern Easter Convention. About six hundred attended that meeting and, after being satisfactorily examined as to repentance and faith, twenty-two were baptized at Go-da. Many more began to study for baptism at a later date. We were gone three weeks, laying the foundation for work among the women and girls, and a series of short-term schools for the more literate.

While Drema Esther and I went south, Eugene and LaVerne went north to the Ta-da convention. Attendance was about nine hundred, with meetings of great spiritual refreshment and reconsecration. LaVerne, now thirteen, was showing signs of becoming a good evangelist, too.

It was that spring that our beloved Swami-pa, our teacher and first evangelist, was drowned as he was crossing the river. He was such a pillar of strength all of those years he worked with us. We are sure his heavenly reward must be great, indeed, for his faithful witnessing, and the many souls brought to the Lord by his labors among his own people.

✝

We began receiving many calls for some of us to come to the Irrawaddy Valley in Burma, where we had several Lisu congregations. The members of those congregations were not

215

Christians when they moved from the Salween Valley to the Irrawaddy. They had learned about Christ from relatives and friends, or from native evangelists, and were eager to learn more. After the Easter meeting in 1942 we sent six preachers over there to teach.

Because we were cut off from that valley so many months of the year we decided to send a permanent pastor, Timothy, with his wife and child, to minister to them. In the fall another earnest preacher and teacher companion went over for the winter months, adding to the evangelistic force. Our mission field area now bordered the Baptist mission field in Burma, with no unevangelized area between.

22
Aiding the Allied Forces

In those war-torn days it was hard to send or receive mail. We were two hard days' travel from the nearest postal agency at Aiwa (Eye-wah), as we were off the postal runner's route. One letter sometimes cost as much as 800 Chinese dollars, and sometimes men were so desperate they would rob just to get the stamps, which they then resold. Much mail was lost. One of our private carriers was beaten and robbed between Pugeleh and Aiwa. Our best method was to seal the mail packet addressed to the Kunming American Consulate, with money to cover the postage. The consulate was good enough to attach the postage and send it on.

About Easter time, 1943, I received a letter from my sister, Helen Howe, telling about the long illness and death of my mother. She had suffered so long it was comforting to know that at last her suffering was over and she was now with the Lord, but I also suffered a great sense of loss. At the time I was all alone except for Ruth and my Tibetan girls. Almost immediately after I received this word, several Christians from Madi came to ask me to come and meet with them for the southern Salween Easter convention to be held in their village, which was a day's travel to the south of us. They offered to carry my pack loads if I would go, so I decided to leave my bereavement with God while I tried to help others. After the convention, I went another half day's travel on to Go-da for some special women's meetings which were well attended and profitable.

✝

In the spring of 1943, Eugene (now 22) and Robert (now 20) began to discuss making a trip over the awesome Salween-Irrawaddy pass into North Burma to teach at Tiliwago (Tee-lee-wah-go) where the N'mai and Ahkyang (Ah-chang) rivers meet. This was the center of a large group of Lisu Christians who had moved there from the Salween Valley. For a long time they had repeatedly been asking that some of our own missionary family come and teach them.

By April, the Japanese had completely besieged China for many months. Burma had fallen, too, and our mission station was cut off from supplies. Our clothes were getting threadbare and our supplies were low. The boys began to talk of going to Ft. Hertz, the northernmost British outpost in Burma, where they thought they could get some supplies, as it was still free from Japanese occupation.

"The more I think about it, the more it seems like the logical thing to do," Eugene said thoughtfully. "We could visit all the churches along the way, and maybe even go all the way to Putao."

"Yes," Robert added, "maybe we could even get some supplies in Putao to replace some of what we lost in the flood."

"Well, if Eugene and Robert are going, I think I should get to go too," insisted LaVerne. "After all, I'm fourteen now, and I could be a lot of help along the way. Besides, it would be good experience for me, and training for the future."

The idea of LaVerne going too had not been even considered before. He was our youngest son, and it was hard to realize he was growing up. But after much prayer, and consideration of the overall situation, we realized that we needed to "let go," and gave permission for him to go with his brothers.

However, we thought of all the dangers of such an undertaking, remembering that nightmarish trip we had made in 1927 when Eugene and Robert were small. We had gone over that same divide but by way of a pass farther north. The route they now contemplated had never before been traveled by a white man, although many Lisu had gone that way. We thought about the difficulties of traveling through deep snow, and the danger of malaria in the jungle region. Also, we considered the fact that perhaps they might be going directly toward the Japanese front lines. But then we were comforted by the words of Psalm 121:5-8:

"The Lord is thy keeper; the Lord is thy shade upon thy right hand. The sun shall not smite thee by day, nor the moon by night. The Lord shall preserve thee from all evil; he shall preserve thy soul. The Lord shall preserve thy going out and thy coming in from this time forth, and even forevermore."

Our need for new supplies was urgent, and with this comforting promise in mind, the boys prepared to leave as soon as the passes were open and before the monsoon rains began. They hoped to return before the worst of the tropical summer began in Burma, with its accompanying epidemics, fevers, and malaria.

✝

They left Pugeleh May 7, 1943 with two native evangelists: Stephen, who went along as their personal aide, and Noah, who was going to take up a pastorate in Tiliwago. There were eight porter loads of equipment, including books, cots, medical kits, an accordion, cooking utensils and food supplies for two months. I had no sewing machine, but by hand I made each boy a pair of trousers out of some denim cloth which Robert had brought from Kunming. The trousers they had been wearing were so old and threadbare they were almost nothing but patches upon patches.

They had to climb 7000 feet, cross the mountain range over the bitterly cold 11,000-foot high snow-covered pass, and then descend on the other side into tropical jungles and heat. So clothes had to be provided for two kinds of weather. Robert described that trip:

"*There was no path, much less a trail, over our proposed route. It would have been impossible even to lead a dog across, to say nothing of a pack animal. Going over in the snow as we were, we knew those alpine peaks and precipices would be an undertaking hard to describe. But being young and adventurous, with much of our ancestors' pioneering blood in our veins, we were drawn on, both by the exciting prospect of something dangerous and new, and by the knowledge that over the divide many were waiting, eager to be taught more of God's love and His way of life. If it were not for the knowledge that we have a Guide Competent to help and protect us at all times we would never have dared to make such a trip and take with us our younger brother LaVerne, a young lad of fourteen. At first we were climbing up through thick forests, over cliffs, through streams, between high peaks, then dropping downward sharply again to 4000 feet, all in three days of hard travel. The trip could very easily be divided into five days, but there is no place to stop on top of the mountains.*

"*By noon that first day we were quite tired and, stopping beneath a huge overhanging rock by the side of a mountain torrent, soon had many fires going with dry brushwood. The pots and kettles either were propped up by stones or hung from sticks, and smoke was in everyone's eyes. Climbing after lunch was more gradual, following the stream up to its source over ridge after ridge. The path was just a series of footsteps; everyone walked in the footsteps of the person before. Soon even this path petered out and we found ourselves pushing our way through underbrush, over logs, snow banks, cliffs, and sometimes even climbing trees. We soon discovered we should depend on our hands as much as our feet.*

"*We finally stopped around sundown under a huge hollow tree in a small clearing. We scattered, with knives and machetes, into the forest for firewood, bamboo, vines, and large leaves to build individual shelters. We three brothers put up our cots in the only level spots to be found, and built up shelters around them to keep off the worst of the bad winds and rain. Even so, we got pretty wet that night. The rest of our group scattered throughout the area and found shelter for the night under overhanging rocks, in hollow trees, etc. Half a dozen big camp fires were started and, as we were up to 10,000 feet, they felt very, very pleasant.*

220

"We awakened next morning to find ourselves in unexpected thick fog as well as rain. Breaking camp at dawn, we continued our climb through alpine forest and snow, plodding on, too cold to stop for rests. At 10:00 a.m. we arrived at the base of the steepest, coldest, and most dangerous part of the whole trip. I've been over snow passes before, and always at this point there is a short pause with almost everybody feeling half desperate and wondering how the adventure will turn out. On almost every such trip the Lisu lose one or more of their group. On one of our trips we lost two, a mother and child, due to the cold and high altitude. Were we going to be as unfortunate on this trip? This question was probably in all of our minds as all were unnaturally quiet.

"After a final check-up of persons and equipment, and assigning of positions we were off in a very thick pea-soup mist, with a guide and myself in the lead. We were on deep snow now, sinking down only six to eight inches because of a hard crust. We climbed steadily and silently up an honest-to-goodness sixty-degree slope. We passed crevices where the snow was sometimes twenty-five to thirty feet deep, and we were scared. When someone would lag behind and disappear in the fog we had a frantic sensation until he reappeared.

"Several times when there were breaks in the fog we saw sheer precipices towering up darkly on every side, and we had an empty feeling at the 'fountain spring of the heart', as the Lisu would say. Then, amid all this, we got lost! It was a dangerous situation because we might go in a wrong direction and suddenly find ourselves falling over a cliff to be buried in the snow below. Only God knew the way, and after prayer we tried using our voices to get the proper echo from a cliff just to the left of the trail. This we found was now on our right so, with a bit of backtracking and skirting several crevices, we climbed to the top. From the front and from below, a gale was blowing what seemed to be a combination of snow and ice into our faces.

"Taking a quick count of our men, holding hands in groups of twos and threes and jumping like kangaroos, we followed the leader as he plunged down the sixty-five-degree hard-packed snowslide. We had to jump to make a dent in the crust, to get a footing, and to keep from freezing. LaVerne especially had a difficult time because he wasn't heavy enough to dig his heels into the *snow-crust and couldn't keep from slipping, but his courage took him through. At one point Eugene and I tried 'ski-ing' down-hill, using our shoes as 'skis' and our sturdy walking sticks as ski-poles. By leaning back on our poles we were able to control both the speed and direction of our descent.*

"When we finally got to the first rest stop below the snow line on the Burma side we were tired out and soaked through. We stopped for a hot lunch around 2:00 p.m. but the difficulty of get-ting wood and making a warm fire and finding shelter from the rain made all of us determined to reach some native hut by night. After readjustment of loads and frequent stops, we pulled into the last village at the head of the Ahkyang Valley on the northeast Burmese frontier just as black night rolled down upon us like fog. We had completed in twelve hours a distance that took us two days to cover on our return trip.

"The village meant two things to us. We were back on a good trail again, this time British-built, in good repair. Actually, the trail isn't more than what we'd call a foot-path in the States, but we had been used to such bad, small trails that this one seemed like a highway. At least, it was big enough for a horse to travel on and well enough built so there wasn't much danger of tripping every few minutes. But what made us feel best of all was the fact that this village, Nyi-ta-di, was the site of one of our congregations. Our fellow-Christians, many of whom had never seen a white man, came together and greeted us heartily, surprised to see us coming over that dangerous pass in such weather."

They stayed at Nyi-ta-di several days, teaching, exhorting, and conferring with the church leaders. Among other things, they discussed the possibility of establishing a mission out-sta-tion, and looked for a suitable site for building a house and planting an orchard.

✝

Soon after arriving in Nyi-ta-di they were given a letter from the British political officer in Ft. Hertz, asking them to come there for a conference regarding the work of the Mission in Burma.. Although the letter was dated almost a year earlier, even before the beginning of war with Japan, they felt that it would be good to comply with the official request, so decided to travel on. For one thing, there was the possibility that they might be able to buy much-needed supplies. However, since the letter was already old, they felt they should follow their original plan of visiting and encouraging congregations, teaching and preaching as they went.

The monsoon season had arrived in full strength, so traveling was difficult and unpleasant, through rain-soaked, leech-infested jungle, and across flimsy bridges over swollen streams. At night they stopped at the British-built rest houses or in villages where there were congregations of Christians. After six days of such travel, they arrived at the village of Tiliwago, where there was a fairly large congregation. Here they held a one-week Bible study/school, performed a wedding, and rested up.

By the time they finally arrived in Ft. Hertz, they had been traveling for more than a month, and were quite bedraggled. Besides that, all three boys had malaria. When they met the British official, one of the first things he noticed was the poor condition of their shoes, so he gave each of them a new pair of British army shoes. Because they had been in such an isolated place they had heard no war news, so were much surprised to hear that the Japanese army was only about forty miles to the south of Ft. Hertz, being held off by the renowned Kachin Rifles, a unit of the British army, similar to the Gurkhas of Nepal.

✝

When officials of the various armed services heard of the arrival of the boys from the "Hump" area, they wanted a conference with them to obtain information about the condition of the roads and people in that isolated, unknown area between India and China.

The boys gave all the information they could, pointed out the roads on a map, and explained that Christians could be found all along that route who would be glad to help any fliers who might bail out. The officers were delighted with all the information and asked them if they would be willing to go to Assam, India and give officials there all this same information. They agreed to go if they were assured of being brought back, which they were.

Our sons were flown by military transport to a British base in Assam, where they were royally received, and served an excellent meal that evening, with cake and ice cream — something they had only dreamed of since leaving the U.S. in 1937. Because of their malaria they were put in the British military hospital, but when it was realized they were Americans, they were transferred to the hospital at the American Air Force base at Chabua. After a few days the severe symptoms of malaria had subsided, and they were able to relax and rest after their long trek through the jungles of Burma, and for the remainder of their three weeks in hospital they enjoyed the good beds, the food, and beautiful music. That time was a real treat and vacation for them.

✞

After their release from the hospital, the boys were interviewed by the commanding officers of all the different air groups based there. These officers were much concerned because the morale of air crews was very low, due in part to the high casualty rate in the rugged mountains, but also to fear of the unknown natives in that wild country. No one knew anything about the area, so they asked for information and suggestions. From their knowledge of the country and the people, the boys were able to make some practical suggestions and recommendations: 1) to change the flight patterns to follow a "safe" corridor over lower mountain ranges and more populated areas; and 2) after explaining that many of the people in the area were Christians and literate, they suggested that a ground search and rescue network be established in the Salween Valley, which would extend from the Tibetan border on the north to the Burma Road on the south. They proposed distribution of letters in Lisu to all village headmen instructing them how to

224

proceed in case airmen crashed or bailed out in their areas, and letters in English to be given to downed crews. Their recommendations were accepted as submitted, and they were assigned the task of organizing the entire search and rescue operation.

✝

When they had fully recovered from malaria, the boys were asked if they would like to go to Calcutta for rest and to do some shopping before returning to their home. This seemed to them to be a God-given opportunity to get some of the much-needed supplies, so they were eager to go. Also, they hoped they would be able to get a new edition of the Lisu Bible Primer printed. They found that due to the war and necessary censorship, most printing shops were closed, and paper was almost impossible to obtain. However, after much prayerful searching, and with the Lord's help, Eugene finally found an elderly Christian printer who told them of an unusual set of circumstances.

"It is a strange thing," he told them. "I have never had a license to print anything but pamphlets, but only recently I had to renew my permit. When it came back to me just a few days ago, it was a permit to print booklets. Now you come asking me to print booklets. Surely God's hand is in this."

Paper was rationed, and not normally available for civilian use, so the boys went to the American Air Force with their problem. There they received the official requisition they needed to get paper, and the books were printed.

In Calcutta the boys stayed at the Lee Memorial Mission Home where many refugee missionaries stopped on their way out of China. While there, some of the missionaries exhorted Eugene and Robert not to take LaVerne back home, but to send him to the Woodstock Missionary School in north India. Being unable to consult with their father and me, they prayed and were convinced that would be the proper course to follow. When Russell and I finally heard about this arrangement we were terribly disturbed. What an experience for a fourteen-year-old boy to be separated from his parents and family, and be all alone that far away. I grieved about my precious son, but had I known at that time how long a time we would be separated (over two years) and what a traumatic experience it would be for LaVerne, I would have been even more heartbroken. I could not go to bring him back, or do anything else to change the situation. I could only pray daily, and trust LaVerne to His care. Meanwhile, I went on with the mission work, with God's comfort and help.

☦

While the boys were still at the mission home in Calcutta, awaiting completion of the printing work, they were also gradually collecting other needed supplies such as shoes, clothing, pencils, chalk, notebooks, medicines, and other things needed for the mission work. Other missionaries who had come out of China because of the Japanese threat were now unable to return even with a small suitcase, so they kept asking the boys how they expected to get back with such a stack of supplies. The boys replied that they weren't sure, but since God had given them the opportunity to buy the supplies, they were trusting Him to help them get them to the mission station. When the printing was completed, they contacted the American Air Force again, and were asked to report at once for an urgent, top-secret conference. Meanwhile, arrangements were made for a big military truck to go to the mission home and collect all their supplies, then take them directly to the airfield to be flown to Assam immediately. Eugene and Robert said they would never forget the incredulous expressions of the other missionary friends at the guest house, when the big Army truck came and picked up all their supplies. Truly, God honored their faith that because He had opened the way for them to get to Calcutta to buy the supplies, He would also provide a way to get them back into China.

At the military headquarters, the officers explained to our sons that they wanted them to serve as guides and interpreters on an overland trip from Kunming to Ft. Hertz (now called Putao) for the purpose of making a survey of the best route to lay a pipe line to carry fuel for their aircraft, instead of transporting it by plane. Our sons told them they had been over that road many times and knew the languages needed and would help all they could. When asked how much pay they would want for their services, they said they did not want any money, but would appreciate having their books and supplies taken to Ft. Hertz.

"Don't worry!" they were told. "We'll see to it that all your supplies will be dropped by parachute at your mission station in the Salween Valley!

You can imagine how surprised and thrilled they were at this news. When our supply of primers was destroyed by the flood, none of us would have ever dreamed that God would arrange to have so many replacements delivered right to our doorstep by air. The boys flew to Yunnan-yi, near Kunming, with the three officers — Major Madson, Capt. Callahan, who was a doctor, and Lt. Musser. From there they began what would eventually prove to be a 3-month trek through the Hump region to Ft. Hertz and return.

Our family in Yea Chi, in 1940, just before moving to Tobalo.

Easter convention in the Salween Valley. Around 1000 attended.

Eugene and Robert were both grown, and preaching and teaching full-time, helping the work to grow.

Because of the work of Eugene and Robert, it was possible to rescue an American crew of 4 when their plane crashed. They spent 54 days in our home before the passes were open enough for Eugene to take them home. Robert is in the center.

In 1944 Eugene and Russell made another trip to India, where they met Dorothy Sterling, a nurse who came to join the work, and escorted her back to the Salween Valley. L-R: Eugene, Dorothy, Russell, and Lisu preacher Barnabas.

23
Mission Rescue

In the meantime, back at Pugeleh in the Salween Valley, Russell and I knew very little about what was going on, as we had received only a brief message about LaVerne. Then a message came from the Mekong Valley saying that Eugene and an American army lieutenant would arrive the next evening, and that Robert and two officers were crossing the Salween on another route farther south. We were full of questions, wondering why army officers would be coming to that isolated region, and could hardly wait until Eugene arrived to explain. He told us very, very secretly about what they had been doing, and that the books and supplies would be dropped by parachute on September 27, 1943.

In the two or three days that he and the Lieutenant stayed with us while waiting for the air drop, Eugene made arrangements for several Lisu Christians to carry their loads to Ft. Hertz (Putao). It had been prearranged that they would meet Robert and the other two officers at a certain place, on the Burma side. Robert's party surveyed the route over one pass, while Eugene's party surveyed a second route. Both routes ended in Ft. Hertz, and from there the officers got air transportation back to their base in India. We later heard from the Lieutenant that he was very impressed with the Lisu carriers who went about their work so cheerfully, in spite of the constant rain, and no matter how many hardships they encountered, but each evening sat around the camp fires singing hymns.

Just a few hours before Eugene and the officer left Pugeleh, the plane dropped forty-three parachute packs with the books and supplies on the mountain side where a big white cross had been made with my sheets. We were quite excited, and the natives talked for many months about the "flying house" that dropped boxes down by "big umbrellas". It was about seven weeks before Eugene and Robert returned from that trip. They traveled every day, all the way to Ft. Hertz (about a month), then returned immediately, in order to get back to the Salween Valley before the snows closed the passes. By then they had been traveling on foot almost constantly for about three months.

✝

After returning from Ft. Hertz and the survey trip, Robert traveled over the mountains and hidden valleys to tell all of the Christians and headmen in each village to watch for planes that might be in trouble, or for fliers who might come down with "umbrellas". He gave each headman a letter, written in English, for them to give to any survivor they might find. The letter advised that the natives were Christians who would direct them to a missionary's house, and that they would be safe. Even on this emergency business Robert always managed to witness for the Lord, preaching and teaching while going through the many villages.

Many of those brave fliers had no time to use their parachutes and hundreds perished. But we personally know of four who were fortunate. On March 29, 1944 some Lisu men came running to call Robert, who was about three hours' travel away from their village,, telling him about four white men with "umbrellas". Robert immediately went to check on them and help. The four had landed in trees, and the parachute lines became entangled in the branches. Later, one of the fliers told Robert he thought they would all be killed when one of the natives unsheathed his knife to cut the parachute lines, which had gotten tangled in tree branches. Then, much to the relief of all four, they were handed one of the letters.

231

Robert escorted them to our home, five days' journey to the north, where they remained for fifty-four days. As soon as they arrived, we had them remove their wet clothing and take a hot bath in our folding, black rubberized bathtub. Somehow, I got together enough underwear for each one, until theirs could be washed. Our good beds had been destroyed in the flood, but we had acquired two double folding cots which they used. Ruth and I slept in the storeroom and Russell slept on a cot in his study. During the day the fliers stayed in our small adobe storehouse just above our bamboo house. They had a stove, table, radio, some books, and some trunks they used for seats.

That was a famine year, but our Christian brethren were very generous in sharing their meager supply of food with us and the flyers. We had milk, some eggs and canned fruit, but many times we had only popcorn for lunch, without butter or salt. We tried every day to attract the attention of low-flying planes, but it was at least a month before we succeeded. A few days later some supplies were dropped but not much that would be of use during the four-week trip that had to be made on foot over the high passes, and on to Ft. Hertz..

✞

Russell had been having a lot of trouble with diarrhea for several months, and it was decided that when the fliers were escorted out he should go along and try to get treatment. So as soon as the passes were open in late May, Russell, Eugene, our young evangelist Barnabas, and a number of carriers escorted the four flyers to Ft. Hertz. It was a difficult and dangerous trip. In the highest altitude, crossing the pass, two of the carriers became almost unconscious from the cold. Eugene's alertness and skill saved their lives. He poured kerosene from a lantern onto some wet bamboo and when a fire was started, this provided quick heat. On one dangerous slope Eugene made a mis-step, and went slipping and sliding down the mountain side, finally coming to a stop only inches from the edge of a deep crevice. Surely God was watching over him.

After four weeks of travel they reached Ft. Hertz. From there they flew to Assam with the four young airmen who were delighted to return to civilization. Russell, Eugene, and Barnabas went on to Calcutta, where they bought medicines and other supplies. Also, Russell was able to get proper treatment, and his diarrhea was cured. They even were able to get some much-needed rest. They had three thousand Lisu hymnals printed, and also contracted for three thousand Lisu Bibles to be printed later by the Bible Society. When their business in Calcutta was finished they were flown back to Assam to await the arrival of a new missionary from America — Dorothy Sterling. The fact that Dorothy was a nurse, and conceivably could help in the Search and Rescue work, contributed to the favorable consideration given by the Air Force.

✝

Although Dorothy Sterling was eager to come to China to assist us as a missionary nurse, she was having trouble obtaining her passport. At that time passports were being issued only to military personnel, but because of our co-operation in the Search and Rescue work, the U.S. Air Force commander in India interceded on her behalf. Not only was she able to obtain her passport but she was also given permission to fly to Calcutta on a military plane. However, she was allowed to take only sixty-five pounds of luggage.

She arrived in Calcutta on September 27, 1944, expecting to find Russell and Eugene waiting for her, so was quite distressed when she learned they had gone on to Assam, and wondered how she would make connections. She had expected to meet our men-folk at Lee Memorial Mission Home in Calcutta, so thought she'd better go there, but had much difficulty finding anyone who even knew where it was. Concerning this experience she wrote:

"One British Captain who seemed to know the city, told me to stop at the Great Eastern Hotel, and there get a cab over to the Mission Home. As he was only going a block beyond the Hotel, he

got off with me and found a taxi for me. Just before the taxi driver started, two Americans jumped out of a jeep across the street and came running over. One was Warrant Officer Martin, of the A.T.C. (Air Transport Command). He asked if I were Miss Sterling, and told me that Mr. Morse had left a letter with him for me. I was to go over to the Mission Home, where they were expecting me, and he would arrange my priority and flight on to Assam as soon as possible. Officer Martin and his friend had been waiting in their jeep for that bus, in order to meet someone from their office. Knowing of my expected arrival, and seeing an American woman getting off the bus from the airport, he guessed it might be me, and hurried over to investigate. I was surely thankful to see someone who at least knew something about the Morses."

Three days later, on September 30th, Dorothy flew to Assam, where she found Russell, Eugene and Barnabas waiting for her. As soon as the weather cleared enough, they all left by plane on October 11 and flew to Likiang, where they landed on the grass airstrip (altitude 9000 feet) at the foot of the snow-covered Jade Dragon Mountain, (altitude 18,500 feet). From there they hired horses, and finally arrived at Pugeleh on November 1, after a two-week caravan trip. When Dorothy's baggage finally arrived in Calcutta by ship, the Air Force dropped it by parachute (beautifully colored nylon ones!) at Pugeleh for her. We were very happy that she had joined us. She had such faith in God and such a pioneering spirit, yet was such a quiet and gentle soul. She was immensely helpful to Russell in his care of the many sick people who came for treatment. In addition she assisted me with Ruth's studies, and began her study of the Lisu language. Because I still had not regained my strength, she examined my blood and found that my hemoglobin level was extremely low and I was very anemic. She gave me various injections to help my condition, and was of great help to Russell in treating me.

✞

When Russell and Eugene went to India they tried to contact LaVerne, but found he was no longer at the school. He had managed to obtain a passport, and then to secure passage

on a Chinese refugee ship which was so crowded that he had to
sleep on the deck. He landed in Los Angeles on July 3, 1944, a
fifteen-year-old boy, alone and not knowing a soul. He remembered the name of a Christian church, and knew that his parents were acquainted with one of the elders there, but couldn't
remember his name. When someone mentioned the name, W.
K. Chamberlain, he remembered that was the man. The Red
Cross helped him until he contacted the Chamberlains, who
then helped him get in touch with relatives. It was so good to
have Christian friends. He was asked to speak before several
groups in Los Angeles, and even en route to Tulsa. In Tulsa he
stayed with his grandmother, Mrs. Ruth Morse, and aunts
(Russell's mother and sisters), and attended high school there
for two years. How we missed him during all those years!

✝

One vital part of the rescue work was the search for crashed
planes and obtaining identification of those who did not survive, to be given to the Air Force commander. Robert was
home just twenty-eight days that first year after he became
involved in the Search and Rescue work. He climbed up, over,
and around almost inaccessible peaks. The natives all listened
and watched for any planes in trouble and got word to Robert
as soon as possible. After Eugene returned from India, he
assisted Robert in that work also. The Search and Rescue unit
had supplied Eugene a radio transceiver, and this was of great
help in keeping touch with the air force.

Later we were very proud to receive a letter from H. H.
Arnold, Commanding General of U. S. Army Air Forces:

"Dear Mr. Morse:

*"To you and your family I express the gratitude of the Army
Air Forces and my personal appreciation for the work you are
doing and have done among the Lisu tribes of West China, to effect
the rescue of American air-crew members who have been forced
down in that area. Search and rescue work initiated by you, and
your efforts to counteract enemy propaganda, coupled with your*

unlimited zeal to Christianize and educate the Lisus, have proved of inestimable value to the United Nations' cause in this war.

"The manner in which you have continued to battle seemingly insurmountable obstacles has won the admiration of all who are familiar with your work. I am sure that when the chronicle of your outstanding achievements can safely be told, this feeling will be echoed by all Christian peoples.

"The Army Air Force recognizes the importance of your work, both to the successful prosecution of this war and to the establishment of better relations between the people of this country and those of the Salween Valley."

> */s/ H. H. Arnold*
> *Commanding General,*
> *Army Air Force*

During Eugene's seven months of travel through Burma, Assam, Calcutta and Yunnan, he had been on the lookout for new and better ideas in mission buildings and we were all eager to see what he could do with native materials and helpers in the Salween. After surveying the mission field, he decided to construct a mission home at Tada, two days journey north of Pugeleh, where we already had a strong congregation. Eugene had a natural genius for construction work, also some previous experience. With his complete mastery of the native language he had enthusiastic co-operation from his helpers.

The house was three stories high, each story over eight feet. The main framework was made of big pillars and cross beams, dressed down from big trees which had to be gotten up on the mountain. A road had to be built without the aid of modern construction machinery. He even engineered an aqueduct so water would flow by the house to furnish power for an electric generator. The natives were simply amazed at what Eugene could accomplish.

Eugene put in many, many hours of prayer, as well as work, in building the house. He prayed especially for the safety of the workers. A Chinese house of that size was seldom built without accidents because of the crude way the materials must be assembled, but during the two and a half years of work no one had so much as a splinter injury.

The burning of the tiles for the roof was another example of answered prayer. The Chinese tile workers were not Christians. They had been making tiles for many years and it was an ancient superstition that before the kiln was opened to remove the tile a ceremony must be performed to appease the spirits. Without Eugene's knowledge, they went ahead and killed a chicken, and recited the incantations, but for all that the first batch was soft and could not be used. The chief tile-maker was a man of good reputation and he felt that his honor was at stake so, before the second batch was mixed, he and Eugene tried to figure out what was wrong. After sampling several clays, they decided to make the second batch the same as the first. When everything was ready the tile-maker asked Eugene for a chicken.

Eugene said, "No, instead of that we will ask all the Christians to pray." God has said He will not put to shame those who trust in Him, and the second batch of tiles was absolutely perfect. The old tile-maker said, "Your God did it".

Even before the house was finished, Russell planted an orchard of three hundred fourteen (314) fruit trees in the adjoining property. All through the months Eugene was at Tada working on the house he was also preaching, teaching, and holding Bible studies.

24
Thinning of the Ranks

I was ill most of 1945 with what we believed was pernicious anemia, but in spite of that I did make several teaching trips to the south, and conducted a two-week Bible school for native teachers and evangelists at Pugeleh. The four adult members of the Morse family were seldom all home at any one time. Our Easter meetings were very successful. There were 650 at the northern convention and 350 at the southern convention at Go-da.

After his Search and Rescue work was over the latter part of 1945, Robert went over to the Ahkyang (Ah-chang) Valley in northern Burma, along a tributary of the Irrawaddy River. Numerous requests had been received from there, asking for teachers to come, so Robert stayed there through the winter months of 1945-46. Lisu evangelists had worked in that area, and Robert felt it would eventually become even more extensive than the work in the Salween Valley. It was amazing how the Gospel had spread, carried not only by full-time evangelists, but by the Lisu Christians as a whole..

Most of the people there were Lisu and Rawang. After Robert had been there for some time preaching and teaching, he received this message from a Rawang village about three days' travel away:

"We, the Rawangs, have ever been classed as a slave tribe to the Tibetans. Is it that our slave-tribe is fated to go to hell in the next life as well as to be spurned in this? Is this the reason you folks refuse to show us the way to salvation?"

What could Robert answer? He was the only missionary in that part of upper Burma. For several months he had tried to meet the overwhelming demands of new churches scattered over an area of twenty-three days journey from north to south and twelve days journey east and west, with no transportation but his feet. In that area some 1500-1800 people had turned from heathenism to the Lord Jesus Christ, and Robert had the help of only five young Lisu preachers in all that vast territory. No wonder he felt overwhelmed! People with centuries of heathen background cannot hear the Gospel just once and instantly accept the Lord. They must be taught constantly, with much love, patience, and wisdom. Bible schools must be held frequently in order to train leaders and teachers for the new churches.

One day, a Rawang chief's son came to Robert, begging him to make a written language in Rawang so they could read about "the Mighty One" in their own language. He said, "The Lisu have a written language, so please make us one". That was to be an indescribably long, hard, tedious job for Robert — but that is another story.

✝

After Isabel Maxey returned to America she continued to study, and to speak and work on behalf of the Tibetan-Lisuland missions. She interested several wonderful young people who became missionary volunteers, including Dorothy Sterling, Jane Kinnett, and David and Lois Rees. While studying further for the mission field, Isabel met and married Warren Dittemore, a fine Christian man. Mr. and Mrs. Rees and Warren all studied Chinese language at Berkeley, California. It was while in California that they had a son, Jonathan., but when he was only a few months old they had the sadness of parting with him when he died suddenly in his sleep. In May, 1945 they were blessed with a daughter, whom they named Janet Leigh. Then in January, 1946, after many disappointing delays en route, Isabel, Warren and little Janet, arrived in Pugeleh. Soon after their arrival, we Morses moved into the stout, new house Eugene had built at Ta-da, leaving the Pugeleh house as headquarters for Dittemores and Dorothy Sterling.

Between the happy arrival of the Dittemores and the leaving on our much-needed furlough July 1, 1946 we held two Bible Training Schools for native church leaders in the Salween Valley. Eugene, Dorothy and I held one and Warren helped with the other. Robert had conducted similar schools for the Upper Burma regions. Warren went on a month's tour of the Mekong Valley churches. Calls for medical and nursing services were keeping Russell busy. We kept saying, "How can we ever leave now!" Yet we knew that we needed to go. A term of almost ten years on that mission field, during which our home and supplies had been lost in a flood, and we had gone through the strains of the war years, had left us mentally, physically, and spiritually exhausted. Our health, the boys' education, and contacts with the homeland all were demanding attention.

For the last three Sundays in June, Christians from most of the surrounding churches came to Ta-da for worship and to hear a farewell message from each member of our family. Our Lisu Christians were an affectionate people. Some wept, all joined in prayers, and there was much entreating from all that we should soon return to them. With tears in our own eyes, we reassured them. Had we not been so very, very weary we might easily have given up the trip.

Walking along the valley enroute to Pugeleh, with a large escort of native Christians, we visited two churches. We remained in Pugeleh for a week of conference and happy visiting with Warren, Isabel and Dorothy. Again, our heartstrings were pulled by the many more native friends from surrounding churches. Warren seemed tired and a bit weak, but none of us had an inkling that his death was but a month away. Dear Warren! Brave Isabel and Dorothy who stayed on with our dear Lisu Christian brethren! I was reminded of Acts 21:5,6 — "And when we had accomplished those days, we departed and went our way; and they all brought us on our way, with wives and children, till we were out of the city; and we kneeled down ... and prayed."

✝

We started out with about twenty Lisu porters who helped carry our loads as far as Ai-wa on the Mekong River, which took three days of walking. After crossing the Mekong in small dug-out canoes we hired pack animals and riding horses. On that side of the river most of the population were Chinese and we were now on the main Chinese-Tibetan caravan trade route. Living standards there were higher, and we could buy vegetables and find shelter where there were stoves for cooking, some furniture, wooden floors, whitewashed walls and tiled roofs, none of which could be found in Lisu villages in the Salween valley. Ruth was quite excited by all of that, as most of her eleven years had been spent among the Lisu. In Likiang, we visited our German missionary friends, the Starr and Seiring families, who would later be of much comfort to Isabel.

It was while in Likiang that we were shocked and grieved to receive word of the death of Warren Dittemore, the lovable and brilliant young man whose coming to Pugeleh had made our furlough possible. He had died on August 5th, from typhus fever. Suddenly we realized that we were a long, long way from either of the places for which our hearts yearned.

At Tali we came at last to the end of the horse road and the beginning of the motor road, leaving behind the old, familiar travel ways of interior China. When we had traveled that section of the Burma Road with Dr. Shelton twenty-five years before, it had taken us two weeks. Even as late as 1937 it had taken nine days. Now, traveling by truck, we were able to make it in two days.

We packed most of our caravan equipment and stored it in readiness for our return to China. Our other luggage was loaded atop a Burmese-owned merchant truck, and we ourselves sat atop that. How thrilling to be flying along at the dizzy speed of twenty-five miles per hour! Ruth was having her first remembered car ride, and our 19-year-old Tibetan girl, Drema Esther, was amazed. Our other Tibetan girl, Anzie Ruth, had remained in Pugeleh with Dorothy Sterling. We were happy to share this experience with Esther, for she had been so patient and helpful all along the way on the overland trip, assuming a heavy portion of the hard work.

✝

Upon arriving in Kunming, we were invited to stay in the nicely furnished home of a China Inland Mission family, who were away on furlough, and we set up our own housekeeping while waiting for passage to the seacoast. We were all extremely weary, and it was wonderful to be able to rest.

Near the end of October, it appeared that a shipping strike in the United States was ended, so Eugene flew to Shanghai to try to arrange passage on a homeward bound ship. In appreciation for the work of Eugene and Robert in the Search and Rescue operations, the American Air Force paid our transportation expenses, both on a plane from Kunming to Shanghai, and on a troop ship to San Francisco.

Just as we were all prepared to leave, our new missionaries David and Lois Rees and their baby son, arrived in Kunming. After having so much difficulty arranging for passage on the plane, all of us except Russell decided to leave as scheduled. Russell felt he could not leave those young people alone in a strange city. The Reeses were anxious to join Dorothy and Isabel at Pugeleh, but both became ill with influenza shortly after arriving in Kunming.

After Warren's death, Isabel went to Likiang to spend some time with the German missionaries there. They were a great help and able to give her much comfort in her bereavement. However, she returned to Pugeleh before the passes closed for the winter.

✝

We took Drema Esther as far as Shanghai to enter her in a missionary school there. We thought she should have more

242

formal education than that which she had at the Chinese school in Yea Chi. During our three weeks in Shanghai we met Miss Jane Kinnett, another new missionary coming to join the work, who planned to join the Reeses in Kunming. After we left, Esther began hearing about the terrible things the Chinese communists were doing and became so frightened she clung to Jane, begging her to take her to Kunming with her. Unable to resist her tearful pleas, Jane let her go along. Once in Kunming, she was a help to J. Russell, and the new missionaries —the Reeses and Jane Kinnett.

We all missed Russell as we thrilled over our journey to America and marveled at the great change in the world's transportation. We had often looked up at the planes flying over our Salween Valley home, so it was exciting to fly over and look DOWN at the the hills and valleys. The ocean voyage, too, was memorable. When we stopped in Japan, we joined the troops on a tour of the devastated city of Tokyo. Our entire journey home was an unforgettable experience.

Eugene, Robert, Ruth and I arrived in San Francisco December 16, 1946. We caught the first view of that great homeland city at 4:30 that morning. As we came down the gang-plank a few hours later, we were surrounded amd welcomed by many friends. They will never know how much joy they brought us, nor how strongly we felt the reality of rope-holders across the sea supporting us in our missionary endeavors.

But the greatest joy of all was when LaVerne stepped off a plane two days later. At first we didn't know him! That chubby little boy of fourteen whom we had last seen in 1943 was now a slender, handsome young man almost as tall as Eugene. However, there was no mistaking Mother Morse who was at the Tulsa depot to meet us Christmas afternoon, nor Russell's sisters who helped make Tulsa the center of our home thoughts during our twenty-five years in China. My own dear mother had gone to be with the Lord three years before and could not greet us, but my dear sister, Helen, came. It was all like a wonderful dream. God had kept His promise to be with us.

☩

Yunnan Province, which lies next to Burma and French Indo-China, was populated by not only Chinese, but by over fifty different tribes, of which a large proportion had never had an opportunity to hear the Gospel. Conditions there were more primitive, and the need greater than in many other areas of China.

Unfortunately, David and Lois Rees were unable to take the bulk of their baggage and supplies with them when they flew out, and it was very difficult to obtain equipment on the Chinese markets. Landlocked Yunnan was in an especially isolated position, presenting a marked change from war time, when almost anything could be purchased. During the war, Kunming (the capital of the province) was a U.S. Army and Air Force base, so transportation was easy and trade flourished. After the war ended, the Burma Road was abandoned, air routes over the "hump" were discontinued, and the old railroad to the seacoast through French Indo-China had not been repaired. Thus, it took a whole year for the Reeses to receive the baggage they had shipped from the States. It arrived just in time for them to get to Pugeleh before the passes were closed. Isabel Dittemore and Dorothy Sterling, had been carrying on alone all of that time. Jane Kinnett decided to stay in Kunming for language study after Mr. and Mrs. Rees left.

Russell, as Director of the Tibetan-Lisuland Churches of Christ Mission, felt a great responsibility for the new missionaries, and it seemed imperative for him to stay on in Kunming to help them. It was at that time he began to see the need for a mission home there, where workers could stay while passing through, or come for a short rest. It could also be used to store bulk supplies. The transaction was completed before he flew to America in the spring of 1947, bringing Drema Esther with him.

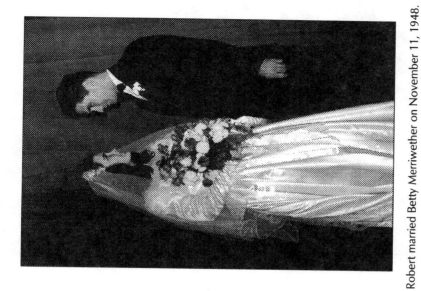

Robert married Betty Merriwether on November 11, 1948.

Eugene married Helen Myers on June 20, 1948.

The two couples sailed together on the
"Flying Dragon" on November 11, 1948
just one month after Robert & Betty were married.

The two young couples joined the work in Kunming, China, where a
congregation of believers had been established. Russell and I were
working with them, and also teaching in nearby villages.

Russell and I were together in Kunming.

Russell and I, Ruth Margaret, Drema Esther,
and Eugene and Helen all lived in this mission home
in Kunming in 1949. Robert & Betty were here also,
before they went up-country.

Eugene & Helen, with 2-month-old David, flew to Likiang, where they landed with their supplies and equipment on an old military air strip at the foot of the snow mountains. Robert & Betty also landed here, as did Dorothy Sterling in 1944.

When Eugene & Helen returned to Kunming after being turned back by the Communists at Likiang, LaVerne was almost ready to leave on his trip through Tibet, and the rest of us, except for Russell, soon flew to Hong Kong. L-R: J. Russell, Gertrude, LaVerne, Helen, and Eugene, holding David.

25
The Expanded Family Returns to Asia

After being away from the United States for nine and a half years, we had a lot of visiting to do with relatives and getting acquainted with new members of our family. Many changes had taken place while we were away. In the spring of 1947, Eugene and Robert decided to study at Cincinnati Bible Seminary for one semester. By that summer, however, the five adult members of our family had scattered over much of the United States and Canada on a very full schedule of speaking in Christian Service Camps and Mission Weeks.

In August, 1947, Eugene and Robert went to Los Angeles, where together with Mr. A. B. Cooke of the C.I.M., they worked day and night on a new edition of the Lisu hymnal, which was to contain nearly three hundred hymns. The hymns had been carefully selected for both their strong Gospel message and for their good music. Many of them were newly translated, and were being eagerly awaited by the Lisu Christians, who loved to sing. (The Lisu language had been put into a written form in about 1908 by a missionary of the China Inland Mission, Mr. J. O. Fraser. With the help of Mr. and Mrs. A. B. Cooke, Gospel portions had been translated into the "Hwa" Lisu dialect in the 1920's, but the entire New Testament was not completed until 1939.)

Christian hymns played a very important part in spreading the Gospel message in that land of hopeless darkness and despair. Living in an environment of cynical fatalism, with little to be happy about and nothing to hope for, the pagan Lisu had no real songs — although they were much more musically inclined than their neighbors. The hymns had the peculiar value of showing that there IS joy and hope in this life through Christ. On our evangelistic tours we were often told of people who became interested in Christianity through hearing and learning to sing the wonderful messages. The demand for hymnals was always greater than the supply.

The difficulties encountered in printing these new hymnals were almost overwhelming. The work needed to be accomplished as quickly as possible because Mr. Cooke, who was in Los Angeles to assist in the project, was scheduled to return to the mission field by October. First, professional typesetters cast each piece of type individually, on a monotype machine, then Eugene and Robert had to manually turn the letters that needed to be upside-down or backward. After that, either Eugene, Robert, or Mr. Cooke had to proofread it, making innumerable corrections. Lisu music uses numbers to indicate the tones, rather than the staff note music we find in our Western hymnals. Dots and dashes indicate the time value of each note, and commas and apostrophes show the high and low octaves. After corrections were made, the manuscripts were sent to another company where permanent plates were made, from which the actual printing was to be done. A third company handled the printing. Nine thousand nine hundred pounds — almost five tons! — of paper were ordered from Pennsylvania for the ten thousand books. A fourth company then made up the books, stitching and gluing, then binding.

All this took much longer than the three months Eugene and Robert had planned to spend on the project, but we all considered it well worth while, even though it was necessary for them to forego continuing their studies in Bible College, and they had to cancel many speaking engagements. They finally finished the work just before Thanksgiving.

✝

One matter of great concern to Eugene and Robert was the problem of finding wives. Both boys had been praying about this for a number of years before our return on furlough, and Russell and I had been praying with them and for them. After all, they each wanted just the right person, the one that God knew would be a real help-mate. Because they were moving around so much, speaking in churches and camps on behalf of the mission, they were not in any one place long enough for them to get really well acquainted with any girls. As the time approached for us to begin preparations for return to the field, each was beginning to wonder if perhaps the Lord wanted them to go back to China alone. But both were seeking the Lord's will, and trusting Him to guide them.

Eugene met Miss Helen Myers, daughter of Julia and Oscar Myers of Terre Haute, Indiana, at the North American Christian convention in Springfield, Illinois. Helen was a nurse, was president of the Life Recruit Group at her home church, and had already made a commitment to missionary service. They met on April 20, 1948, and exactly two months later, on June 20, Russell and I, together with his sister Eva Melton, and my sister Helen Howe, attended their wedding in Terre Haute, Indiana. Helen's mother, Mrs. Myers, became the forwarding agent for Helen and Eugene. Later, when Russell's dear mother went to her Heavenly reward in 1953, "Mother Myers" became forwarding agent for all of the Morse families, and served in this capacity until just before her death in 1976.

✞

Russell and I had wanted to return to China the latter part of 1947, but our doctor emphatically told us we should rest another six months. We did, however, accept some speaking dates around the country until time to go to Los Angeles. There we spent the last few hectic weeks, purchasing and packing supplies, and taking care of last-minute business. LaVerne decided to stay and finish his second year at Minnesota Bible College.

During our time in the United States, we had been on the lookout for new recruits, and had been joined by two young ladies: Miss Imogene Williams and Miss Lora Banks. Both were Bible College graduates, besides which Imogene had also had some nurses' training, although she was not a registered nurse. Both had dedicated their lives to full-time Christian service, and seemed to have the qualities needed for missionary service. Both were in California when we arrived there, working along with Eugene and Helen and Robert, buying supplies and packing, looking forward to starting their journey to the mission field.

We sent off most of our supplies on August 6, 1948. Russell and Eugene, with the help of friends, loaded all the boxes onto a truck, including the big boxes of Lisu hymnals, which each weighed over 300 pounds. Then they had to unload everything at the dock, so they were all very tired. Russell, Ruth, Drema Esther and I left Los Angeles by freighter on August 15, 1948. We went by way of Manila, where we visited with some of the missionaries, and arrived in Hong Kong on September 8. During our stop-over in Manila, I was told by a doctor that I should enter the hospital there for more rest, but I felt I should go on to Hong Kong. I knew that when I arrived there I could rest while Russell purchased additional supplies and made arrangements to go on to Kunming.

Our 10,000 Lisu hymnals, Lisu phonograph records, medical supplies and other equipment and supplies weighed about 24,000 pounds, and we knew it would be expensive to ship by air from Hong Kong to Kunming. But Russell personally met with Quentin Roosevelt, vice-president of the China National Aviation Corporation, (CNAC) who was instrumental in getting us the very best discount possible. Finally it was decided that since we were shipping three plane loads of goods, we could also transport personnel by weight as freight, instead of charging passenger fares, This did save us money, but because the plane was designed for freight, it had only the metal "bucket" seats down each side, so it wasn't very comfortable.

Also, it had neither heat nor oxygen on it, and we all developed severe headaches. Because we were going from the heat of Hong Kong through the freezing air above the mountains, we suffered from the intense cold.

When we arrived in Kunming on October 8, we found the city crowded with refugees from the Communist-controlled northern part of China, and heard reports that many more were coming. Most of the people were very frightened by developing conditions and there was war talk on all sides. We felt that if there were any prospects for missionaries continuing anywhere in China, Yunnan Province was the most likely place.

✝

While attending Cincinnati Bible Seminary in 1947, Robert had met Miss Betty Meriwether, of Baton Rouge, Louisiana. In the summer of 1948, they both enrolled in the Wycliffe Summer Institute of Linguistics course held at the University of Oklahoma. Because Betty was still rather young (only 18) and also because of unsettled world conditions they originally planned to wait a couple of years to marry. Then Robert was delayed by a shipping strike, and after much prayer, and seeking the Lord's will, they decided that it would be all right if they went ahead and got married. The ceremony took place in the Cincinnati Bible Seminary Chapel on November 11, 1948. After a brief honeymoon of only 3-4 days, they went directly to Los Angeles to join Eugene and Helen in preparing to return to China. The next three weeks were crowded with such things as securing a passport (necessary for foreign travel) and visas for Betty, making ship reservations, and buying and packing supplies. We knew it sometimes took up to six weeks to obtain a passport, but with the Lord's help Betty received hers in only a little over two weeks.

On December 11, 1948, exactly one month after Robert and Betty were married, the two young Morse couples left the United States for the mission field on the "Flying Dragon", a freighter which also had accommodations for twelve passengers.

For both Helen and Betty it was an "initiation" and introduction to traveling abroad. After a stop in Manila, Philippines, where they visited the missionaries, they arrived in Hong Kong on January 4, 1949. For the first few days they stayed in a Chinese hotel, which was quite an experience for the new brides. This was necessary because there was no room for them at the Basel Mission Guest House where they had hoped to stay. Later, they were able to move to the Christian Guest House. On Januuary 8, Imogene Williams and Lora Banks arrived in Hongkong, and just twelve days later, on January 20, 1949, they flew to Kunming together with Robert and Betty. Once they arrived in Kunming, Imogene and Lora soon settled down into a routine of Chinese language study, while Robert and Betty began their preparations for proceeding on to the mission station in the Mekong Valley. Eugene and Helen flew to Kunming on February 18, bringing the balance of the supplies left in Hong Kong.

On March 18, after a few weeks of rest, Robert and Betty flew to Likiang on the first stage of their journey to the Mekong Valley mission station. It took only an hour in the Lutheran Mission plane known as the "St. Paul" to cover a distance which would have taken three weeks by horse caravan. As a "bonus", Eugene flew up with them and cane back on the return flight. From Likiang, however, Robert and Betty had to travel by horse caravan. A few days out of Likiang, Betty was thrown from her horse, and suffered a slight concussion, from which she recovered gradually. Aside from that, they encountered no difficulties other than the usual hardships experienced on a caravan journey. However, after arriving in Dratsilo, one of our mission stations in the Mekong where Isabel Dittemore was holding a Bible School, they faced another kind of difficulty — one not related to the communist threat. The Tibetans and Chinese became embroiled in border warfare, and fierce battles erupted. The Tibetans burned the village of Yea Chi to the ground and killed many, many people. They also devastated

Kang Pu, destroying our mission post there, and either drove out or killed the entire population.

✝

Eugene and Helen remained at the mission home in Kunming awaiting the arrival of their first child, — a son, David Lowell Morse, who was born on March 19, 1949. On May 19, when David was two months old, Eugene and family flew on the "St. Paul" to Likiang, where they began preparations for the caravan journey to Ai-wa in the Mekong Valley.

Likiang had been "liberated" by the communists July 2, but Eugene and family were allowed to leave on July 21, as scheduled, with a caravan of thirty-five horses carrying all their goods. However, when they stopped in Shigu the second night of the journey, three soldiers came to find out who they were, where they came from, and where they were going. The next morning about twenty soldiers appeared and insisted on inspecting everything in each of their 35 horse loads of boxes, trunks and baskets, ostensibly looking for guns and ammunition. After two days of unpacking and repacking, and another two days of waiting for word from the Communist headquarters, the caravan was ordered to return to the Mission home in Likiang. When they arrived back in Likiang, they were detained under house arrest. For over a month, they were subjected almost daily to groups of soldiers entering their house and going through their possessions at gun point. Each group took what they liked, with the comment, "We can use that". They even took the baby's vitamin drops.

During those troubled days a C.N.A.C. cargo plane, and the"St. Paul" were the only planes coming to the Kunming airport. The St. Paul was flying twice a week from Hong Kong to Kunming to evacuate missionaries and their belongings. Not knowing whether it would even be possible to get the St. Paul to come to Likiang, Eugene finally asked the communist officials if the plane would be allowed to land at Likiang and evacuate his family and two other missionary families — the last foreigners still in the city. He was told that this could be arranged if the plane would bring up some personnel and supplies for them (the communists). Of course Eugene agreed to this plan. When, at last, he was able to get word to us about the situation, Russell immediately chartered the plane and began trying to arrange for the "pay loads" to help defray expenses.

LaVerne had flown to Kunming in June after his school term ended and he was now of enormous help in this undertaking. He and Mel Byers, a young missionary who had been with Harold Taylor at Tali, went around Kunming on bicycles arranging for additional "pay loads" to fill up the plane. Then LaVerne went along, listed as "engineer" to help unload and reload the plane. So far as we know, this was the only place in China that the St. Paul landed in Communist-held territory to evacuate missionaries. Three trips were made to bring out the three missionary families and all their baggage. Although Helen didn't want to leave Eugene, she and David and one other missionary family, who also had a small child, came out on the first trip. Eugene and the other family came on the third flight, three days later. When the plane returned for this third trip, they found soldiers lined up in front of the passengers and their belongings. The crew immediately suspected they planned to confiscate the plane, as this was the last trip.

LaVerne began talking with the soldiers in a friendly way, admiring their caps with the red star, and asked if they could get him one when he came back, leaving the impression that another trip would be made. The plane was allowed to leave. By the end of August, Eugene, Helen and David were all back in Kunming. Eugene was very thin, and both were extremely nervous and exhausted from their ordeal. However, they took satisfaction in the fact that they had been able to save most of the supplies they had with them in Likiang.

✞

During the summer, the situation in Kunming also had been very tense, first with rumors that a Communist takeover was imminent, followed by reports that the Nationalists were firmly in charge. Everyone was puzzling over what to do. We had been urgently advised to send our 15-year-old daughter, Ruth, back to the United States because of all the terrible tales we were hearing. In mid-August, she flew back in the company of her English teacher from the Kunming Mission School. She was met in Los Angeles by Helen's mother, Mrs. Julia Myers, and returned with her to Terre Haute, Indiana. She entered her first year of high school there, and for the next three years made her home with Mr. and Mrs. Myers and Helen's younger sister and brother.

Because of the reports from areas already under communist control, many of the missionaries felt there would be little or no possibility for Christian work under a communist government, and large numbers of them were leaving Kunming to go to other mission fields. After some discussion, it seemed advisable for Imogene and Lora to leave also. Imogene decided to go to Thailand, where she joined C.W. and Lois Callaway in the new mission work they were beginning. Lora returned to the U.S., where she soon married Willis Harrison, to whom she was already engaged, and together they began a music ministry.

✝

In September, 1949 LaVerne, together with Mel Byers, decided to try to reach Burma by a round-about route, starting in Kunming, going up through Tibet and down through the Salween Valley. LaVerne hoped he could help Robert and the others there if they had not been able to escape.

When they arrived in Kangting, they met several young missionaries who had been delayed there more than a year and a half, waiting for some way to get from China to India. It finally seemed possible for all of them because a powerful Tibetan chief, trader and caravan leader named Pangdat Tsong had recently made a trip into China and was returning with his small army of soldiers guarding his part of the caravan, with rifles, pistols and machine guns. They heard that he was not a

257

believer in Buddhism and the lamas, and had many times befriended foreign missionaries and travelers. He was known in India as one of the two top men in Tibetan finance, and was reputed to control eighty percent of the wealth and the fighting force of Tibet.

LaVerne and Mel arranged for an audience with this Tibetan chief the day after their arrival. Imagine their surprise to find that this powerful official was the same wealthy merchant, Bangdat Tsong (Buh-ra-gah), who had made possible our memorable trip to Tibet in 1925! "Bong" as he was familiarly called, was equally surprised. He even remembered Eugene's and Robert's names. Could it have been mere chance that led LaVerne and Mel to that fortunate meeting? We don't think so. We believe it was God's answer to prayer. Bangdat Tsong then led them through a great part of their journey. But even so, there would be many months while they were traveling that we would have absolutely no word from or about them, and would not know if they were even alive.

26
Leaving and Loss,
Patience and Progress

During the summer of 1949, Robert and Betty, Isabel Dittemore and daughter Janet, David and Lois Rees and two children, and Jane Kinnett were all at mission bases in the Mekong Valley. At Dra-tsi-lo, Robert was awakened early in the night of August 28, and secretly told that the communists planned to arrest him the next day. Hurriedly gathering a few supplies, he and Betty and Isabel and Janet left in the middle of the night with a few trusted helpers. Much equipment, food, and mission records were abandoned. Betty was now an expectant mother, and Robert managed to arrange for a hwagan to carry her. Isabel rode her horse when possible.

Before leaving Dratsilo, Robert had managed to secretly send word to Mr. and Mrs. David Rees and Jane Kinnett, who were at Ai-wa. They also hurriedly gathered up their supplies, and left for Pugeleh. When all of the missionaries arrived from the Mekong, they had a conference and it was decided they would all have to try to reach Burma. The only word they had received from the outside world was that Eugene and his family had been forced to return to Kunming, and there were some rumors that the United States had entered the struggle on the side of the Nationalists.

Traveling down the Salween valley for two days, the party finally reached the rope bridge crossing, only to find that the rope bridge over the river had been destroyed, so it was necessary to use boats. Robert explained to a rather suspicious official that because of her condition Betty needed Dorothy Sterling's attention and care, so they were allowed to go on to Burma. Going over the same route by which Eugene and Russell had taken the air force officers in 1944, where they had to go across the 11,000-foot pass between China and Burma, they experienced terrible hardships. It was especially difficult for Betty, as there were many stretches where the hwagan could not be used, and she had to walk. After crossing the pass between China and Burma, they rested a few days in the first village in Burma, Nyi-ta-di, before going on another five days' travel to Tiliwago, where they finally arrived on September 17. It was there, only about three weeks later, on October 8, 1949, that their son, Jonathan Russell (Joni) was born, with Dorothy Sterling attending.

☦

In Kunming the situation remained very tense, with rumors flying thick and fast. We scarcely knew from one day to the next who was in charge of the government. We were all in a quandary as to what we should do. We wondered where we would go if we really had to leave Kunming. Russell had applied to the Burmese government for permits to work in Burma, on the basis of recognition granted to the mission in 1946, but had not received a reply. As summer turned to autumn, the situation had become increasingly disturbed and critical. Then in mid-November, residence permits for all the family were received, entitling them to work in Burma. The question was whether conditions in Burma were settled enough for us to move there. Finally, on November 24, Eugene's family and Drema Esther flew to Hong Kong, to wait there while Eugene checked on conditions in Burma, to see if it was safe for them to go.

As the situation in Kunming continued to deteriorate, Russell insisted that I, too, go to Hong Kong because he felt that my health could not withstand great hardships and we did not know what might lie ahead. On December 7, 1949 I flew from Kunming to Hong Kong, never suspecting that I would not see Russell again for two and a half years. He planned to follow in a few days, but was unable to do so, because the night after I left Kunming, a group of Nationalist airmen looted the airfield and flew off with three C.N.A.C. planes, one of which crashed and killed all on board. The "St. Paul", the Lutheran mission plane on which I had flown to Hong Kong, was unable to return to Kunming on its scheduled flight. Conditions were really chaotic. Then on December 9, the communists took over completely. Russell was not allowed to leave the city, and was restricted to the mission compound. However, he could go to church, preach, teach, and care for the ill who came to him. During the next fifteen months we received only a few brief and carefully worded messages from him, and then nothing for the next fifteen months. His account of what happened during those years is included in a later chapter.

In Hong Kong I was met by Helen, David and Drema Esther. There I learned that they had received word that Robert and the others of our group who fled from the Salween Valley had arrived safely in Burma. On December 2 Eugene had gone to Burma to investigate conditions, to meet with Robert and party, and to help them in any way possible as they faced new problems. He also had to decide whether it would be possible, or even wise, for the rest of the family to go. Tentative .plans had been made for all of us to go by ship to Rangoon, but a telegram from Eugene in Rangoon advised against it, so those plans were canceled.

✝

On Christmas Day we were shocked and grieved to receive a telegram from Eugene with word that our "adopted" daughter, Anzie Ruth, had died in Putao, North Burma, on December 23. Drema Esther was specially grieved, for she had been eagerly anticipating the reunion with her sister Anzie. I, too, felt a great sense of loss. I remembered how Anzie had been with us almost from birth, first with her dear mother,

Duje, who had been both helper and friend, and then with Drema Esther as our adopted daughter. She had become an important part of the mission work, not only as a teacher in her own right, but as a translator for the new workers who could not yet speak Lisu. She had spent much time working with Dorothy Sterling, especially after we left on furlough.

In tribute to her, Dorothy Sterling wrote:

"Anzie Ruth Morse was my co-worker, companion and loyal friend from January, 1947, until her death. Anzie had a rare talent for making friends among the Lisu. She was loved and honored by the many, many students in our Bible schools because of her ability in translation, and her patience in teaching and the rare tact and insight with which she was able to help straighten out personal and home problems of the individual students. She had a God-given talent for teaching children and, because she loved them, won their love and adoration. Discipline was never a problem.

"Anzie had her heart set on going to America with me for several years of schooling to prepare herself to help with opening a hospital in Lisu country. Together, we planned our furlough. After crossing the mountain peaks from Pugeleh to Tiliwago, we started down-country to apply for Anzie's passport and to go on furlough. Just one week from Putao, we stopped to treat the people in a village where sixteen had already died in a typhus epidemic. It was there that Anzie contracted the disease which two weeks later caused her violent illness, and her death just twelve days later in Putao. It seemed incredible that after all our happiness and sorrow and work together she should be taken just when the longed-for opportunity for study in the States was about to be realized. Until the day when we meet again, the memory of Anzie Ruth and her unselfishness, love, and loyalty will live in the hearts of all of us."

✝

Because of the great turmoil and chaos in the entire far east, and with conditions changing so rapidly it was impossible to make plans very far in advance. By the time Eugene returned to Hong Kong in mid-January, it seemed it would be safe for

Helen, David, Esther and me to travel with him to Muladi, our mission post a few miles from Putao. However, there was still work to be finished up in Hong Kong before we could move over to Burma.

While waiting in Hong Kong, we had to repack and ship off some of the things we had brought out from China, but which we would not be taking to Burma. Also, Eugene was hoping it would be possible to get some revised Lisu New Testaments printed, together with the Psalms, which had just been translated into Lisu by Mr. Allyn B. Cooke of the China Inland Mission. But the Cookes and the manuscripts were still inside communist territory. It had become increasingly difficult for people to get permits to leave the "liberated" areas. Just as Eugene was ready to place an order with the Hong Kong Bible Society for another edition of the old, unrevised version of the Lisu New Testament, word came that Mr. and Mrs. Cooke and family had reached Rangoon and had brought his manuscripts of the revised Lisu New Testament and the newly translated Psalms.

As soon as Mr. Cooke arrived in Hong Kong, the printing was started through the Bible Society. Their work was subsidized, and this substantially reduced the cost per book. The China Inland Mission designated Mr. Allan Crane, one of their missionaries who had worked with the Lisu in China, to do the proofreading and supervisory work. Mr. Crane had recently completed translation of the book of Genesis, and Eugene asked his permission to have some copies of this printed also. A new edition of the Lisu Gospel Primer was also greatly needed. But because we were planning to leave soon for Burma, we needed to find someone who could do the proof-reading if we were to print a new edition of the Primer. At that time, all books were typeset with lead type, and all had to be proof-read — especially in Lisu, where some of the letters had to be turned upside-down or backward. Then Isabel Dittemore and daughter Janet arrived in Hong Kong from Rangoon, Burma, where she could not get an extension of permission to stay. She offered to stay in Hong Kong long enough to finish the proof-reading, and see to the packing and shipment of the Primer and the edition of Genesis. We appreciated her help so much, because we had already had to spend four months waiting in Hong Kong. We had received our residence and entry permits, and we were eager to start for the mission post in North Burma.

✞

About ten days before we all planned to leave Hong Kong, we were informed there was a problem in getting an entry permit for Drema Esther. It was necessary for me to fly to Rangoon to expedite obtaining an entry permit for her, even though she already had a residence permit. A few days later, I arrived in Rangoon, just at the time of the annual Water Festival, when government offices were officially closed and most people stayed at home to keep from getting soaked, as fire hydrants were opened up and water seemed to be every-where. Although the offices were closed, some young ladies at the YWCA where I was staying volunteered to take me around to the homes of the officials. After a week of going from one to another, I finally was successful and sent the permit by wire to Hong Kong. It arrived just the day before they were scheduled to leave Hong Kong.

On April 18, 1950, which was Eugene's 29th birthday, he and his family and Drema Esther flew from Hong Kong by way of Bangkok, to join me in Rangoon. We had heard that going through customs in Rangoon could be very difficult, and expected we might have to pay quite a bit of duty. We had been praying about the matter, though, and the Lord certainly answered. Only two suitcases had to be opened, and no duty was charged at all.

We had heard of some people having to wait as long as two or three months for a flight from Rangoon to Myitkyina (Mit´-chee-nah). We were also concerned about obtaining cargo space for our baggage on the plane. Again we prayed about the problem, and again our prayers were answered! Eugene walked into the airline office and was able to make reservations for space right away. We were allowed to take a thousand pounds, or a little more if we wished.

✞

After almost five months in Hong Kong, we were at last on our way to our mission work! We expected to be able to fly only as far as Myitkyina. However, through the help of the Public Works Department, we were given permission to go on a chartered plane which they were sending to Putao — but there would not be space enough for our supplies. We could take only our suitcases. Eugene stayed behind to arrange transport for the baggage, while Helen and David, Drema Esther and I flew to Putao on May 11, 1950. We landed on the grassy airstrip, which had been used as a temporary landing strip by the military during World War II. There we were met by Betty (Robert's wife) and Jane Kinnett, and learned that Robert was away, on a trip to Tiliwago. Because it was late afternoon when we arrived, we stayed overnight at the government bungalow in Putao, and the next day made the all-day trip on foot to the mission base in Muladi.

It was about ten days laater that Eugene arrived. From Myitkyina he had traveled by jeep for two days, covering about 130 miles, to reach Sumprabum. In Sumprabum he was unable to hire either horses or load carriers, so to our surprise he arrived in Muladi with four elephants carrying our loads. They came right up to our door to unload.

It was during the first part of his journey, when traveling by jeep, that there occurred one of those incidents, or "accidents", which are common in Asia. The 100 lb. bag of sugar which was to last us for a year was packed in a burlap bag. Somehow, it "happened" to be placed next to the tins of kerosene, and one of them leaked. We removed the portion which had been next to the leak, but the entire bag was tainted, and for the next several months we had to use kerosene-flavored sugar, for no

265

amount of airing took away either the smell or taste. The alternative was to do without, and that we couldn't quite do, although our taste for sweets was reduced.

Robert, Betty, and Joni, together with Jane Kinnett, had been living at Muladi much of the time since fleeing from China. When we arrived, Robert had been away for more than two months, visiting Tiliwago and Nyitadi (right on the Burma-China border), and then visiting churches in Rawang country, continuing his study of the language and doing translation work. He also had arranged for a house to be built in Tiliwago, so he could take his family there to live, once the rest of us had arrived and could take over the work in Muladi. We were happy to see Betty again, and to see 7-month-old Joni for the first time. He and David had so much fun together. About a month after our arrival, Robert came from Tiliwago to get his family. He and Betty and Joni left in early July, moving to Tiliwago. A month or so later, Jane Kinnett left to go on furlough, traveling by elephant as far as Sumprabum, where she could get a jeep to go on.

☦

It seemed at that time that our family was scattered in all directions, with Ruth in America, Russell in Kunming, some of us in Burma, and LaVerne — we weren't sure just where he was, because we hadn't heard from him for several months. So a few weeks after our arrival in Muladi we were all very happy when we received word that LaVerne and his fellow traveler Mel Byers had arrived safely in Tiliwago in May, 1950. They had many interesting tales to relate, including some of narrow escapes from the communists.

Anzie Ruth. We were terribly grieved to hear of her death, for we had been looking forward to seeing her again.

Drema Esther. She especially grieved over the loss of her sister, whom she hadn't seen for two years. Both girls were very much part of the family, and both helped greatly in the mission work.

Robert returned from Tiliwago to Putao to get his family and take them with him to Tiliwago. Joni was about 8 mo. old.

LaVerne spent the last part of 1951 supervising the construction of a "mission" house at Tiliwago, where we had an outstation.

27
Earthquakes, Evangelism, and Education

We will always remember Tuesday, August 15, 1950 as the day of a devastating earthquake, said to be centered in Assam, India. On that day, Eugene and I were out on preaching and teaching trips, on our way to hold a Bible school in Nam-hte-hku, a village on the mountain not far from Putao. I was at the home of the headman of a very small village where I was going to spend the night. Eugene had gone on ahead to Nam-hte-hku to complete arrangements for the Bible school. The quake, (7.8 on the Richter scale) struck about 8:00 p.m., while we were eating our evening meal. The tremors were so violent we could scarcely sit upright, and liquids in pans on the fire sloshed back and forth over the edges. One of the most frightening things about the quakes was the deep rumbling that preceded them, which seemed to start some distance away, roll under your feet, and move away.

The house of the headman, who was a Christian, was much more substantial than most native houses, and the terrified villagers came running and crowding into it. They had never before experienced an earthquake like this, and they thought it was the end of the world. They came to me crying, "Pray for us, pray for us, Mama (the Lisu word for "lady teacher")! Pray that God will forgive us for our sins". They were new Christians and were afraid their prayers would be inadequate. They said, "We want to stay here all night so we can be near Mama."

Aftershocks continued for twenty-two days. Some of the more than two hundred aftershocks (we counted 220 in just the hours when we were awake) were so hard that the people could not stand up. The earth cracked in many places, big landslides up in the mountains destroyed houses and fields which were in their path, and also turned the rivers into giant mudflows, which choked and killed all the fish. Hard rains accompanied the earthquake, and as the rivers flooded, many bridges were destroyed and giant trees were felled. Huge boulders came tumbling down the mountainsides. Helen, David and Drema Esther were alone at the mission station in Muladi. It was impossible to get word to or from them, but we trusted them to God's care constantly.

The next day, I continued on my trip. Traveling was extremely difficult going up the steep mountain and over the swollen streams where the bridges had been damaged or completely destroyed. Paths were blocked by fallen trees and enourmous boulders. In spite of everything, Eugene and I succeeded in holding the Bible School as we had planned. Although no one was killed in the Putao plains area, people were frightened. As a result, many who had not believed in God now turned to Him, and asked us to pray for them.

✠

In September, 1950 Robert sent word from Tiliwago that they would soon start a Lisu-Rawang Bible School and wished I could be there. Because I was so worried about Russell, I welcomed any opportunity to keep my mind busy and my body tired, so I decided to go and help. I completed that 100-mile journey over steep mountains and across streams in ten days, with one girl helper and two baggage carriers. Sometimes the traveling was very difficult. One day we had to wade a very swift, deep stream, and I got wet to the waist. It was not very pleasant to travel a half day in wet clothing. In one village where we stayed overnight, it seemed most of the people there were sick, and I think I gave out about 600 tablets of malaria medicine. One night we even stayed in a cave. Along the way, I taught in the evenings about seven times. It rained some days, which made traveling difficult and uncomfortable, and brought out the leeches, so we all got many leech bites. The last day of the journey I rode LaVerne's horse, which he had sent to me with one of the Lisu preachers. But the last hour or so I had to get off and walk, because the road was too steep to ride. I hadn't realized that there were such high, steep mountains in that area.

We all helped in the school — Robert, LaVerne, David and Lois Rees, Mel Byers and I. We noticed a real change for the better in most of the students as the weeks went by. LaVerne arranged for the young men students to go out to the nearby villages to teach and preach each weekend, then to meet and compare notes on their return.

The school ended December 17, 1950. We had a Christmas convention at Tiliwago, then our mission forces prepared to go work in other sections of our field. Robert and Mel Byers attended the Rawang Christmas convention at Rawangtang, two days journey south from Tiliwago. After the convention, they evangelized in that area. Mel had learned a little Rawang, so he helped Robert in many ways.

✟

LaVerne went to the Latago Christmas convention near the China- Burma divide, then over a mountain pass to Mon-di, where a small church had been established by Lisu evangelists from the Ta-da congregation in the Salween Valley. It was on that long trail we followed in 1927, when we walked out by way of Ft. Hertz, now called Putao. I was amazed at how many, many churches there now were along that trail, clear to Putao.

When we walked out over the Himalayas in 1927, after eight long days of travel through absolutely uninhabited mountains, we finally arrived at the village of Mon-di. We were very glad to reach that small village where we rested two or three days. Later, in 1940, an earnest Lisu preacher, from the Tada church in the Salween valley, went to that village as a missionary. He preached the Gospel, and taught them to read the Lisu script, until they were able to read the Lisu Bible. They were well-grounded in their faith in Christ, and carried the "good news" to other tribes who, seeing their joy, were anxious to hear. The nearby villages began sending messages to the Mon-di church, saying, "We are not just animals, but human beings just like you. We, too, want to be free, and become followers of Wu-Sa (God)."

Thousands of primitive tribespeople, including Lisu, Rawang, Kachin, Shan, Chinese and Tibetan, until a few years before had never heard of God. Most of them had lived for generations in dreadful fear of evil spirits, but it seemed that in the area around Mon-di they were especially enslaved to their fear of the spirits. They were extremely poor, and eked out a living by clearing out small patches of jungle with crude homemade tools. They planted mountainside fields of corn, rice, buckwheat and millet, and were often drunk with home-made rice wine. They did not wash or take baths more than once or twice in a year, and their faces were black with soot and grime. Their eyes were darkened because of ignorance, and fear of demons and evil spirits, which had to be appeased with sacrifices when offended.

When crossing a high mountain they were very careful to be quiet, not talking above a whisper, so as not to disturb the demon of the mountain. They believed that if the demon were awakened, it would be angry and bring a sudden, fierce blizzard roaring upon them. They constructed many altars around their bamboo houses on which offerings of boiled rice were placed, which they believed the spirits would eat.

The awful climax was the hopelessness seen at the time of death, when the relatives and friends wept and wailed all night, beating gongs. But after they became Christians, they sang hymns telling of the joys of heaven, and there was a wonderful spirit of hope and joy. Mon-di became a strong center for evangelizing.

✟

Eugene sent word to Tiliwago that a Beginners' Bible School would be started at Muladi on January 7, and he would

272

like for me to help. The trip back was interesting, for I found work to do at every village along the way, speaking at meetings, talking with mothers about home problems, and conferring with elders and preachers about the conduct of the church. I was astonished at the spiritual growth of the people. The verse, "My Word shall not return unto Me void", certainly applies to the fruits of the Gospel among these people.

Leaving Tiliwago on the return journey to Muladi, our destination the first evening was the village of Kobudeh. You would understand Lisuland a little better if you could see how that village (Kobudeh) was located. I arrived at the point where the mountain trail to this village breaks off from the main horse path about 4:00 in the afternoon, but I did not get up to the village until about 7:30, an hour or more after dark. The last part of the climb was almost impossible. It was so steep that I simply could not get a toe hold, so the carriers dug little notches for me to climb upward in the pitch-black darkness. With the Lord helping, after resting and eating a bit, I was able to preach to an attentive group.

We climbed a long, steep pass the next day and arrived after dark at the official bamboo rest house. The Burmese government maintained those rest houses along the graded horse paths at intervals of about a day's journey. They were very convenient, as the villages were few and far between. Travelers had to gather their own firewood from the surrounding jungles. As we went along the trail, we heard the barking deer nearby, and then, in the distance but coming our way, some Lisu boys singing Christian hymns. It made my heart sing, too.

In the next village they had a church building, but they were so far away from the convention centers that none of the people had been able to attend, so I worked among them for three days and most of each night. Some, who lived a long way off, brought their bedding and food and slept in the church yard beside their campfires. When I wasn't teaching or preaching, I was busy with the sick, most of whom had malaria, and to whom I gave our standard dosages of quinine or atabrine, which was all we had in those days.

My journey wasn't as lonely as it might seem, for several people escorted me a long way from the village, and two young men who were on their way to the school at Muladi stayed with me all the way. The next church was a bit over two days' journey away, but we were met on the way by people who came to help me, and carry my loads. They sang and laughed and visited with me as we walked along. It was almost like a homecoming.

✝

While I was in Tiliwago helping with the Bible School, Eugene had been working on laying out a new village site back in Muladi and helping to build a new church building. It was 90 feet long by 36 feet wide, built up on stilts about six feet above the ground. The walls were ten feet high, and there was unobstructed floor space because the roof was supported by bracing, instead of having poles at intervals. This was an entirely new concept in building for these people. The roof was covered with thatch made of the tall "elephant" grass which grew all around us. It took just nineteen working days from the time people started getting materials together until it was finished. And the only actual cash outlay was $3.00 for some nails. The new church building was finished in plenty of time to be used for the Christmas convention held on December 24, which was attended by more than 1000 people. They also built a special "cook house", where meals for the convention were prepared, and there was plenty of room around the church for people who had come from a distance to camp out.

In addition to the church building, Eugene planned and built a new house, beside the river, in the new village of Muladi. They had hoped to surprise me, and have it finished by the time I returned from Tiliwago, early in January, 1951, but it took longer than expected. But when finished it was very nice. It was built in two "wings" — really two separate houses,

connected by a covered passageway. One wing contained bedrooms and a "family" living room, and the other had the
kitchen and dining room, plus a room for receiving Lisu guests,
and a place to give out medicines to sick people.

✟

After the Lisu beginners' school at Muladi was finished, we
began preparing for the Bible school for the preachers, to be
held in March and April. David and Lois Rees, LaVerne,
Robert and Betty all came from Tiliwago to assist with the
teaching. For the first time, ALL THREE of our sons were
together in teaching at a Bible School.

At the end of the school, we held an Easter convention
which lasted three days. Many conventions were held throughout Lisuland churches, but that one held at Muladi in April,
1951, was the largest. It was attended by over 1300 Christians,
many of whom came from as far as six days' journey away.
Muladi had the largest church in Lisuland, and it was such a
thrill to see so many fervent Christians come together for services which were sometimes held in three languages: Lisu,
Rawang, and Kachin. Some non-Christian officials who visited
the convention were very much surprised that a group of
people whom they considered primitive, and near-aboriginals
could conduct themselves "in such a creditably civilized
manner". After the Easter convention, David and Lois Rees
and Mel Byers left for the U.S. because they could neither
extend nor renew their visas for staying in Burma.

Because of the request from the Rawangs for a written language of their own, Robert had started work on a Rawang
alphabet, with the help of the chief's son, Tychicus. The
Rawangs formerly were a practically unheard-of tribe in northern Burma who were now hearing the Gospel for the first time,
and the growing work among them was almost more than we
could keep up with.

Robert devised the Rawang alphabet by listening to
Tychicus slowly pronounce words, noting not only the sounds,

but the tone, or pitch, of each one. When the alphabet was completed, he started work on a Rawang primer. When he came to Muladi in March, he conferred with several leading Rawang men to check on the dialect used in the primer. There were differences in the dialects of the various Rawang sub-tribes, and he wanted this primer to be read and understood by all of them. By the end of the convention, the primer was ready for the printers.

We were happy to welcome Dorothy Sterling back from the States with her three-year-old foster son, Mark, whom she had rescued from starvation when he was an infant. She arrived just in time to help with the last part of the preachers' school.

✟

On May 3, 1951 Robert, Betty, and Joni went to Rangoon, starting on their way to the U.S. Once there, Robert enrolled in Wycliffe Bible Translator's Summer Institute of Linguistics at the University of Oklahoma. Both Robert and Betty had studied there in 1948, and now Robert needed to confer with them about the Rawang alphabet. He also wanted to take further training which would help him in translating the Bible into the Rawang language. Robert took with him some tape recordings of Tychicus speaking Rawang, so his instructors could listen to it for analysis.

The plane that took Robert and Betty to Rangoon also brought a letter telling of Russell's arrest in Kunming. Ever since leaving Hong Kong, the only way we had been able to get news from Russell was through Howard Phillips, a young missionary in Hong Kong, who was about the age of our boys. For several months Russell was able to send carefully worded letters or telegrams to him, and he in turn relayed the messages to us and to Russell's mother. The Kunming congregations had been greatly strengthened by the work that Russell and his Chinese helpers had been able to do since other members of his family escaped the incoming Red armies. For security reasons, we were advised not to contact him personally. We prayed for him constantly, and still hoped he would soon be allowed to leave China. Then the United States entered the Korean war, and we received no further word from him.

Russell's last letter had been written in February, 1951, and was an S.O.S. appeal to all prayer-bands and individual supporters of the Mission to pray that the rulers of China would speedily grant him an exit permit from Kunming to Hong Kong, and that he might safely rejoin his family and other mission associates working in Upper Burma. And now came the word that the Communists had arrested him in March.

Sometimes it seemed that I could endure the suspense no longer, with no letters, no word of any kind from Russell! Month after month I just couldn't stop thinking and wondering about him. I was quite sick for about a month after I received the news of his arrest. My old anemia had recurred, and I was very, very weak. Still I knew Russell was in God's hands, and I prayed for strength and faith to trust Him to care for Russell, and for the ability to accept His will, whatever it might be.

✝

On May 24, Eugene and his family went to Rangoon to await the birth of their second child, and to arrange for the printing of the Rawang primers, taking Tychicus along. They had hoped to reach Rangoon well before Robert and Betty had to leave, but because the plane was delayed in coming to Putao, they had only two or three days with them before they left for the U.S. LaVerne also had gone to Rangoon with Robert, and stayed on to continue to help. He and Tychicus did much of the proofreading, while Eugene assisted in the technical aspects of the printing. The printers were not equipped to set up the type for hymns, so Eugene typed twenty hymns, using the Lisu typewriter for the music (which is written in numbers and music symbols), and the English typewriter for the words. Tone marks had to be added by hand.

On July 22, 1951, Eugene and Helen welcomed their second son, Thomas Eugene Morse, who was born in Rangoon.

He did not get off to a very good start, as he was born with malaria. The doctor said that happened very, very rarely. Eugene and Helen were thankful to be in Rangoon, where it could be detected early (four days) and treatment started at once.

LaVerne returned from Rangoon on August 9, after he and Eugene had made arrangements for printing the Rawang primers. Rawang preacher Tychicus waited until the printing was completed, and on September 27, flew to Putao with the first 100 copies of the Rawang primer. Eugene and Helen and boys waited in Rangoon until all the finished books had been received and shipped to Putao. They also bought a Gestetner mimeograph machine to bring with them when they returned to Putao on October 11, 1951.

☦

Dorothy Sterling had gone to the village of Kobudeh after the Easter convention, and that left Esther and me alone at the Muladi mission home to carry on the work. Because the Lisu refugees who fled from the Salween Valley, had to leave their crops in the fields in China, and had not yet harvested any new crops in Putao, there was a famine among them in northern Burma. The Shan people of the area had enough food and were willing to sell some, but at a rather high price. Because the people had no money, the mission provided work for the refugee Lisu so they could earn enough money to buy a small amount of food. We also bought some extra rice for emergencies among other refugees who might come later.

There was much sickness, too. The children seemed specially susceptible to things like dysenteries, malaria and other tropical diseases, as well as childhood diseases such as whooping cough and measles. These "common" diseases were often complicated by "simple" colds which developed into pneumonia. We missed Russell's help so terribly. Dorothy had shown Esther how to give intravenous injections of quinine for malaria, and she was quite good at it. Helen, who was a graduate nurse, had been kept busy attending the sick before she went to Rangoon, and, of course, after her return also. The Lisu people were afraid to sleep even one night in the Putao plains area for fear of getting the virulent, often fatal cerebral malaria which was so prevalent. They would walk far into the night to get across the plain, and avoid sleeping in the lowland area — nicknamed "Death Valley" by both tribespeople and the Allied soldiers stationed there during World War II.

In the fall of 1951 we took the first steps in an anti-malaria campaign by clearing off weeds and overgrown jungle around the villages on the Putao plain. Somewhere Eugene had read an article about malaria control methods in other countries, including a description of how the homes were sprayed with insecticide, so while in Rangoon, he had bought Gammexane powder which we mixed into a solution and test-sprayed our own homes. In early 1952 as soon as the mosquito season began, we began using it to spray all the homes in the village. Word of the good results spread, and soon other villages were asking to have their homes sprayed also. As a result of this spray program, malaria was almost eradicated from that area in a few years. Later, the government carried on the spray campaign, using a different chemical.

☩

LaVerne had returned from Rangoon the middle of August and soon began visiting the many churches, preaching and teaching in the Upper Burma area. After Eugene and Helen arrived from Rangoon in October, we were all busy with evangelistic work, and helping the colonies of Lisu refugees settle into villages and get organized into strong churches.

Eugene, our "engineer" and builder, designed and supervised the building of a simple suspension bridge across the Mung Lang River (sometimes called the Nam Lang) which used bamboo poles for flooring. The Government helped by supplying the cables and the hanger wires.

As soon as people finished harvesting their crops, Eugene began work on irrigation canals for the rice fields in that vast, untouched plain just across the river. The main canal drew water from across the Mung Lang River. Soon people from other villages began begging Eugene to come and help them too. This he did while on evangelistic trips in their area.

✝

Robert, Betty and Joni returned from the States on November 8, 1951. By then, the Rawangs were begging for schools and books in their own language. Robert began immediately on translation of the New Testament into Rawang, amid constant interruptions. The people had no concept of the meaning of "privacy". When they heard he was working on a Rawang book, they wanted to see to satisfy their curiosity. But they wanted his advice on other things too. For instance, a few elders would arrive, saying, "Teacher, help us figure out how to get necessary goods by plane from Myitkyina (the state capital)" — or "Teacher, we need advice on how to carry on a shop" — or "Quick, teacher, lend me your gun — there's a tiger!" But Robert was always considerate and understanding, knowing that dealing with people is a very large part of missionary work.

There had been some delay on starting the translation because Tychicus, who had been on loan for one year from his work as pastor in one of the churches, had returned to active ministry. He was doing a very good job, teaching the newly printed Rawang Gospel Primer and Hymnal. While waiting for another assistant, Robert did some work on translation of the Book of Proverbs. Betty did some teaching, with Esther acting as interpreter. Helen and Esther ministered to the many that were sick, and Helen did a lot of typing of Lisu and Rawang teaching materials.

Around the end of the year, Robert acquired another Rawang assistant — Preacher Stephen, who had been evangelizing a new area far to the southeast of Putao. One afternoon he began feeling the symptoms of malaria, and by evening he was unconscious. Although we had no laboratory equipment,

experience told Robert that Stephen was suffering from cerebral malaria, which was almost always fatal unless treated immediately. Treatment was started at once, but on the second day,
complications set in. Stephen's convulsions and frothing at the
mouth were horrible to see, and people were too frightened to
come near for fear it was contagious. Esther did a brave job of
nursing him through that period, but just when he seemed to
be improving, he suddenly seemed to go insane, — shouting,
talking, and throwing himself about — and his family gave him
up for lost. But claiming victory in prayer, and persevering in
his treatment, we saw him restored to consciousness before the
week was out. Cerebral malaria patients usually take several
weeks to convalesce, but just ten days after he first got sick,
Stephen walked into Robert's office, ready to start on translation work. All recognized that though Satan wished to take
him from the work, the Lord preserved him in answer to
prayer. Later, Stephen, too, returned to his church and congregation. The Lord blessed Robert abundantly by sending still
another capable translation helper, Magaltaq Peter, who proved
ideally suited for the task.

28
Bible School in Wawudo

On December 1, 1951, Eugene and I, with several Lisu preachers, left on a six-week trip to Wa-wu-do (Wa-WOO-doe) in the Taron Valley, to hold a Bible School. On that long, long walk over the Himalayas in 1927 when the boys were small, it was there we had encountered natives who wore almost no clothing. Now, the little six-year-old boy of that trip was grown up, and going with me to help teach in a Christian school for those people! Some of the older Christians remembered seeing the white family with the two little boys carried in baskets. That had been the first time they had ever seen white women and children — possibly the first time they had seen white men, too.

On our first day of travel out from Muladi, we went through the tall grass of the Putao plain, through beautiful forest. I was on a pony which I could ride most of the way to Wa-wu-do, and Eugene walked. At the end of that first day we crossed the river by dugout boat and arrived at Nam-si-baum village, where there was a church. At that first stop we found quite a number of people ill with malaria, and quickly gave them medicine. They were much improved by Monday morning when we left. Saturday evening, and again on Sunday, we held regular services. An earnest elder there had been doing the preaching, and we found the people faithful in their worship, and eager for teaching.

On Monday we started the climb of the low divide between the Putao plain and the Taron Valley, and went through more beautiful forest containing many varieties of trees and other foliage. We noticed that the higher we went, the trees we saw were larger and larger, and near the top Eugene estimated it would take six men to reach around the base of some of them. Such large trees made it difficult for the people to clear the land for fields. Rats had eaten much of the small amount of food they had been able to raise, leaving them in rather straitened circumstances. That evening we reached Nam-tee, and stayed in the elder's home. He was quite ill with malaria, so we gave him medicine which helped him.

The next day we continued the climb through the beautiful forest for about three hours, and arrived at the top of the divide about noon. From there we could see the great landslides caused by the earthquakes in 1950. The trail down was too steep to ride the pony, so I walked with Eugene and the others. At the foot of the pass, we climbed over and around great boulders and trees brought down in the landslide, and arrived at a bamboo rest house about evening. At this guest house we noticed small packages of food tied up to the ceiling and upon inquiry we were told that travelers often left some food along the way to be used on their return journey. As there were no caretakers at those places, it would seem there were no thieves.

We had only six miles to go the next day, to get to Lo-meda (Nogmung), where a friendly Christian official lived. We were on level ground again, going mostly through bamboo, and what a relief! The monkeys barked excitedly and the birds sang — it was good to be alive and enjoy God's beautiful world. Upon arrival at the large wide river beside Lo-me-da, friends from the village came after us in small boats, even though the river was shallow enough to wade across.

☦

It was voting day, and about a thousand people had come from all the surrounding country. As our boat neared the other side the people lined up to shake hands with the white teachers.

It seemed that nearly all of the thousand were Christians. Some were from the Church of Christ, some were from the Baptist church of that village. We were led to the guest house, where we were scarcely settled when sick people began coming for medicine. In the evening the official, who was our very good friend, came for a long visit. We talked over various plans for helping the refugees from the earthquake areas, as well as those suffering from damaged fields due to the rat plague. That good man was really interested in the welfare of his people.

A number of Christians who had come to vote were glad to help carry our loads, and an elderly man took the responsibility of making all necessary arrangements. After attending the crowd of sick people the next morning, we bought some note books and pencils at the little store. When we left about noon, many school children and Christians escorted us out of the village and begged us to come back soon.

Our stage that day was a short one of about seven miles. A stage is one day's journey, or the distance between two rest houses. These rest houses, first built by the British and maintained by the Burma government, are found every seven to ten miles along the frequently traveled roads. Because the bamboo bridges commonly used everywhere rot quickly and need repairs often, the official had sent a group of people ahead to patch up several bridges. They also had to cut away some logs or trees that had fallen across the trail.

On the sixth day we started early because we knew it would be a long, hard, steep climb. Evidence of the recent earthquake was everywhere. There were large cracks in the ground along the ridges, and the landslides were immense. They broke away abruptly and slid down perhaps two thousand feet to the stream bed below. One of our companions said, "It looks like a picture of hell, except there is no fire at the bottom"! But in other directions, the view was grand, with a breath-taking view of snow-capped ranges stretching in every direction. Snow mountains towered up on the Tibetan side, snow-covered peaks loomed between us and China, and to the west, marking the Burma-India border, snow-crowned, jagged mountain peaks reached up into the sky like icy fingers.

After a steep descent of several hours we reached another church center beside a rushing stream, and met some Christians from one of the churches on the Tibetan border which was near the earthquake center. The continuing landslides were destroying their fields, food was a problem, and they needed to move.

On our last day of travel, even before reaching our destination, a large number of Christians came to escort us to the church at Wa-wu-do where we were to hold the school. Leaving the main trail, we wound up the rocky stream bed, climbed around and over immense boulders, tree trunks and rocks of all sizes, and waded back and forth across the river for about four hours. Finally we reached the village, and found that a great crowd of smiling, welcoming Christians had turned out to greet us. They led us to the nice bamboo house we would call "home" while there.

☦

There was a neat little bamboo church with rows of log benches on one side for the women and on the other side for the men. In front was a little table with a chair, all made by one of the young men with his crude, home-made tools. On one side was a blackboard, which was "painted" with a combination of raw egg white mixed with the black soot (accumulated from use over an open fire) scraped off their cooking utensils. This "paint" worked well, and was used in many of our schools.

Our school began on Monday with around 80 students, including about 15 elders. We had four groups — two by age, and two by language (Lisu and Daru). Two of our evangelists taught along with Eugene and me. The school lasted a month, with a three-day break in the middle. The Lord abundantly blessed, as the school was undisturbed even by sickness. Over and over again I thought of the change which had come to them since 1927. What hath God wrought! How we thanked Him for making them new creatures in Christ.

At the end of the school, we had the Christmas convention, with about 400 attending. We were amazed to learn there were that many people living in those seemingly empty jungles and mountains. Some of them traveled from nine to fourteen days to attend. Nine of the Daru and Lisu preachers helped in the convention. There were seven main preaching services besides several classes for those who were to be baptized. Then there was hymn singing between the services. Although the water in the river was icy cold, having come down from the snow mountains, sixty-nine people were baptized at two baptismal services. While people were gathered by the river for one of the baptismal services, a small deer ran past. Some of the men immediately gave chase, and caught it. It made a welcome addition to the convention meals. Also, three couples were married, including two of our Daru preacher boys. It was indeed a time of rejoicing. There had been three hundred new converts in that area in the past six months.

After the convention, we had the farewell worship service and handshaking. I gave out medicine for four hours while Eugene conferred with the elders and packed. It was about 1:30 in the afternoon before we finally were able to leave, amid many tears. The Daru and Rawang people had a custom of beating gongs when friends left. One of our evangelists who was delayed a bit told us afterward that the whole village was wailing and beating gongs after we left. We thanked the Lord for the time of sowing precious seed and trusted it would bring forth fruit for His glory. We arrived home from that long trip on January 15, 1952.

✟

While Eugene and I were away holding a school in the extreme northern area of the work, LaVerne had been very busy in the area to the east. At Tiliwago, besides being busy with mission work, LaVerne had supervised the building of a house of bamboo, grass, and poles similar to the government rest houses. This house was much more substantial than the usual Lisu or Rawang bamboo houses which are discarded after only two or three years. While overseeing that work, LaVerne made many trips between Tiliwago and Kobudeh, a day's journey away, where local Christians were putting up two houses for the church and school there. This was his first experience as a builder, but the houses turned out very well. Kobudeh was also the place where Dorothy Sterling had established a mission station.

Dorothy Sterling's dream was to start a full-time school, in addition to the regular Bible schools, for a selected few who would be willing to study several years. Later they could go to outside schools for specialized training which would enable them to teach and help their own people. She had ten students, for whom she had purchased ten sets of the Calvert School course, beginning with pre-kindergarten, and going through the fourth grade. School opened in Kobudeh on January 9, 1952.

In addition to supervising the building work at the two out-stations, LaVerne also spent much time in both places conferring with local church leaders. In a personal letter, Dorothy wrote: "LaVerne has a fine ability to get along with people and to speed up construction. I have sat with him through long, tedious conferences with church elders and community headmen and marvelled at his patience. He courteously hears out all the arguments, and then reviews the situation, and presents his solution in such a way that both sides are satisfied".

Before helping with those buildings, LaVerne taught in the Bible School at Wuning, a day's journey south of Tiliwago. One hundred and four (104) students studied for two months. They came from all parts of Northern Burma, even some from just south of the Tibetan border. Assisting LaVerne were two fine Rawang preachers. One was Tychicus, a natural leader, an earnest Christian and a powerful preacher, who was such a help to Robert in devising the Rawang alphabet. The other was Sergius, another outstanding Christian and excellent teacher and preacher.

Upon our return from Wa-wu-do, Eugene supervised construction of a bamboo house for Robert and Betty. Then Eugene, Helen, Esther and the two little boys went on a short trip to visit some of the congregations in the plains area, which were within two or three days' travel time from Muladi. As soon as they returned, we began preparations for the usual two-month Bible School which began March 3, 1952. At the close of the school we held the Easter convention.

I was in Muladi, alone except for Drema,
when the others went to Rangoon.

When LaVerne decided to go back to school in the U.S.,
I decided to go with him., and Rangoon was the first stop along the way.
We were delayed there about a month, and we wondered why.

In Hong Kong we began to understand our delay in Rangoon. God took us from Burma to Hong Kong at just the right time, then worked a miracle in bringing Russell from the prison in China to meet us there at just the right time.

29
God Still Works Miracles

After the Easter convention, LaVerne decided that he should return to the United States to finish college. I had not been sleeping well, and when I was awake, I couldn't stop thinking and wondering about Russell. There seemed to be absolutely nothing I could do to reach him. Mother Morse had received word from a "reliable" source that he was alive, though still in prison. We didn't know whether he was sick or well, being mistreated or not. I felt I could stand the suspense no longer, but just had to do SOMETHING! So I decided to go as far as Hong Kong with LaVerne, and try to find someone who might have news of Russell.

We left on May 12, 1952 and after a stop-over in Myitkyina to take care of some business there, we went on to Rangoon on the 15th. But in Rangoon we met with one frustrating delay after another, going from one government office to another and being told to "come back tomorrow", as we tried to get re-entry visas. If we left without these visas we would not be allowed to return to work in Burma. After spending a month in Rangoon, we finally got the visas and on June 15 were able to go on to Hong Kong.

In Hong Kong, we stayed at the only mission guest home still open. The others were all closed because most of the missionaries in China had already left for their own homelands. The administrator of the mission home suggested that we visit all of the Catholic convents in Hong Kong to find out if any priests or nuns had recently come out from Kunming and ask if they had heard anything at all about J. Russell Morse.

Howard Phillips, our missionary friend, graciously offered to take us around to the convents. We had plane reservations to leave June 21st, but in that city of about 3,000,000 people there were lots of places we wanted to go, and we had not quite covered them all. Therefore, LaVerne and I decided to delay.

✝

On June 20, While LaVerne went to the airline office to change our tickets, I went on back to our rooms. About an hour later, I heard a knock on the door. When I opened it, there stood Howard Phillips and MY DEAR HUSBAND!!! I could scarcely believe my eyes! Oh, how I praised God who so gloriously answered all of our prayers. My heart almost broke, when I saw how terribly thin Russell was. His clothing was ragged, and he had only white rag strings for his shoes. When LaVerne returned, there was more rejoicing! Surely the Lord's ways are past finding out! We had not heard from each other for fifteen months, and had come from two different countries, yet were both there in Hong Kong!. We understood then why we had been delayed so long in Rangoon: If we had come to Hong Kong earlier, we would have missed meeting Russell. Only our God could perform such a miracle.

We learned later that Russell's living-link congregation, Inglewood Christian Church, Inglewood, California, where Ted Hurlburt was minister, had held a twenty-four-hour-a-day, week-long prayer chain. That had ended the same day Russell was notified that he was to be taken to Hong Kong and released. He had traveled sixteen days by bus, boat, train, again by boat, and the last stretch by train. We learned that many other people had fasted and prayed for him also. After returning to the United States, he was introduced to a little seven-year-old girl, who thrilled his heart when she said, "I want to meet the man I prayed out of prison".

On Sunday, the day after Russell arrived, the parents of Howard Phillips invited us to dinner and we sang "We've crossed over Jordan to Canaan's fair land, and this is like heaven to me". They furnished him some clothes so we could go shopping for some new ones. The old ones went into the trash immediately!

30
Fifteen Months in a Communist Prison

The following is Russell's account, in his own words, of his imprisonment by the Chinese Communists.

"I wasn't afraid. For almost thirty years I had labored for the Lord in Southeastern Asia, and I felt that I knew the people there. But I didn't know Communism.

"Most of the workers of our mission had left for other fields where the future promised more certainty but Mrs. Morse and I continued to labor for Christ in Kunming. While we evangelized in the homes we also watched the creeping menace of totalitarian government threaten to overwhelm the peoples of that part of the world. When one province after another fell and it became evident that resistance in Yunnan Province was impossible, we felt Mrs. Morse should leave.

"The communists took over Yunnan Province just two days after she left on December 7, 1949. I was able to provide a refuge at our mission home on the outskirts of the city for many victims of the warfare. I had a good supply of medical materials and thus was able to minister to many poor people who could not get to the Kunming hospitals. Later, I helped in starting a little mission school as a refuge for wandering waifs from families that had been forced to live from hand to mouth. Many of the parents — hundreds of them — were even committing suicide, leaving their children to be cast out on their own.

"The Christians were treated fairly well for a time, and for several months the churches were not molested. But in November, 1950 the Chinese Communist armies entered the Korean war and were eventually defeated. That caused them to "lose face" and their suspicion and hatred of all Americans became pronounced. The persecution of Christians now began. Most of the few remaining missionaries applied for permission to leave. Some applications were granted. Others, including mine, were refused.

✝

"On March 22, 1951, I was standing on the porch of our mission home in Kunming when the place was suddenly surrounded by about sixteen men in plain clothes who announced themselves as having been sent by the communist government. They brought from under their garments American-made Thompson machine guns. Some drew pistols and others had bayonets fixed on the points of their rifles.

"'Come along. You've been accused!' they said. There was no use to argue. Even my request to be allowed to take along some clothing and bedding from my house was refused.

✝

"As I was being marched away, with those guns and bayonets pointing at me, my heart turned, in a feeling of human helplessness, to the Lord Who had never failed me; Who, despite my own weakness and often poor judgment, had been faithful to overrule whatever evils had threatened. I turned to Him and said. "Lord, enable me to be an overcomer."

"At once these words came to my mind — words from the fourth chapter of Paul's prison letter to the Philippian church, the members of which had been persecuted, and had seen some of their fellow Christians killed -

> *"Rejoice in the Lord always; and again I say, REJOICE . . Be careful for nothing, but in everything by prayer and supplication with thanksgiving let your requests be made known unto God. And the peace of God, which passeth all understanding, shall keep your hearts and minds through Christ Jesus."*

"During the months that followed, I was to need the assurance of those words. They were a haven of refuge to me. The trials of that fifteen month period which began with my arrest were not great because of the awful physical things they did to me, as much as because of the spiritual and mental torture that threatened to drive me mad — torture that made me wish I could die by some means less terrible than those being used every hour of the day and night, within hearing distance of my prison cell, to bring suffering and often death to hundreds and hundreds of the several thousands of my fellow prisoners. Later, after my release, I learned that I was by no means the only foreign missionary who had been imprisoned and tortured, and that many had become mentally unbalanced to such a degree that they will never again be normal.

✝

"That first night after my arrest, with my hands manacled behind my back, my guards took me to a great stone prison about which other guards with machine guns were marching. We passed through successive iron gates and eventually I was put into a room about ten by fourteen feet in size. It was devoid of furniture except a stool and a battered and much repaired cot. I was allowed to sleep on that cot for several months but after I had refused to confess to the amazing false, faked charges that they brought against me, it was taken away. My small amount of bedding was dumped onto the dusty floor and from then on I slept on some boards on the hard-beaten floor.

"About eight o'clock on that first night, guards came to my door and motioned for me to come out. After a hood with small slits to see through, was placed over my head, I was handcuffed and marched away between two soldiers. I was taken to a tribunal of four men and, as I stood before them, guards with drawn pistols and sub-machine guns stood on each side of me. There I was — the only Christian in that group, without a friend except the Friend in heaven above. I thought of the words of the poem, "The Charge of the Light Brigade," which I had learned as a small child:

"Cannon to the right of them, Cannon to the left of them,

Cannon in front of them, Volleyed and thundered.

Stormed at with shot and shell..."

"My accusers brought charges about my being one of the main minds in an American spy ring and also being an agent of the FBI. They tried to get me to tell them where I had received orders and what those orders were, how many parts of my mission had already been accomplished and what yet remained undone of the things I had been ordered to do. They also charged that I had a secret radio transmitter in my home, and that I went out every night after other people had gone to sleep, and released three savage dogs that I kept on my place to keep people away while I sent out radio messages to the American government. The truth is, I do not even know how to operate a radio transmitter.

"They said I had been accused by various ones, and that there would be no use for me to deny the charges. All they wanted, they maintained, was for me to make a clean breast of the matter and then join them in their activities. They would help me by giving me instructions, and then I could work with them as a communist. But first, I should go to school and become a good communist.

"Finally, after long hours of grilling for information, during which I was at my wit's end, one of the men said, "Give me a rope! He's just a big bully. We'll give him a taste of what it's like!" They took my hands and twisted them behind my back until I thought that my arms might be wrenched out of their sockets. The pain and the nervous shock were such that the perspiration poured out of my body. While refusing to make a false confession, I tried, throughout four long hours, to explain what my work actually was and what I had been doing. They didn't want explanations. They simply wanted to force me to confess to the charges they made so they could use my confession for their purposes of propaganda. Then I was told, 'You may go back to your cell and think it over. We'll give you a chance; but tomorrow night you come prepared to talk.'

☩

"When the next night came, some benches, boards, and ropes were brought in and they said, "Now, if you don't talk, we're going to crack your head." The 'nutcracker', as it was called, was fatal. I was saying a prayer in my heart when I first heard that. Then I began to talk. I've forgotten what I said to those men, but finally one of them motioned to the others and they went into a near-by room. I heard them talking in high, angry voices but all I could understand was: "Well, if we kill him, then he is of no more use to us. If we keep him here in this prison, ultimately he may tell us some things that will be of some use."

"They came back and said, 'We'll give you a chance to write the history of your mission and of your work of the thirty years you have spent in China — all of your connections at any time. If this is satisfactory, your life will be spared.'

"Well, I welcomed that, because it had been put into my heart during that second day after my arrest that I should seek to endure, and if I could endure long enough, the Lord would raise up forces for my defense — that my friends on the outside would hear of my imprisonment and pray that I might be released.

"Months passed. I wrote and wrote. Five hundred pages. The only history of our missionary work in West China, Tibet and Burma that had ever been written. After it was presented and discussed among themselves, I was called again before the tribunal and asked, "Why did you write all of this stuff? It's no use to us at all! You haven't told us a thing about the American spy system, the FBI, and what they're trying to do here in China."

"I told them again, as I'd told them before, that neither the United States government nor the FBI ever had approached me with a request to do anything against the Chinese government, any people, or any party in China. I was taken back to my cell.

During the days that followed I paced up and down wondering whether my dear old mother would still be alive for a last reunion should I later be released, wondering whether I'd ever see my wife and children again, and battling against the fiery darts of the evil one in remorse and self-pity and frustration.

"The verses from God's Word that I had learned as a child were my resource again and again. I had asked for my Bible. It was refused. But in that difficult time I remembered many of the promises, and one of those was, "If any of you lack wisdom, let him ask of God, that giveth to all men liberally, and upbraideth not."

☩

"The thought came to me that I should show my captors my open-mindedness. 'Now, if communism is right,' I told them, 'if it is for the benefit of humanity, I'm not opposed to it. I want to study your teachings, your practices. I'm willing to accept communistic principles if I become convinced that they are right.'

"For months I appealed for some literature about communism that would show me the truths and benefits of it. Again and again I was refused or put off with some excuse. But, finally, after about eight months, one of the "higher-ups", I suppose he was, brought to me twenty copies of communist periodicals in English. Among these were the Daily People's World, published in Los Angeles, California, and the National Guardian, published in New York City, which told what the Chinese communists were doing here and how they were working against conditions displeasing to themselves.

"In those papers I read stories of accused communists in the United States arrested because of subversive activities, and of their appearing before courts and talking of their constitutional liberties, their civil liberties and their privileges under the Bill of Rights. They asked to be freed, even after they had been accused and arrested — asked to be freed on bail and released from prison. And I knew that they were allowed, before being convicted, to have free and open trials, with full legal facilities, and allowed to come face to face with their accusers.

"I said to myself, 'Surely the Chinese communists must have some system of justice.' And I sat down and wrote a petition, explaining in it that communists in America were receiving justice through the privilege of fair trial. 'You also must believe in justice. I want a representative, a fair trial, with legal facilities such as have been given to the accused communists in the United States. If I can have a fair trial, I'll not be afraid of anything. Let me come face to face with these people you say have accused me, and let me give my position and answer them personally. Give me several lawyers to help me on my case. I'm not experienced in communist law.'

"The only answer I got to that was a sullen rebuke by one of the judges. Several other times when I referred to my position, I got only a cold shoulder. And I learned what the iron curtain is. It's really iron — a curtain let down between truth and freedom, trying to divorce them. And I learned that the communists' dictionary is entirely different from ours. I heard double talk and triple talk until I couldn't believe anything that the communists said.

✝

"For the last eight or nine months of my fifteen months in that prison, the only way I was able to cut my hair was with about one sixth of a safety razor blade which one of the guards — perhaps at the risk of his life — had secretly slipped to me. I'd pushed it into a piece of broom corn which I'd broken off a whisk broom used to sweep my cell. Using my hands and that little fragment of blade, I cut my hair.

"One day a guard who was trying to eliminate the little bit of light that had been coming into my cell, put the top of a fifty gallon gasoline drum outside the window. I noticed that on the side of it were two metal flanges, and that the whole thing was quite rusty. When the guard went down the corridor, I reached out my hand, twisted one of those flanges, broke it off, and kept it until I could sharpen it on the stones in the cell. This was the razor I used in pulling out my whiskers, usually one by one, but sometimes five, six or seven at a time. In that way, for about eight months toward the end of my imprisonment, I kept down my beard. Somehow the communists never seemed to wonder why my beard was not long. Perhaps it was because the guards changed every two hours and possibly the new ones didn't notice such things.

"The torture continued. Of some of the things I underwent I dare not tell, even to my own family. Then there were experiences so fantastic that if I should tell them in public, I doubt that what I should say would be believed. One day after about six hours of torture and questioning, when I went back to my little room. I realized there was no one to help me — except God. I sang the song that I was to sing hundreds of times in that place, "Jesus, Lover of My Soul", the words of which became my daily prayer while in that prison:

> *"Other refuge have I none; Hangs my helpless soul on Thee;*
> *Leave, O leave me not alone, Still support and comfort me.*
> *All my trust on Thee is stayed, All my help from Thee I bring.*
> *Cover my defenseless head With the shadow of Thy Wing."*

"Once when I had finished a song, I thought I was hearing an echo. I finally realized it was another prisoner two cells away. We developed a system of one person singing a verse of a hymn and the other responding with the next, when we knew the guards were at the other end of the prison.

"My singing partner had watched me being led past his window several times and was sure I was either American or English. One guard was more sympathetic than the others and was persuaded to bring me a note. My prison mate proved to be a Methodist missionary from England named Vernon Stone. We exchanged a few more notes, giving each other addresses of relatives to be notified by whomever was released first. He was released a few months later and notified my mother that I was alive and in prison. I had no idea where the rest of my family was at that time.

✝

"Vividly I recall many times during the fifteen months of imprisonment when great chains were fastened to my feet — chains weighing fifty pounds or more. Sometimes I was handcuffed, often with my hands behind my back, and left to spend the night thus shackled. Only after begging was I released so I could attend to those things that normally required the use of my hands. All these things and much more they did.

"I remember that in my frustration I turned even to the simplest of things in order to divert my mind from the unpleasant situation. I thought about the sparrows, for every time I saw them outside the words of Jesus came to me: "Fear not. Ye are of more value than many sparrows." And I'd answer, 'Lord, I'm so weak! My faith is so small! Increase my faith! Enable me to trust in your promises, Lord.'

"I recall studying the insect life in my cell. I killed hundreds of bedbugs. Then I noticed that there were five different kinds of spiders that came in and out of my quarters. Some were so small I didn't pay much attention to them until one day one of them attacked a bedbug, sucked the life out of it, and finally left its shell there upon the wall. Then I thought, "HERE IS MY FRIEND — KILLING INSECTS THAT TORMENT ME."

"Another day I noticed a very large spider, about as big as a silver dollar. He must have been the granddaddy of them all. At first, I resented him because he looked so fierce and reminded me of the communists. I took a piece of paper and struck him, knocking him to the ground below, where he doubled up and was still. Why, if he had been a man, that fall would have been equal to a fall from the top of a twenty-story building. I thought, "That poor spider! he wasn't menacing my life, he just came to kill other insects." Then I regretted my act, and resumed my pacing up and down in the cell. After a while I noticed that the spider put out its legs and started walking around and finally wobbled over to the wall and climbed it. I prayed, "Lord since that spider could survive the blow I gave it, give me faith and I'll survive the fall I've had in this prison."

"Another time a big rat came barging into my room with two guards after him yelling, "Kill that rat!" They shut the door, and around and around they went. My first inclination was to help them. The next moment I was on the sidelines secretly rooting for the rat. I found myself praying, "Lord, don't let them kill him — I'm just as helpless as he is!" The rat did lose his tail, but when a third guard opened the door to see what was going on, the rat made his escape. I saw him foraging around for several months.

✝

"There were periods when, day after day, I prepared to die. That was after I had heard that my whole family had been accused of being spies. The reason given for the accusation was that during the second world war our family had stayed on the mission field on the border of Tibet and Burma — an area of no strategic importance at all!

"It was true that we had stayed there. Also it was true that years before the second world war we and other missionaries had been working there on that border of Tibet and Burma. About 7,000 natives had been won to Christ in a region stretching about one month's journey from east to west and about twenty-five days' journey from north to south. Here our missionaries had been working some 1900 years after Jesus Christ had given His commission to go and make disciples of all nations — working in a place where the gospel never before had been preached.

"We did participate in a Search and Rescue work. The rescues were made by the Christians living on those Himalaya Mountain slopes and in the valleys. The planes did sometimes drop supplies by parachute. The communists accused me of being an American spy because, they said, "Unless you are a 'big shot', airplanes just don't drop supplies to you like that." I just did not know how to convince them of the truth.

"Back in my prison, I prepared to die and I followed a procedure that I feel sure was followed by thousands in the early New Testament Church. I remember they had been admonished to forsake not the assembling of themselves. Also, in regard to the Lord's Supper, they had been told, "This do....in remembrance of Me", as they partook of the emblems of the Lord's broken body and shed blood. As they themselves faced death, they partook of them, remembering that He had been scourged by Roman soldiers; a crown of thorns had been pressed down upon His head; He had been forced to carry the cross upon which He soon was to be nailed to die there. And Jesus had said, "A servant is not greater than his lord." He had said also not to fear men who are able to kill the body, but who, after that, are able to do no more.

"Daily, for months, I partook of those emblems, using steamed bread and water, which I had saved from my meals. And each day I prepared myself for that death which I thought might come at any hour. I knew, too, that unthinkable tortures might precede my death. Those in charge of the prison were constantly, day and night, doing terrible things to others. For example, in many cases before killing their victims, they poured scalding water on them and scraped the hair from their heads as a butcher scrapes bristles from a pig.

"I don't know what happened to my thinking one time when I attempted to escape, and actually did get out of my room. But the communists never knew that I not only left, but got down to the prison wall — to the place where I thought I could get through. I thought, at that time, I'd rather be shot trying to escape than to die by the terrible means which they used in killing hundreds of other people. But down there by the prison wall I felt rebuked for my lack of faith in God. I crept back into my room before I was found out. During that period of my imprisonment, a great mental struggle threatened to overwhelm me all the time.

"On June 2, 1952, two guards came to my cell, told me to get my things together and to come with them. They again took me to the military tribunal and gave me the money that had been taken upon my arrival at the prison, and also gave me several pieces of clothing that they had taken from my home. The two armed guards took me to the railway station, where they bought tickets, using my money. Then they went with me about a hundred miles by train. How thrilled I was to see the green grass and the trees, and other growing things!

"At the end of the journey by train, we took a bus to Chungking, and after a few days, a river boat to Hankow. On the way I asked the guards to buy for me a few little necessities, which they did, but I was scolded if I bought any "extra" food — perhaps because they looked forward to possessing whatever of my money was left at the end of the trip. On the boat to Hankow some Chinese started to talk to me, but the guards scolded them sharply, and after that none of them dared to speak to me.

"The trip by boat ended, we took a train for the last lap of the journey in communist country. On the way I saw an American — the only one I had seen on the whole sixteen-day trip. "Are you an American?" the man, a missionary, whispered. The guards saw him speaking to me and scolded him. To me they said, "If you want to keep your head on your shoulders, keep your mouth shut! If you communicate with anyone, or allow anyone to communicate with you, we shall not be responsible for what happens to you."

"At last, on June 20th, we reached the "bamboo curtain" border, which is a little over an hour's journey from Hong Kong. Here the guards and Chinese customs officers examined my belongings and took about one hundred of my United States dollars, leaving me with $1.70 with which to get to Hong Kong. Then I crossed "No Man's Land", which is about 150 yards wide. What a relief as I passed beyond the barbed wire fences!

"'You don't need to be afraid any more', the British immigration officer told me, and gave me a drink of cold pop. A French priest gave me four egg sandwiches and another bottle of cold soft drink.

"When I got to Hong Kong I had barely enough money for one night in a hotel room. There I took a bath and changed my ragged, dirty clothes for some equally ragged but comparatively clean ones that I had washed with my own hands in just a little bit of water that had been difficult to obtain. Then I went downstairs and asked the manager to please call Howard Phillips at the Ebenezer School for the Blind. Mrs. Phillips answered the phone, and when I said 'This is J. Russell Morse', she became quite excited and called to him, 'Howard, come quick, this is Russell Morse.'

"Soon Howard was at the telephone saying, 'Brother Morse, I can't express the joy we have to learn that you're alive. We've been praying for you.'

"I said, 'Howard, where's my family? The communists have tried to make me believe they've all been captured and maybe some of them killed.'

"He said, 'Why, man, none of them is in prison, and just six days ago your wife and LaVerne arrived here in Hong Kong. They've been inquiring every place for you. Where are you?' I told him, and then he said, 'Just stay where you are. Within an hour I'll be over there, and I'll take you to them.'

"On our way to the place where my wife was staying, Howard said to me, 'Your wife thinks you still may be in Kunming, and seeing you suddenly might be quite a shock to her. I'd better go in first.' When we arrived, Howard climbed the stairs and I, with my rubbery legs, weakened during fifteen months of inaction and sickness, climbed slowly after him. I heard him knock and tell Mrs. Morse who he was. I heard my wife say, 'Just a minute.' By then I had reached the top of the stairs, and when she opened the door — there stood Russell!"

"*Peter therefore was kept in prison: but prayer was made without ceasing of the church unto God for him.*

"*And when he had considered the thing, he came to the house of Mary, the mother of John, whose surname was Mark; where many were gathered together praying. And as Peter knocked at the door of the gate, a damsel came to hearken, namely Rhoda. And when she knew Peter's voice, she opened not the gate for gladness, but ran in, and told how Peter stood before the gate. And they said unto her, Thou art mad. But she constantly affirmed that it was even so. Then said they, It is his angel.*

"*But Peter continued knocking: and when they had opened the door, and saw him, they were astonished. But he, beckoning unto them with the hand to hold their peace, declared unto them how the Lord had brought him out of the prison.*" *(Acts 12:5,12-17a)*

31
Recovery, Return, and Reunion

After buying some new clothes for Russell and allowing him to recuperate some, we flew to the United States, by way of Japan and Alaska, and arrived in Seattle July 3, 1952. While there, we visited briefly with Russell's sister, Louise, then went on to Los Angeles. Ruth Margaret had gone to California soon after the end of her school term in Terre Haute, Indiana, so she was there to meet our plane. What a joyful reunion! We had not seen her for three long years.

We visited Russell's living link church and the minister, Bro. Ted Hurlburt, at Inglewood. As always, we enjoyed the hospitality of our very close and dear friends, Mr. and Mrs. Ray Partridge, members of the Christian Church of Inglewood. Their home was a "home away from home" for any members of our family passing through Los Angeles.

Russell's ninety-two-year-old mother, Mrs. Ruth Morse, flew to California to welcome her son for whom she had so earnestly prayed during the many months of his "silence." She had not known whether she would see him again in this life, but she had never wavered in her faith. She was with him during his surgery for a hernia, — a condition probably caused by his mistreatment while in prison.

LaVerne went to Cincinnati, soon after our arrival in the States, to enroll in the Cincinnati Bible Seminary, where he was a junior. On the way to Ohio he filled several speaking engagements at the School of Missions at Lake James and Cedar Lake, Indiana, as well as other camps and a number of churches.

After Mother Morse returned home, Russell and I were offered the use of a home on Big Bear Lake in the mountains of California, which we gladly accepted. What a beautiful place to further rest and recuperate. When we felt strong enough, we went to Oklahoma to visit relatives. I went first to Oklahoma City to spend some time with my only sister, whom I had not seen since 1948, then joined Russell in Tulsa.

✝

In September, Russell, his mother and I attended the National Missionary Convention at Dodge City, Kansas, where he delivered the opening address to a capacity audience and told of the trials of his imprisonment. Mother Morse also gave a talk, her last one before such an audience. At the close of the convention in Dodge City, I went to Springfield, Illinois to visit my living link church, Westside Church of Christ, and spoke to a number of groups there before joining Russell in Cincinnati. Russell and his mother returned to Tulsa, where he addressed the Midwest Christian Convention before going to Cincinnati to preach the opening sermon of the Conference on Evangelism at the Taft auditorium.

Ruth Margaret had also decided to attend Cincinnati Bible Seminary, so Russell and I decided to make Cincinnati our headquarters. I wanted to be near our children as long as we remained in the United States. Ruth had already made arrangements to live in a dormitory, and LaVerne had rented rooms in the home of Professor Rupert Foster of the Seminary. We found a small apartment next door to the Foster's home. Russell spent the greater part of his time away on speaking engagements, but I wanted to be with my children as much as possible, as I felt I had been away from them for far too long. I sometimes "sat in" at Professor Foster's class as an observer.

During the summer, while visiting his living-link church, First Christian Church at Joliet, Illinois, and attending the Missions Week program at Cedar Lake, Indiana, LaVerne had met Miss Lois Elliott, who was working in the office of Lake

Region Christian Assembly at Cedar Lake. Lois's parents, Professor and Mrs. George Mark Elliott, were well-known for their outstanding work with the Cincinnati Bible Seminary. Following that eventful meeting, their acquaintance and friendship grew and deepened throughout the fall and winter at the Seminary. On March 27, 1953, they were married at the Cincinnati Bible Seminary chapel.

An interesting sidelight to this marriage was that Lois's grandfather, G.W. Elliott, had been an evangelist in South Dakota many years before, when LaVerne's grandparents also lived there. It was G. W. Elliott who baptized Russell's father, Frank E. Morse. G.W. Elliott was also the minister that Russell's mother asked to pray for her, that she would have a son who would become not only a preacher of the Gospel, but a missionary, and win many souls to Christ. Who could have known that some 55 years later G. W. Elliott's grand-daughter would marry the son of the child-to-be for whom he prayed.

After a furlough of ten months during which we had time to recuperate and visit Christian friends throughout the United States, we left Inglewood, California, on May 1, 1953 , headed for the mission field. It was an especially hard parting for Russell and his mother. She called the night before we left to tell him good-bye. As he paced the floor in the kitchen of the Partridge home, he said, "My mother said she didn't expect to see me again, but she didn't say I should stay." That seemed to comfort him. Just twenty days later, on May 20, Mrs. Ruth Morse died, following an illness of influenza.

Following an overnight flight out over the ocean, we arrived in Honolulu where we were met by Glen and Ruth Powell, missionaries in Hawaii. From Honolulu, we soared across the blue Pacific, and reached the tiny coral island of Wake in time for breakfast. After a short stop in Tokyo, we flew on southward toward Hong Kong, but the fog there was so dense that after circling for two and a half hours, we had to detour across the South China Sea to Manila. The next day was bright and clear, so we were able to fly back to Hong Kong. After a few hours, we continued on to Bangkok, Thailand, where so many missionaries were doing such valiant work.

I had a valid permit to enter Burma, but Russell's papers had all been taken away from him when he was arrested, and were not returned when he was released. I proceeded on to Rangoon alone to make arrangements with the government for an entry visa and a new copy of his stay permit. I reached Rangoon on May 8, and for over a month I went daily from one office to another, being referred from department to department. Each day it seemed that surely the next day would bring the desired approval, but each day I was told, "Come back tomorrow".

In the scorching tropical heat, my faith and determination alone sustained me. Then a recurrence of malaria made me very ill, and I felt so alone in that big city. In spite of that, I continued day after day to make the rounds of the Immigration Office, the Kachin State Ministry, then back again to the Immigration Office and on and on. Finally, on June 15th, the visa was granted, and Russell arrived in Rangoon June 23rd. We really wanted to get to Putao before the monsoon rains so that Eugene, Helen and family could go home for a furlough. It took yet another week in Rangoon to obtain a copy of Russell's permanent residence permit.

We flew from Rangoon to Myitkyina without incident, but when I stepped onto the plane which would take us from Myitkyina to Putao, I had the strongest feeling — like God was there and would take us through. We had clouds all the way and could not see the mountains. The planes being used in Burma at that time were DC 3's left over from World War II and were not equipped with radar. We just prayed that God would guide the Chinese pilot of the plane! He could not see the landing field because of the clouds, but after about an hour and forty-five minutes, a hole seemed to open in the clouds and we landed safely. Praise God, He saw us through! We learned later that when our plane was overdue, Eugene had asked the crowd of 400-500 Lisu friends who were waiting to greet us, to pray for our safe arrival.

Although Eugene had rigged up two hwagans for Russell and me, at first we walked along with the others. When we arrived at the river, where the flood had previously destroyed the bridge, we found that Eugene and the Christians had built a new temporary one. The floor was made by tying together several lengths of bamboo poles laid side by side— only two poles wide — and these were suspended from two steel cables from the old bridge. The river was about 300 feet wide, in flood, and really rushing below us. The bridge was slippery, and the footing precarious but, inching our way along, we finally made it across.

✞

Drema Esther came to meet us just before we reached the bridge, and waiting for us on the other side were Helen, David, Tommy, and a long line of Christians. When we reached home, we had a chance to meet one of the two new grandsons with whom we had been blessed. Eugene and Helen's third son, Ronald Keith Morse was born at home in Muladi on November 9, 1952, with Dororhy Sterling in attendance. Stephen Anthony, second son of Robert and Betty Morse, was born in Rangoon, at the Seventh Day Adventist Hospital, on November 19, 1952. So there were five grandsons for him to meet — and four of them he had never even seen!

The next day was a holiday, with a thanksgiving service at the church in Muladi. Many people came to welcome us back. Russell and I spoke to about five hundred then, and again on Sunday we spoke to a large crowd. Bible School started on Wednesday, with over a hundred students. Eugene, Helen and I taught, with Esther translating for Helen.

Russell immediately became involved with ministering to the sick, day and night. The daily clinic was always full, with as many as a hundred patients a day treated by Russell with Drema Esther's help. Patients had no other means of getting medical treatment for the very serious diseases prevalent in the area. In this sub-tropical climate where the annual rainfall often exceeds 200 inches per year, malaria, tuberculosis, and dysentery were the most common threat to the missionaries and also the national Christians in more than 150 congregations.

☦

On January 4, 1953 Robert and Betty had left Muladi to go to Kobudeh, to hold a Bible School with Dorothy Sterling. They traveled ten days over roads which in many places had been destroyed by landslides. Just after their arrival there was a big snow storm, and the temperature dropped to freezing. It was impossible to keep a bamboo house warm in that kind of weather! Everyone had to wear sweaters and jackets even inside the house, and spend a lot of time huddled around the open fire in the center of the house.

The two-month Bible School began the first week in February, with 117 students, later increasing to 125, with almost equal numbers of Lisu and Rawang students. Robert taught in Lisu, with Rawang preacher Peter translating into Rawang. That was easier than for Robert to try to teach in both languages, speaking a few sentences in Lisu, then repeating in Rawang. Students not making passing grades were sent home after the first month.

Early in February, Dorothy added another member to her family. A non-Christian Lisu man brought his little 2½-week-old baby girl to Dorothy. The baby was suffering from malnutrition and was just skin and bones, because the mother had died, and the father had been keeping the baby alive mostly on native rice wine. Dorothy agreed to adopt the baby, and she became known as Judith Kobudeh Sterling.

☦

After the school at Kobudeh ended, Robert and Betty went to Tiliwago, where there was such a desperate need for workers. Our former co-workers — Isabel Dittemore, Jane Kinnett, David and Lois Rees, and Mel Byers — had been unable to obtain permits to return to Burma, and no new misisonaries were allowed to enter.

One evening while Robert was passing through a Rawang village, he was stopped by the headman who asked him to come in for a chat. Over a cup of bitter tea, he then proceeded to render Robert speechless as he said, "Teacher, I've just returned from a conference of all the leading Rawangs — headmen and church elders. This is what we decided: Although we have learned to know Christ somewhat from the efforts of missionaries to the Kachins and to the Lisu, no one teaches us in Rawang. We have to study the Bible in either Lisu or Kachin, and many of us don't know these languages. Yet, we are one of the main tribes in this part of North Burma. We have resolved to be recognized as a separate group, the Rawang Christian Churches, and we want a separate missionary all to ourselves.

"Teacher, since you are the only one who has learned our language, and you have already given us Rawang books, WE PETITION YOU to leave your missionary work among the Lisu and come and devote all your time to us Rawangs. We need our own Bible Schools, our own Christian literature, our own preacher training schools, in order to really reach our people."

Robert could hardly believe what he was hearing! What a change from the attitude shown a few short years before, when half-wild, hostile, suspicious Rawangs wanted nothing to do with the Christians, much less a missionary. Robert could make no commitment, but he promised to think and pray about the request.

☦

It is impossible to tell of all the difficulties which faced many of the people who wanted to become Christians, or the problems and actual physical dangers confronted by the preachers going into unevangelized areas. One of those new Christians was Zau Ma Aung, a Shan village headman, who became a Christian and was persecuted for his faith by the Buddhist priests.

While on a preaching trip in early 1953, Eugene had stopped overnight at a Lisu village only half a mile from a Shan village. He stayed in the home of the preacher, Levi. While he was giving out medicine the next morning, the headman from the Shan village brought his four-year-old son for treatment. Not having the necessary medicine with him, Eugene sent them to Muladi for treatment, where it was necessary for them to stay for several days. Preacher Levi accompanied him, and during that time talked with him about the New Testament, using four languages alternately: Shan, Kachin, Burmese, and Lisu. By the end of a week, Zau Ma Aung believed in the Lord and wanted to be a Christian and have a Bible name, even though he knew he would be facing much hardship and persecution from his own people for turning away from Buddhism. Levi had not minimized the fact that we must often suffer for our faith in God and His Son. This "babe in Christ" took the name of Paul, for like the apostle of old, he had persecuted and ridiculed the Christians, and he knew he now would be facing the same treatment. And like the apostle, he was eager to go and tell his people of his Saviour, of the God who hears and answers prayers, who is always with His children, the God who is a Father. He said, "I cannot but tell them so they too can know Him". A special delegation of Buddhist priests was sent to Paul's village on a special campaign of teaching Buddhist doctrines. When he heard they were coming, he hurried to Muladi, asking to be baptized.

As he was about to be baptized, he stood in the center of a group of people gathered at the river's edge. He spoke to them, with young Preacher Levi translating, "In the Bible it says that for Jesus we must leave our home and family. Today I am doing that. From now on, you are my brothers and sisters and, with you, I will feel at home. I am a new Christian. There are many things I do not know. But what I do know, I want to tell my people. Please pray for me."

While the group sang "Whiter Than Snow," Shan Paul and two Lisu preachers, Titus and Ashur, waded out into the river, and Paul was baptized. As he came up out of the water, the group on the bank sang "Oh Happy Day". Immediately following this baptism, the regular church service was held, and Shan Paul, for the first time, shared in the observance of the Lord's Supper.

Shan Paul's conversion was an answer to three years of praying by the Christians in the Putao area, praying for an opening to give the Gospel to the three thousand Shans who were Buddhists and who had firmly resisted all past attempts to present the Gospel message to them. While they had not been openly hostile to the Christians, the Shans oppressed and persecuted them politically, in matters of taxes, obtaining land grants, etc. When Shan Paul returned home he took with him a phonograph and several Gospel records, in order to witness to his people. Many were interested, but the priests increased their persecution, threatening to tie him up and beat him. An effort was made to separate him from his wife and children, but Paul remained constant in his testimony.

We had brought several thousand records back with us in 1948, with several small portable phonographs. These had often been the key that opened doors in previously closed areas. People were curious about the "talking box", and that curiosity led to their listening to the Gospel records and later letting the preachers and evangelists speak. Paul was able to record some for use on one of these records in his own language.

✟

It was in March, 1953 that Eugene and the headman found a good location for a suspension bridge. Such a bridge was needed now that a new village was being planned for the north side of the river, so that people could easily go from one side to the other. An official came up from Myitkyina to inspect the

316

site, and as a result the government donated the cables and hangar wires for the bridge. Not only that, but it was decided to make not just a foot bridge, but one big enough that oxcarts could go across. During the discussions of the bridge enlargement, it was pointed out that a motor road from the airfield, about 7 miles to the north of our village, to join up with the Myikyina road, about 10 miles to the south, could easily be built. The government agreed to give the contract for the road building to our village, but expressed concern that it would not be possible to finish it before the rainy season. Eugene reassured the official, and offered to supervise the project, without pay, in order to make sure that it was finished on time. When the entire 17 miles of road, as well as the bridge, were all finished AHEAD of schedule, well before the rainy season, the officials were very much surprised .

☦

In August, 1953 Robert and Betty returned to Muladi. That was another joyful reunion! Robert had not seen his father since early in 1949. Early in November, 1953 Robert and I went to Tiliwago to hold a three-month Bible School. Because of famine conditions in the area it had to be shortened to two and a half months. Betty had been unable to accompany Robert and me to Tiliwago because she was expecting their third child in February. Also, she needed to go to Rangoon a bit early because Jonathan needed dental work. After the school, Robert joined her there, and on February 23, 1954, their third son, Robert Howe Morse, Jr. was born. This little boy later became known as Bobby, a nickname to distinguish him from his father, who was always called Robert.

In December, 1953, Eugene, Helen, their three sons and Esther went to the Christmas convention at the village of Namhte-hku, which was nestled beside a river in a beautiful, peaceful valley. In many respects that convention was like any other, but the different part was the presentation for the first time in Lisuland of a Christmas play, telling the Christmas story. All parts were acted out by school children, except those of Joseph, Mary, and King Herod, and these were played by some young adults. Esther worked very hard on the play, first translating it from Chinese to Lisu, adapting it when necessary to fit Lisu settings, and then coaching the players. The results were worth the effort. In that audience there were nine hundred and twenty of the quietest and most attentive Lisu we had ever seen. The play lasted an hour and a half, but small fires here and there kept the people from suffering too much from the cold.

During the monsoon rainy season in both 1952 and 1953 we had experienced severe flooding at our mission base in Muladi Village. Eugene began laying out another model village on the higher ground across the river, with three main streets and ten cross streets, and we began preparations for moving. Two roomy mission residences with bamboo floors and walls and grass-thatched roofs were completed, and all of us got moved to the new location before Eugene and his family left in June, 1954 on their overdue and well-deserved furlough. A small temporary chapel, and a clinic for treating the sick were also built, using the same type of construction. Applications for homesites (four lots to each block) from Christians from the famine-plagued mountain regions came in faster than the land could be cleared.

LaVerne married Lois Carol
Elliott in Cincinnati, OH
in March, 1953.

Russell bid farewell to his 92-year old mother in early May, 1953,
not knowing that she would be called Home only three weeks later.

A big crowd had gathered to welcome us at the Putao airfield.

There were five grandsons for Russell to meet,
four of whom he had never even seen.
(L-R: Jonathan Russell and Stephen Anthony sons of Robert & Betty);
Ronald Keith, Thomas Eugene, and David Lowell (sons of Eugene & Helen).

The bridge was 420 feet long, and 40 feet above the river. It was a dangerous undertaking, but by God's grace not a single person was injured during construction.

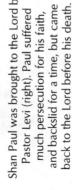

Shan Paul was brought to the Lord by Pastor Levi (right). Paul suffered much persecution for his faith, and backslid for a time, but came back to the Lord before his death.

Robert completed translation of the Gospel of Mark, Eugene typed it all on stencils, it was mimeographed, and made into booklets. This was the first part of the Bible ever to be translated into the Rawang language. (1st 1962 NL)

People came from long distances to the medicine house for treatment from Russell.

Eugene supervised the building of our house, and we moved in, in February, 1954.

32
Tractors, Refugees, and Broken Bones

As one looked out over the grassy Putao plain, an area approximately 20 miles long and twelve miles wide, the grass looked velvety-soft and lovely — from a distance. In reality it was the tough, wiry elephant grass which grows ten to twelve feet tall. The tangled mat formed by the tough roots extends several inches below the surface of the ground. The tribal people living in the area owned only crude and ineffective home-made ploughs which could not cut through these tough roots, and thus this fertile plain could not be cultivated. Instead, people resorted to hacking out small fields on the steep mountain-sides, clearing out the trees and bamboo clumps. We realized that with such a concentration of refugees around the Muladi area there would soon be a serious shortage of nearby areas for fields, as well as bamboo and other building materials for houses.

When Eugene and Helen were in Rangoon in December, 1952 they met an American, Mr. Don Carter, who was the Technical Advisor to the Kachin State Agriculture Department. He was stationed in the Kachin State capital, Myitkyina, and was very interested in the prospect of opening up new lands for cultivation in the Putao-Muladi area. In late 1953 when Eugene went to Myitkyina to buy supplies he met Mr. Carter again. Don visited Muladi in April, 1954, and after testing soil samples he was very optimistic and enthusiastic over the prospects for agricultural development and crop improvement.

✝

In 1953, while visiting the church in Newberg, Oregon, Russell had met Mr. C. F. George, who generously offered to supply funds for some mechanized farm equipment. When Mr. George heard about the possibilities of development in the Putao plains he gave $5000 for purchase of a Massey-Ferguson 25-horsepower tractor, with plows and harrows. This equipment was designed specially for use in underdeveloped areas such as Putao and many other parts of Asia. There were no motor roads from Myitkyina to Putao, but after prayerful careful consideration, it was decided to fly the equipment from Myitkyina. The tractor and accessories arrived in Putao by chartered plane in February, 1954, along with an instructor who taught Russell, Eugene, and two Lisu drivers about operation and care of the equipment. There was great excitement as the instructor showed how the plow could cut through the tough elephant grass!

Actual plowing wasn't started until early in March, 1954, but by the end of May one hundred thirty acres of new land had been plowed, harrowed, and planted. More than fifty families benefited from the two-acre plots assigned to each. In addition some fields were worked by all the people of the village for the church, to provide grain for convention time, for helping any families whose crops failed, and for the local preachers and their families. Two Lisu drivers learned to operate and maintain the tractor. Later, two more tractors, with plows, etc., were added, more drivers trained, and eventually more than two thousand acres were brought under cultivation, providing good fields for the people of ten or twelve villages. The tractors were also used in road making, leveling house sites, and other village development.

Russell was a great help to the people in the agricultural phase of their development. In addition to his medical and evangelistic work he was vitally interested in improved methods of cultivation, and also had long been experimenting to find ways to provide a greater variety of food to those under-privi-leged people. He wanted them to have the additional fruits and vegetables which would improve their health and give them the physical strength to equal their zeal in carrying on the Lord's work. With God's help this hope was realized as the plains area was developed. Just as he had done in the Mekong and Salween Valleys, he started planting fruit trees — especially dif-ferent varieties of citrus trees, as the weather seemed particu-larly favorable for that. Gradually he taught many different people how to plant and care for the young trees, and also to graft cuttings from older trees onto the young seedlings. After several years of this work, almost every home had at least three or four citrus trees around them, and some even had small orchards. Grapefruit seemed to be a universal favorite.

✝

Eugene, Helen and family finally left Muladi June 14, 1954 to start home on a much-needed, well-deserved furlough. Arriving in Los Angeles on July 5, they were met by Helen's parents, Mr. and Mrs. Oscar Myers, and her brother, with a group of other relatives and friends. During the summer they visited relatives, their living-link churches, attended the Week of Missions at Cedar Lake, Indiana, and spoke at several camps and churches. Eugene then enrolled for the fall term at Lincoln Bible Institute (now known as Lincoln Christian College) in Lincoln, Illinois.

✝

That summer of 1954 we had a very disturbing and emo-tionally exhausting experience. Early in August, suddenly and without warning, hundreds of Lisu Christians came pouring over the high mountains from China into Burma. They had fled from their homes in the Salween Valley because of severe persecution from the communists. They had been threatened with brain-washing and even liquidation because they refused to renounce their faith in Christ. Knowing of the comparative peacefulness and freedom of North Burma, in their desperation they fled there to seek asylum — an asylum which was denied outright. Among the refugees were entire families, ranging in age from old, white-haired grandmothers down to new-born babies. Four young mothers gave birth to babies during their journey, but only two survived the harsh conditions.

It took the refugees from thirteen to nineteen days to get from the last habitation on the China side to the first village on the Burma side! When they arrived, all of them were starving, emaciated, and sick from exposure. Yet they could not stop until they had gone another seven days' walk to report to the Burma officials. Although the Burma-side Christians had suffered crop failure, they took pity on the refugees, and shared what little they had, so that no one died of hunger, but they suffered terribly.

In the uproar that followed their unexpected entry into Burma, the refugees were divided into groups, and the weaker women and youngsters were secretly forced back across the border. Some of the sickest were allowed to go to Dorothy Sterling at Kobudeh for treatment. Later, although they were still sick and had to be led or carried, they were forced to return the eight to ten days' journey to the mountain pass nearest to China, and left there to the mercy of God and the weather.

One group of ninety-three had come across the border and had written an appeal to the Burma government. They were confidently awaiting a reply when they heard of the forced return of the others. Such was their faith in a free, democratic government that they now went to the Putao official for confirmation of permission to remain in Burma. About twenty of the leading Christians of the Putao area churches guaranteed their bonds while the government considered whether to let them stay or send them back to the Chinese communists.

Dorothy Sterling was called from Kobudeh to Putao to answer spurious charges that she was harboring over one hundred sixty illegal entrants. She was then refused permission to return to carry on her school and continue medical and missionary work in the eastern sector. She moved her school to Muladi.

✝

There were widespread rumors that all Lisu refugees would be put out of North Burma and that all foreign missionaries would be expelled. Uncertainty, distrust, and fear were spread among the Lord's people who had remained faithful through all those years behind the "bamboo curtain". Even the non-Christian Burmese soldiers guarding them at one place were moved to tears as they heard the almost-starving Christian refugees continually singing their hymns of hope and dependence upon God. The Lord used them to strengthen the faith of many and to awaken all the churches. After six months of deliberation by the Burmese government, the group of ninety-three Christians who had applied for permission to stay in Burma were told they would have to return to China.

"If we allow you to stay," the Burmese officials said, "the Chinese would accuse us of 'stealing' their citizens, and if we help you, it would be considered an 'unfriendly act' toward China."

One of the families told to return to China had lived very near our home in Muladi. During the time they were there a son was born to them, and they did not want to take their baby back to China, for fear he might either be killed or taken from them and educated to be a Communist. Drema Esther asked if she could care for him, and they agreed. She named him Samuel, and raised him as her own son.

We were told that many of the guards felt sorry for the refugees and "looked the other way" as they neared the Chinese border. Thus, practically all of them found their way back to the jungles of Burma. Some moved farther west and established a village in the wild, uninhabited area near the Burma-India border, but within India, which was later named Vijaynagar.

✝

In spite of the unsettled conditions that summer, I had been going around and teaching in churches within several days' travel from Muladi. In October, 1954 I was returning from such a trip, and was within about two hours' travel from home when the horse I was riding scented a tiger which apparently had just gone through a nearby village and crossed the road. The horse wheeled around sharply, causing the saddle to turn and throw me violently to the ground. A native Christian girl remained with me while one of the carriers went to Muladi for help.

Russell and Robert came immediately in the tractor and I was taken home in the "transport box." Russell then scanned his medical books to find out how to treat my injuries. The main impact was to my right arm and shoulder. Russell and Robert decided from their examination that there was both a dislocation and a broken bone, and were concerned that they might not be able to set it properly. But they prayed, then did all they could, and surely the Lord guided them. After setting it as best they could, they bound my arm to immobilize it, and treated my many scratches and bruises. Then we prayed, committing the injury to our Great Physician and trusting Him for healing. I stayed in bed, as quietly as I could, for about three weeks, until I could move around without too much pain. Some of the Rawang Christians brought me some herbal medicine which was especially for bone injuries. Very gradually I started moving my arm a little at a time. About three months later, when I went to Rangoon with LaVerne, I went to an Indian doctor, an orthopedic surgeon. An X-ray of my shoulder and arm proved Russell's diagnosis correct: my shoulder had been dislocated and the bone had been broken just below the shoulder joint. The doctor said that although he was sure I had suffered great pain, the work Russell and Robert had done would be considered an excellent job of setting a broken bone, even by the medical profession. It had healed perfectly, even though it had not been in a cast. Truly the Great Physician had provided the best possible care and cure! We truly praised the Lord for His care.

✝

After LaVerne and Lois were married in March, 1953, they continued their studies at Cincinnati Bible Seminary. When LaVerne graduated in May that year, he had the honor of being selected Class Orator and gave one of the commencement addresses. Lois completed her junior year at that time. Sometime during that summer Lois recalled having spent many happy hours in her childhood reading a set of books called LIFE OF CHRIST VISUALIZED. Thus began a dream — a dream of printing those books in Lisu, Rawang, and Burmese, and even in the languages of many other countries, to be used in evangelizing the people of those lands.

Checking with Standard Publishing Company in Cincinnati, they were advised that if the missionaries over the world would place orders for at least 100,000 copies of ONE of the three books, Standard would print them for approximately sixteen cents each. When this idea was presented at the Sixth National Missionary Convention, in the autumn of 1953, many of the missionaries enthusiastically hailed it. Orders were received for 165,000 books to be printed in sixteen languages. Thus was a dream fulfilled.

LaVerne and Lois left San Francisco by ship on November 5, 1954 and arrived in Bangkok, Thailand on December 8. They spent Christmas with missionary friends in Chiengkam in northern Thailand, then LaVerne flew to Rangoon to apply for a visa for Lois, who had to remain in Thailand.

After a week of intensive efforts, without any apparent results so far as a visa was concerned, LaVerne made a quick trip to Muladi to confer with the rest of the family. He had with him one hundred ninety of the first copies of the LIFE OF CHRIST VISUALIZED which had been printed in Lisu. His arrival could not have been better timed, as it was just two days before the close of the preachers' Bible School. About two hundred preachers and potential leaders from all over the mission field in Burma had gathered as students at Muladi, some having walked about eighteen days to attend. With students leaving school for their homes, this was an excellent opportunity to introduce those first copies of the book to every valley, mountain, and jungle area in northern Burma. The bulk of the books arrived later.

✝

On March 11, 1955, while Eugene and Helen were still on furlough in the U.S., our daughter Ruth Margaret was married to Frank Johnson, son of Mr. and Mrs. Floyd Johnson of Austin, Indiana. Because Russell and I were on the field in Burma, her "big brother" Eugene acted in our stead and gave her in marriage. Ruth was a junior at Cincinnati Bible Seminary, where Frank was also a student.

About a month later Eugene and family left the United States to return to Burma. It was a difficult time for Helen, because she had to leave her mother in the hospital, slowly recovering from a serious illness. On May 9, 1955, they arrived in Rangoon, where they were reunited with LaVerne. He was still working on a visa for his wife Lois, who was still waiting in Bangkok, Thailand. On June 24, Eugene and Helen's fourth son, John Lawrence (Larry) was born. This little one was the source of much concern, for he was born with a malfunctioning lymph system, which resulted in poor circulation and caused swelling of his hands and feet. This problem made it difficult for him to walk, and also made him very susceptible to respiratory infections and other diseases.

It was about this time that the matter of a new name for the mission work arose. After the Communist take-over in China, it was, of course, impossible to continue missionary work there. Since the base of work was now moved to Burma, we decided that the old name — Yunnan-Tibetan Christian Mission — which had been used for twenty-six years, was no longer appropriate. Russell and I, and Robert and Betty had discussed this when LaVerne came to Putao, and now he and Eugene and Helen talked it over also. The name unanimously

chosen was "North Burma Christian Mission". Before register-
ing the new name, the Kachin State Ministry of the Union of
Burma requested a detailed report of the extent and nature of
our mission work. Because we were working in a politically sen-
sitive area of Burma, we emphasized the fact that our work was
strictly Christian missionary work, and that all work was within
Burma, not transgressing any international borders, so there
were no more questions or problems.

Anyone who has known the Morse family or read their
newsletters knows that all of us have referred often to the monsoons. This term is often used with reference either to monsoon rains or to the monsoon season. However, the dictionary
defines monsoon as a wind. It is the wind that brings on the
torrential rains so often called monsoons. The monsoon winds
are seasonal, blowing from over the tropics and the Indian
Ocean in a steady, northeasterly direction across southeastern
Asia, for about six months. Beginning in March, and increasing
in violence as the warm, moisture-laden air from the Indian
Ocean meets the cooler air masses coming off the snows of the
Himalaya Mountains, the monsoon is most violent from June
to August. These winds correspond to the trade winds of the
western hemisphere. Each is caused by rotation of the earth in
its annual orbit around the sun. If the Rocky Mountains lay
from east to west across the United States, all the lands south
of the mountains might also have regular cloudburst-type rains.

In the Putao plains, where our mission base was located,
the rainfall of the monsoon season is never less than 200
inches. (The annual rainfall in the United States averages about
40 inches). The violent monsoon wind twists and beats and
pounds with slashing rain in almost cyclonic fury, making travel
dangerous. Roadways are washed out, and airplanes are blown
about like leaves in a high wind. No one seems to know how
high these storm clouds may be. After the first violence, there
are brief intervals of calm. In spite of the destruction, the mon-

soon rains are welcomed, for they bring relief from the intense heat, fill water reservoirs and flood the rice paddies. The humidity of the monsoon air is overwhelming. We were told that an air conditioner in Rangoon might condense as much as four quarts of water in a twenty-four hour period. Keeping these facts in mind, perhaps you can understand better what Eugene and Helen and family faced in returning to Putao from Rangoon duirng the monsoon season.

✟

Eugene and Helen's baby, Larry, was just one month old when they and their four children, together with Drema Esther, left Rangoon by plane. Drema Esther had gone to Rangoon in June for minor surgery and was now returning. They were able to fly only as far as Myitkyina because planes were not flying from Myitkyina to Putao due to the monsoon rains. The 218 miles from Myitkyna to Putao had to be covered by overland travel, and the heavy rains made that very difficult, too. They were able to use a jeep for about the first hundred miles, but so many bridges had been washed out that the final eight days of the journey had to be on foot, slogging through knee-deep mud and crossing rivers in "tippy" canoes with a month-old baby and three small boys, ages two, four, and six years old. Drema Esther was of inestimable assistance, helping with the children and providing much-needed encouragement during that hard trip.

While speaking of Drema Esther, I should add that all of us felt we would scarcely have known how to get along without her. In her quiet, humble way she helped all of us in more ways than we can count. She usually taught the children's Sunday School, and took care of procuring supplies and preparing medicine kits to give out to preachers at the preachers' Bible Schools. Besides teaching some classes herself, she also translated for those of the mission who had not yet mastered the Lisu language. She was an excellent teacher, and the students had a sincere love and respect for her. She dispensed medicine and helped Russell in taking care of many of the sick, who often numbered as many as a hundred patients a day. Her love and sympathy for the people were shown by the careful and patient way in which she worked. Her faith, kindness, and zeal to do the Lord's work was as nearly perfect as possible and produced many good results. She was a full-fledged missionary and co-worker in her own right. Without her faithful help in our home, I could never have gone away on such long teaching trips. She surely was given to us by God.

✟

After six long months of waiting alone in Bangkok, Thailand, Lois was finally granted her visa and joined LaVerne in Rangoon on June 28, 1955. A residence, or "unrestricted stay" permit had not yet been granted, however, so they had to remain in Rangoon two or three more months. Originally LaVerne had had an "unrestricted stay" permit like the rest of us, and when he went to the States to complete his work at Cincinnati Bible Seminary he was told by the Controller of Immigration that he could have the same permit after his return, even though he overstayed the one-year validity of the re-entry permit. He stayed two years, also was married, and upon his return found changes in immigration personnel and policy. He was really fortunate to be readmitted at all. After months of delay, three-year permits were finally given to both LaVerne and Lois. In the meantime they were allowed to go to Muladi. While still in Rangoon, their first child, Marcia Louise Morse, was born August 30, 1955. Marcia was our eighth grandchild, but the first grandDAUGHTER. Lois, LaVerne, and Marcia also had to make the last two hundred twenty miles of the journey to Muladi by the overland route, although by the time they came in November the monsoon season was over.

Don Carter came to Muladi, took soil samples,
and evaluated the area for agricultural potential.
L-R: Pastor Sa-Yohan, Eugene, Don Carter, and Pastor Asher.

The first tractor was brought up by charter plane,
and was a source of great wonder to everyone.

Demonstration of what the tractor could do attracted
a crowd of onlookers, and caused great excitement.

When the tractor was plowing, it disturbed the nest
of a big python, which the villagers killed.

Russell introduced many different varieties of citrus fruit,
and taught the villagers to graft cuttings and start their own orchards.

During the summer of 1954, many Lisu refugees came from China. It was a
heart-breaking experience to know they had to return to a Communist society.

Dorothy Sterling had to move her children's school to Muladi, because false
accusations made it impossible for her to stay in Kobudeh, east of Muladi.

I visited many villages riding my horse, but it got frightened one day when it
smelled a tiger nearby, and threw me from the saddle, breaking my shoulder.

33
Translation and Teaching

One of the most powerful forces in winning people to Christ is the example of those who have already become Christians. It is a wonderful testimony to the heathen to hear native Christians joyfully singing, "What a Friend We Have in Jesus", or "When We All Get to Heaven". In the Salween Valley the singing echoed back and forth between the narrow canyon walls, while in the plains area the sound carried throughout the villages. In either place, the message of Christ was being carried in song. Whether they were working in their fields on the mountainsides, or sitting cross-legged beside their fireplaces in the evenings, the Christians were happy and enjoyed expressing that happiness by praising God in song. Hymn books and Bibles were never left in the churches, as is often the case in Western countries. Even today each family or individual has their own books. When they travel to another village, or go out to their fields, the Christians nearly always carry a book bag, containing the Scriptures and hymn book in their own language.

By 1954 the entire New Testament plus Psalms, and the book of Genesis had been printed in Lisu. Only the Gospel of Mark was available in Rawang, but Robert worked whenever possible, often late at night, on translation of the Gospel of Luke, as well as other material. In the summer of 1955 Robert moved his family to Dukdang (Dook-dahng), a Rawang village about four miles from Muladi, so he could be with Rawang

338

people all the time and thus be able to do better translation work. By that time he had completed the Gospel of Luke and most of Acts, as well as a Gospel primer with some hymns for people to use in learning to read the new Rawang script. He also prepared another primer for use in schools for teaching children to read.

✞

In December, 1955 a conference of church leaders of the Lisu and Rawang Churches of Christ was held at Muladi. About one hundred fifty elders, deacons and preachers assembled for three days of rich spiritual fellowship and discussion of problems and needs throughout the field. Some came from as far as seventeen days' journey away. For some it was their first time down from the high mountains to the Putao plains, and there was much to wonder at: a flat field stretching out farther than a bow could shoot; a long, straight road wider than their ridgetop houses were long; a strange-smelling and noisy contraption that plowed more land in ten minutes than they could hoe in a day.

Most wonderful of all was the open-hearted fellowship between so many Christian brethren from such widely separated areas and far-flung outposts, speaking more strange dialects than any of them had ever heard at one time. It was a rewarding time for the missionaries, too, realizing that only a few years earlier some of the tribes and clans represented there had been mortal enemies.

This was the second such conference to be held in the north Burma field. The first one had been in 1945, when about thirty men gathered for a ten-day period of conferring with Robert on church problems. There were only about a dozen churches then, and a half dozen or so Lisu evangelists who made visits from the Salween Valley, and three full-time Lisu preachers.

Now, ten years later, in a different area, the needs and calls seemed to be just as great. A large group gathered around the

339

fireplace in our home, including young and old, Lisu and Rawang, most from outlying districts. They had brought their local family and church problems to the missionaries, trying to find solutions which would pioneer a forward step in social adjustments for their new Christian communities. They had no history of Christian customs and traditions to draw on, only a discarded primitive animistic background. The unending conferences with the missionaries were essential to help them translate basic Bible precepts into practical everyday life. The missionaries had to be careful not to suggest solutions based merely on western cultural tradtions, but a Christian answer which would fit into the tribal culture.

Problems were varied, as this sampling shows:

Some non-Christians demanded the daughter of a Christian man in marriage. Insulted by a refusal, they tried to solve the problem by abducting the girl; how should her family react and what should they do?

a mixed Lisu-Rawang congregation with a bi-lingual preacher had won a few converts from a nearby Kachin village who needed to be taught in their own language, so could the missionary find them a TRI-lingual preacher;

as non-Christians they had sacrificed to appease the evil spirits before starting their farm work and gathering their harvest, so now that they knew God and were freed from the chains of fear, shouldn't they offer something to God instead?

Another problem was determining the age of the children so as to know whether they were old enough to marry. It had been decided that girls should be at least eighteen and boys should be at least twenty. A census of the children was begun, figuring their age by relating the time they were born to some important event. From then on, each church kept a record of all children born in that village.

Finally, sometime after midnight the conference was brought to a close. Immediately all those from outlying villages clustered around Russell asking for medicine, not only for themselves, but usually for half the people in their village. That would have to wait until morning. Earlier, Russell had spent some time telling them about the advantages of having their own fruit and vegetable gardens to give them a healthy diet. They had become convinced by the practical demonstration provided through his agricultural and horticultural sideline. Now they wanted to discuss it with him.

The scene at the mission station the next morning was typical. Long before sunup people began to collect on the porch, waiting their turn to be served. After eating an early, hurried breakfast, Esther went over to the clinic to help take care of the people who had minor complaints. Usually several native pastors or evangelists were waiting to have their medical kits refilled. This was one of many services which Esther rendered. Each of the sixty or so workers had been trained in the use of about a dozen different remedies for the most common and widespread ills, and each was furnished with a medical kit containing remedies for superficial infections and to treat cases of malaria, dysentery, etc.

Meanwhile, back at the house, Russell was treating a couple of urgent cases carried from other villages on stretchers and laid out on the porch. They were treated on the spot while housing was being arranged. A three-room "guest-house" had been built especially to take care of such "in-patients" from outlying areas.

By the grace of God, Russell had regained most of his health after his harrowing experiences in the communist prison, although he was not able to return to the strenuously active work of former years. The Lord opened up new fields of endeavor which kept him just as busy, just as exhausted at the end of day, right at the home base. His relaxation, after a long, hard day, was to work in his gardens and orchards.

✟

At the 1955 preachers' "retreat", the church leaders brought up the subject of the women needing more teaching and discussed various ways for them to get teaching and fellowship such as the men had been getting in the many workshops, conferences and schools.

"I'll go to each village and teach the women," I told them, "IF you men will stay home and take care of the children and take over the household chores." After some discussion among themselves, they agreed to those terms.

Most of the villages were not too far apart, and I tried to arrange my itinerary so that in each place I could teach for three days, six hours during the day and one hour at night. After the last day of teaching, I would leave in mid-afternoon and walk for about four hours to the next village. After resting awhile and eating, I would teach for another hour that night. Eventually, I visited about thirty-five villages, going home occasionally for fresh clothing and a good meal. Many times the paths led through marsh lands where I waded in ankle-deep water. Usually the streams were only about waist deep so I just waded across them.

I taught the women first about the way of salvation, using pictures with the lessons, and how to become a good Christian, emphasizing that they must be born again. Then, using the book of Proverbs, I taught them how to be good wives and mothers, explaining as much as possible about good sanitation and nutrition. After several months of teaching the women in those thirty-five villages, I returned home completely exhausted. I had to rest for several weeks before I was again well and strong enough to help with the mission work as before.

About that time a branch of the Rawang tribe, speaking an altogether different dialect, had come in contact with some of our Christian Rawangs and they were so impressed by their Christian way of life that they sent a call for someone to come and teach them. That resulted in almost four hundred conversions within the past year in an area where, only a few years earlier, the Gospel message had never been heard.

The need for more teachers and pastors was desperate. Bible schools were in progress in various locations much of the time, as part of the effort to train new leaders and workers. Many new villages were being established as each year more people moved down from the mountains, where famine conditions occurred at least part of each year. Each new Christian settlement sent a call for Eugene to come and help them lay out an orderly "model" village, on the order of the ones at Muladi and Dukdang.

✟

From the time we first started working among the Lisu, it was our practice to establish self-supporting churches. This was continued through co-workers and later by our three sons when they became old enough to help in the work. We trained teachers, evangelists, elders and deacons to carry on the work of local congregations. Except in rare cases, baptizing was done by national workers, so there wouldn't be a problem because the "white teacher" baptized some and not others.

Church buildings were built and financed by the local Christians. The two large church buildings in South Muladi and North Muladi were designed and supervised in construction by Eugene, but all the bamboo and grass was cut by the congregation. They paid for any materials that had to be purchased, and contributed all necessary labor. The churches at Muladi sent out their own evangelists and missionaries, who helped establish new congregations in other places, and these, too, were supported by the congregation.

Work on a new church building in North Muladi was begun in November, 1955. It was in the shape of a cross, and was 100 ft. long and 40 ft. wide, except at the transept, where it was 80 ft. wide, and 37 feet high from floor to ridge-pole. Supports were all from trusses, so there were no columns in the center to obstruct the view. It would seat about 1500-2000 people, sitting on the floor, Lisu fashion, with the men on one side and women on the other. For that building Eugene was able to obtain some timbers from a recently established saw mill at Putao. The walls and floor were of lime concrete, which Eugene taught Lisu workers to make from locally available slaked lime, sand, and gravel. The supporting posts were set into the concrete so the termites would not destroy them so rapidly. All the labor was contributed by the congregation, with men doing the actual construction work, and women cutting and carrying in the bundles of grass for the roof, as well as helping carry baskets of rocks, or dirt, or other materials. The building was completed in the spring of 1956, just in time for the Easter convention.

Much time and effort on the part of LaVerne and Lois
resulted in copies of the Life of Christ Visualized <u>in Lisu</u>
being delivered to Lisu villages, where it was eagerly read.

During the fall of 1954 we held a 1-month Bible School, and held classes,
as well as Sunday service, in the recently completed chapel building.

Eugene and Helen's fourth son, John Lawrence (Larry), was born in Rangoon on June 24, 1955.

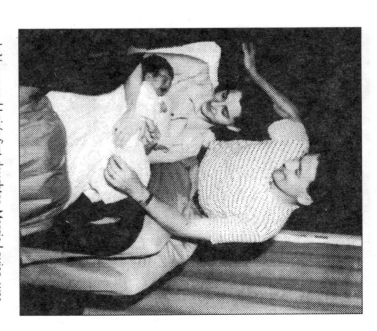

LaVerne and Lois's first daughter, Marcia Louise, was born in Rangoon on August 30, 1955. She was our eighth grandchild, but the first grand-daughter.

I went to many different villages, teaching the women. Sometimes Rawang
girls carried my loads and helped me.

Eugene started building a new church in November, 1955.
Seeing the framework going up was exciting.

The church was finished in time for the Easter convention in 1956.

After the closing service of the convention, everyone came out
and formed a "friendship circle" around the church building.

34
Threatened Invasion

Robert and Betty and family were due for a furlough, and in late January, 1956 they went to Rangoon to try to arrange to leave the country. It was not easy at that time to get a re-entry permit, but they did not want to leave the country without the assurance of being able to return. Plane reservations were also difficult to get for a group, but they were unable to make a firm reservation until after receiving their re-entry permits. Adding to their stress, was the need to get their tickets before their youngest son's second birthday, so they wouldn't have to pay extra. As they prayed for the Lord's guidance and intervention, they were comforted by their daily Scripture readings, especially those from the Old Testament, which said, "...the battle is not yours, but God's. ....stand ye still and see the salvation of the Lord..." (2 Chronicles 20:15,17) These verses reminded them of God's power, and helped them to be able to wait with peace of mind. About a week before the deadline, they received their re-entry permit, then obtained the needed plane tickets, and were able to leave in good time. Right up until time to leave, Robert and his helper, Magaltaq Peter, had been working almost day and night on translation of the book of Acts into the Rawang language, and just barely got it completed before Robert had to leave.

We had known about Gospel Recordings, Inc. for several years, and Eugene and Robert had helped make some recordings in Lisu in 1948. The records had attracted much interest, and had been very effective in helping present the Gospel message when we went to preach. So we were very glad to have Vaughn Collins, from Gospel Recordings, come in January, 1956 to spend a week with us and make recordings in different languages.

In December, 1955 Eugene and Robert began to look for people who spoke different languages used in our area of work, who could help with the recording. Eugene and Drema Esther and Robert had the task of translating scripts from English into Lisu. These translations were then distributed to various ones who could re-translate them into Rawang or Kachin. Then these were again retranslated into still other languages, such as Shan, Duleng, Kwinpang, etc. Most of the informants, or speakers, could read and write these different languages, but a few could not. When two persons were required for a script and only one could read, that one would read the script sentence by sentence and the other would repeat his part for recording. It was a slow process, espcially when it was sometimes necessary to go through four interpreters in order to make an informant understand what was wanted — for example, English to Lisu to Kachin to Shan. In some cases it took as much as an hour to complete the recording of a script which, in its final form, took only three minutes to play. Informants had to practice their lines, sometimes repeating so many times they almost memorized them before they were able to say them without mistakes.

But in one week, in spite of delays, interruptions, and difficulties of translation, it was possible to complete twenty-five sides (12 ½ records) in eight different languages. Eugene recorded the last half record — one side, in Lisu — when he went to Myitkyina with Vaughn. The languages recorded included Lisu, Hkamti Shan, Rawang, Zewang, Masang, Didong, Krangku, and Duleng.

Truly, "faith cometh by hearing." and we were thankful for the work done by Gospel Recordings and workers like Vaughn

Colllins in making the Gospel message available to people in their own language..

✞

One day, in late July, 1956, while listening to a news broadcast from Radio Australia, we were jolted into sudden attention by the announcement that Burma had been invaded by Chinese communists, who held positions from Putao to a point below Myitkyina! We had heard nothing of any such thing locally, and our first reaction was to discount it. But a news broadcast from Rangoon an hour later said the same thing, and added a government statement refuting the report as untrue concerning the Kachin State, but saying it was true that Chinese troops had established outposts in the Wa State, near the China border.

The next night we heard a similar report on Voice of America. After that, we heard no additional news. A few days later a special messenger came from up on the northern border, saying that large numbers of troops were massed there. We were told that as many as three hundred soldiers had actually been seen, and barracks and camps had been built. According to some reports, the troops said they were not there to harm anyone, but only to "liberate" the people from Burmese oppression. (That sounded ominously familiar!) Others said they were told there was no use trying to run away because wherever they went they could be found. It was reported that the soldiers said they were coming down to Putao by harvest time or before. Most of the Putao plain was under cultivation and harvests were bountiful.

We had heard reports of invasion plans every summer since we had been there, but that was the first time Chinese soldiers had been reported inside Burma territory. Even Eugene, who usually discounted all the various reports, was impressed this time that perhaps they really meant business. LaVerne was holding a Bible school with three hundred students, many of them from the reportedly invaded area, and there was a great

351

deal of questioning and anxiety among them. What did it all mean? What about their families ? What was going to happen? What were the missionaries going to do?

We all felt that we should be prepared to leave, if necessary. The local headmen and village elders also thought we should be ready to leave on short notice, but we had little heart for packing. The very thought of leaving was almost more than we could bear. The people were very upset over the idea that we might be leaving, and wondered what would happen to them. The whole community was in a state of turmoil. Many of them had already had a taste of communist government and had no desire to experience any more. Because we were so reluctant to leave, we welcomed the advice of one of the Putao officials, who advised us not to make any hasty move, but wait a while to see what developed. The matter had been brought before the Security Council of the United Nations and he thought the immediate urgency would be alleviated, at least temporarily.

Our whole congregation at Muladi gathered to pray against the coming of the communists. Several days later, some Lisu hunters found two large baskets of communist road markers. Investigation revealed other markers leading to the Chinese border. Evidently, infiltrators had been marking out a secret trail through the backwoods jungle for the invading Chinese soldiers to follow. Then an unusual early and heavy snow began to fall on the high mountain passes, even though this was in mid-summer, in August. Some of the natives heard the Chinese say that was a bad omen, so they must have become frightened and abandoned the project. That was probably the route they intended to follow to Putao at harvest time. Again God answered the prayers of His people, and sent the off-season heavy snow to change the plans of the communists.

LaVerne finished with the Bible School at Dukdang on August 13th. Their loads were already packed and ready to go, and the existing circumstances made it seem wise for him and

Lois to go on to Myitkyina, traveling overland, because air service had been suspended due to the monsoons. This would at least establish a link with the outside world. Some of the students had even waited over to carry their loads as far as Sumprabum, (the home area of the students) about half-way between Putao and Myitkyina. Also, the Gospel of Mark in Rawang needed to be reprinted, as the previous supply of 4000 copies had been exhausted and more were urgently needed.

When Laverne and Lois arrived in Myitkyina they found suitable living quarters, and Lois taught typing four hours a day to several Lisu and Rawang students while LaVerne went to Rangoon to expedite the printing work. He was able to see to reprinting the Gospel of Mark, and also managed to arrange for printing of the book of Acts, which Robert had recently completed translating into Rawang.

The rest of our families decided to remain in Putao and continue working as long as possible. In August, 1956 the mission received a government order limiting the activities of the foreign missionary personnel to an area within a fourteen-mile radius of Putao, because they "could not guarantee the safety of foreign personnel" outside those limits. Later we heard that the Chinese government had pressured the Burmese government to do this, because they did not want the foreign missionaries working close to their border!

✞

The 1956 Christmas convention was held at Hpama Village, and Eugene suggested that since it was on the main road to Myitkyina, it would be practical to take the tractor and trailer, thus eliminating the need for carriers for the children. On the morning of December 21, Russell and I left with Eugene's family of six, and four helpers from our two households. Esther and little Sammy stayed at home with one of the native girls to look after things. Getting that tractor and trailer down the steep bank, onto a large raft floating on empty 50-gallon diesel drums, and across the river was really quite an accomplishment.

When we arrived in Hpama, we went down the one street of the village, passed through a short stretch of jungle, and came out into a clearing where numerous little straw, leaf, and bamboo shelters had been built. Pastor Titus met us and led the way to the shelter the church folks had prepared for us. We were amazed when we saw the nice place they had fixed up — a little house, divided into three rooms, with partitions and roof made of big leaves and rice straw on a bamboo frame. A thick layer of rice straw was all over the ground, just like a soft carpet.

Almost immediately people began bringing us gifts: eggs, a chicken, a piece of pork, and four big fish. We knew these were expressions of their love and their gladness that we were there, and we thanked God anew for the privilege of working among such people as the Lisu and Rawang.

As usual in that area, about half of the fifteen hundred people who attended were Lisu and the other half Rawang, so all services were conducted in both languages. After the evening services each night groups could be heard from all directions, singing far into the night until nearly dawn. One of the highlights of that convention was on Sunday night, when a group of about two hundred young people went all around the camp ground, where more than two hundred shelters were scattered about, and sang Christmas carols. It was so beautiful that we felt almost as if the gates of heaven had opened and we were hearing an angelic choir. We would remember it for a long, long time.

As at all the conventions, whether Easter, Thanksgiving, or Christmas, the food brought by those attending was combined. The rice was all cooked together, and individual portions were wrapped in large leaves and placed in a basket. Individual portions of meat and vegetables were also wrapped in leaves and placed in another basket. As the worshippers left the service, each person received a packet from each basket. Then they took their food and sat around on the ground in small groups, to eat and visit. After the final farewell service on Monday morning, everyone shook hands all around. Most conventions at this time were attended by one thousand to three thousand Christians.

✝

If you could have looked down into the northeastern corner of the mission field, into the village of Nyitadi, around December 19, 1956, you would have seen three young men starting out on a long trip. Each one carried a basket on his back containing his clothing, bedding, and rice. Tied on top were a couple of pans for cooking their food along the way. As they traveled southwest, they began to meet other young men, also traveling, and all carrying similar equipment. Farther along, as they turned more to the west, they met more young men, and some young women, too.

Besides the loads they carried, all those travelers had something else in common — their destination. All were on their way to attend the six-week Bible School to be held at Muladi, beginning January 7, 1957. A large number of students were coming at the same time from other directions — from the north, almost up to the Tibetan border, and from the south, too. They all came with hearts eager to study and learn.

LaVerne and Lois had arrived back in Putao just the day before Christmas, 1956 so he was on hand to teach, together with Eugene and myself. Robert and Betty were still on furlough. We had planned to hold a school in the eastern sector of the field, but that was made impossible by the government ruling that the missionary staff must remain within fourteen miles of Putao. Rather than disappoint the many young people and preachers who had planned to study there, it was decided to hold the school at Muladi, even though it meant long journeys for many of the students. So many students came, (around 400) that they had to be divided into three groups: (1) Advanced students, such as preachers and elders; (2) those who had been to school, could read and write, but had not been to Bible School before (the largest group); (3) those who could neither read nor write, even in their own language (which included quite a large number of girls). There were too many classes to be handled by just the foreign missionaries, and several of the older preachers helped in teaching the beginners. Next to the actual Bible teaching, one of the most important things was to meet with individual preachers and prospective Christian leaders, and to encourage, advise, and exhort them, and to build them up spiritually.

The Christians had all been taught about tithing, and now, with the Putao plain under cultivation, the harvests were more bountiful. The tithes of those crops from the many churches helped to feed the many Bible School students from distant mountain churches who could not carry enough rice for the three months of school. The traveling evangelists, also, were dependent upon these tithes for their needs, and of course any who were in need of food (such as widows, or families whose granary had burned , or whose crops had failed) were also helped.

The young wives (Helen, Betty, and Lois) always assisted as much as they could in the different schools. Betty taught English, Lois taught music, and Helen typed, cut stencils, and mimeographed materials and literature used in the schools and other phases of the mission work. But when the need arose they all helped each other. Helen and Betty also spent much time teaching their children, using Calvert School courses.

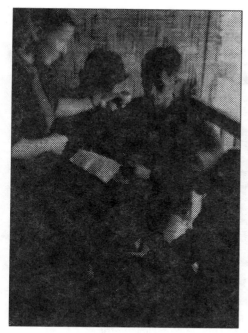

Helping make records for
Gospel Recordings was a
tedious and tiring job, but very
rewarding.

In January 1957 a Bible School was held with around 400 in attendance.

At that time, the foreign mission staff consisted of just our own families.
Back - L-R: Robert, Eugene, Russell, LaVerne
Front - L-R: Betty, Helen, Gertrude, Drema Esther, Lois.

I taught an evening Bible study class in our home, which was well attended.

35
Frontier Evangelism

When we first began preaching the Gospel in the Salween Valley, a young Lisu man named Heh-pa-sha, living high in the mountains of the northern Salween gorge at Mi-le-wa, heard about foreigners preaching a strange new religion. Being inquisitive, he soon learned more about "The Jesus Way", which promised life eternal and release from the terrible bondage to evil spirits under which he and his people were suffering. As an enthusiastic young convert, he was soon actively spreading the Gospel himself, although he suffered from a disability which made him avoid strangers. This conflicted with his urge to go out and spread the good news, but he finally grew bold enough to ask the Lord to touch his body and remove the handicap. He became one of a number of victims of epilepsy in Lisuland who had their affliction taken away in answer to prayer.

When Russell held the very first Lisu Bible School in the Mekong Valley, Heh-pa-sha was one of the first to attend, even though it was some five or six days' journey away from his home. As the years passed, Heh-pa-sha continued to study and witness. He took the name of his favorite Bible character, Paul, then married, and became pastor of the church at Ta-da. He built up the membership of the Ta-da congregation to about four hundred members by evangelizing in more than fifteen surrounding villages, and it became the largest church in the valley. After looking around for new areas to evangelize, he went across the high mountain range into the Taron Valley of

North Burma as a missionary to the Daru tribe. He and his wife, Susanna, with their young children, endured many years of hardship and privation ministering to the Daru tribe on the Tibetan border. Their culture was so primitive that even the Lisu considered them wild. They dressed in next to nothing, and their food usually consisted of various jungle roots and herbs. When Paul returned to the Salween Valley with some of his converts, they were wearing clothes for the first time in their lives!

During World War II, when the mission field was cut off from fresh supplies from the outside, Paul needed more primers and hymnals for teaching new converts. Being of an inventive turn of mind, he fashioned a crude kind of printing press. He found a deposit of good workable lead from which he cut lead plates, and after some trial and error managed to carve out type for printing, a page at a time. He made his own printing ink by experimenting with combinations of various fruits and berries and other jungle plants. This Lisu minister/missionary had such a burden for sharing the Gospel message that he applied himself to the task with great industriousness, and exercised every bit of inventiveness the Lord gave him in order to facilitate production of teaching materials.

After his mission field had seen well over a thousand conversions, and several young Timothys were headed for the ministry, a series of epidemics broke out which claimed many lives, including Paul's. His wife was so devoted to the work that she stayed on for many months, teaching the Daru Christians, until other volunteers could be sent from the Salween Valley to relieve her. When she finally returned to their home congregation at Milewa, Susanna brought with her their three remaining sons and two daughters. She had lost two sons as well as her husband on the mission field.

In November of 1954 Susanna, now remarried and with six children, had been part of the large group who migrated from Chinese communist persecution. We renewed old acquaintance, and Robert was especially interested in fourth son, Jeremiah, because of his patient, long-suffering air and quiet, earnest ways. He looked very much like his father. Robert and Betty arranged for little Jeremiah to live with them, be a companion to Joni, and go to the Christian Day School.

Jeremiah proved to be smart and diligent and soon learned Kachin, Burmese, and English. By 1957 he was in the second grade, making good grades as well as making up for former years of privation in bodily growth. His family had migrated on westward into the jungle, about ten days away, in a no-man's land between the Naga hills and Mishmi hills of Assam. When one of his brothers made the journey to Putao to get salt and other supplies, the three years of separation from his family was too much for Jeremiah, so he went back into the jungle to be with his family.

✝

We had heard of the notorious head-hunting Naga tribes, and the fierce Mishmis. They were greatly feared by fliers crossing the "Hump" during World War II, and with good reason. They were animists, in deep bondage to Satan. They offered human heads as sacrifices as a part of their animistic rituals. A large party of Naga hunters met up with some of the Christian Lisu hunters deep in the jungle. Their languages were mutually unintelligible, so getting acquainted was slow until Jeremiah, now one of the Lisu hunters, found he could use the Kachin language he had learned in school.

The Lisu invited the Nagas to visit their settlement, which was near. The Nagas were surprised to find that in all the Lisu settlement there was no sign of demon worship or appeasement, nor any observance of taboos or use of fetishes. They wanted to know why. How could this be?

Soon Jeremiah, with his limited knowledge of Kachin but solid practical experience of Christianity, was trying to tell the Nagas about the one true God, explaining about the "Jesus Way" and its freedom from the fetishes and taboos of animism.

361

The Nagas were intensely interested and even invited the Lisu to come to their village and teach them more! Thus a friendly contact was established for the first time between Lisu and Nagas. The Nagas had never heard of God, nor of Jesus, nor of Christianity, but it was so interesting and wonderful to them that they never seemed to tire of hearing more. They kept the Lisu men up all hours of the night, asking questions, listening to explanations, wondering, and enjoying the happy hymn singing. And those Lisu can really sing!

Because there was no previous planning, we knew it was the Lord who arranged these circumstances so that the Gospel would reach the unreached, savage and aboriginal Nagas. When little Jeremiah came to live with Robert's family, we never even dreamed that he would someday follow in his father's footsteps, and become a missionary to help take the Gospel to people of a different tribe and a strange tongue. Here the witness of their own lives was of more importance, and carried a greater impact than the medium of words, to get across the message of redemption which is in Christ Jesus.

✞

About this time I began having an evening Bible study in our home. I taught those who came some of the basic doctrines of the Bible, and also some of the most often told Old Testament stories. Attendance was good, so was the attention, and everyone seemed to enjoy the classes.

✞

On September, 28, 1957 we were blessed by the arrival of a second grand-daughter. Margaret Elaine Morse was born at home, the first daughter for Eugene and Helen. This was a very special event for them in that Eugene acted as "doctor", and had the privilege of delivering his first daughter. They already had four sons, so it was a special joy for them to have a daughter at last. Margaret was a very pretty baby, with reddish-gold hair, blue eyes, and a "peaches and cream" complexion.

✞

In late October, 1957, LaVerne went on a preaching tour of about eight churches around the northern half of the Putao plain. For the end of his tour, three churches were to meet together at the village of Nam-shyeh, but no one seemed to know a direct route through the jungle, across the plain, and over several streams to the village.

After traveling and back-tracking for several hours, and seeing fresh tiger tracks on the path frequently, LaVerne, and his companions suddenly came to the end of the trail at a desolate river bank. In desperation they began wading down the river. Just as it was getting too late to go on, they came to a Hkamti Shan village.

LaVerne had never been in one of their villages before, so was both surprised and encouraged by their cordial reception and invitation to stay overnight. He asked their hosts if they would like to see some slide pictures showing the death, resurrection, and ascension of Christ. To LaVerne's surprise, the host was not only willing, but seemed glad of the opportunity, and called the entire village together to see them. Two of the three Christians with him spoke Shan and Kachin, and were able to interpret as LaVerne explained the pictures.

This was the first time the way had been open for preaching Christ in a large meeting to the Hkamti Shan tribespeople — an isolated pocket of what, a thousand years ago, was one of the powerful kingdoms of Southeast Asia. The Hkamti Shan people are closely related to the Thai people. Many of these people were opium smokers, and it was almost impossible to free them from the enslavement of addiction, except through Jesus Christ.

The next day LaVerne thanked his Shan hosts, and set out for his original destination, Nam-shyeh. He had been concerned about being a day late, but when he reached there he found he need not have worried. The Lord had provided for their need. The three congregations had gathered together as scheduled, and Preacher Daniel (who grew up in our home, and was the son of our first Lisu evangelist, Swami-pa) had arrived, unscheduled, in time to preach for the first two meetings. Truly, God directs and guides our ways beyond our knowledge and beyond our foresight, for His Gospel's sake. Surely all things do work together for good to them that love God, just as the Bible says.

☩

Visitors from abroad rarely got to visit the Putao area, so it was a very special and unusual event when we had foreign visitors at Christmas time. In November, 1957, Eugene and Helen had received a letter from Dr. Robert Drummond and his wife Dorothy, who were teaching at Mandalay University, asking if they could visit us during their Christmas holiday. When they arrived, it was a great surprise to find that they came from Helen's home town, Terre Haute, Indiana. They had a good time comparing notes, and learning of mutual acquaintances. The Drummonds went with us to the Christmas convention in Ma-muh Village, crowded into the trailer of the tractor. They and Eugene and Helen stayed in a straw-walled, straw-roofed shelter prepared by the village people out in the rice fields, amidst the temporary shelters of the Lisu people who had come to the convention. They seemed to enjoy the convention, especially the singing, with which they were very impressed. As they were leaving, they said the trip to Putao — and especially the convention — was the highlight of their time in Burma.

36
A Death in the Family

On April 14, 1958 Betty went to Rangoon, for medical care. She was expecting their fourth child in mid-May, and hadn't been very well, so it seemed she should go on ahead and try to get treatment. Robert stayed with the boys until he went to join Betty on April 28. Betty had to be in and out of the hospital several times, but on May 15, 1958 they welcomed a little daughter, Dorothy Drema, known as DeeDee, who was a very special addition to the family, after three boys. The timing of her entry into the world was not the best, though, for just two days earlier, Robert had been admitted to that same hospital for what was supposedly a "routine" hernia operation. However, the "routine" operation had complications, and Robert developed traumatic meningitis following the surgery. He was so very ill that he was unable even to see his new little daughter for several days. With both Robert and Betty in the hospital, and in a weakened condition, it was a very traumatic time, and recovery was slow. We were glad that the three boys were in Muladi with us and Eugene and Helen's family.

Robert and Betty were finally able to travel and return home June 25. We were very happy to see them safely back, and to see little Dee Dee, but we were shocked when we saw Robert. He was very thin, having lost almost fifty pounds during his illness, and very weak and nervous. His hands trembled when he tried to hold things. The doctors told him to strictly limit his activities, until he recovered his strength.

✝

May, 1958 was also a very traumatic month for Eugene and Helen, as well as for the rest of us. Their fourth son, Larry, was almost three years old and had overcome many of his physical handicaps. In answer to much prayer, he had become able to walk, and almost every morning he visited each of us who lived in the same compound, always greeting us with a sweet, sunny smile. But his little body was so frail that Eugene and Helen always felt they just had him "on loan", and that God would call him at an early age. However, he was called Home due to a cause unrelated to his physical weaknesses.

Larry had just learned to pull chairs and boxes around so he could climb on them. On the morning of May 21, 1958 he pulled a box up to where he could reach a shelf on which there was a bottle of a new, tasteless type of malaria medicine thought to be safely out of his reach. He emptied the bottle of the tiny tablets onto the bed and proceeded to eat — how many we do not know.

In just a few minutes the other children found him and immediately called Helen. Larry greeted his mother with a big smile, and seemed so pleased with what he had done. Everything possible was done to rid his stomach of the medicine, but then he began having violent convulsions and great difficulty in breathing. Helen and Eugene brought him next door to our house, and Russell did everything he knew to do to try to save him. But in spite of all our efforts, and much prayer on his behalf, Larry slipped away peacefully about 10:30 p.m., just eleven and one half hours after that awful ordeal began. Concerning Larry's "homegoing", Eugene and Helen wrote to their living link churches:

> "Our hearts throb with the loss of our sweet Larry, whom we laid to rest 'safe in the arms of Jesus' just yesterday. Our dear, dear Larry who was always such a bundle of sunshine and love has gone to be with Jesus. Now he is freed from the limitations of his frail little body. Now he is rejoicing with the angels of heaven, singing

the Redeemer's praise, more gloriously than he ever could sing "Jesus Loves Me" when he was here with us. He will be there waiting for us, beyond all the tears, fears, handicaps, and pain of this life. For him we rejoice, but Oh! what an empty place he leaves behind — a place which can't be filled by anyone else. His sweet ways, his sweet smile, his winning personality, all come rushing down the halls of memory. Everything in the house speaks to us of him — his chair at the table, his bed, his toys. He left so suddenly!"

At the funeral service the next day Pastor Stephen gave a very comforting message. Even the village school was dismissed early, and all the 200 or so children came. There must have been that many more of the village people who came also. Larry was laid to rest in a simple wooden coffin on a bluff overlooking the river, surrounded by his grandpa's fruit trees. His grave was marked with a simple wooden cross with his name, John Lawrence Morse, the date of birth and death, and the words "Safe in the arms of Jesus.".

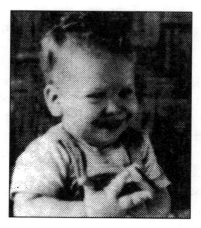

John Lawrence (Larry) Morse
June 24, 1955–May 21, 1958

37

Troubles, Travels, and New Babies

It was in 1958 that we began hearing more and more reports of the relentless persecution of Christians by the Chinese communists, especially among the Lisu in the Salween valley. Adults who were able to work were allowed only two ounces of uncooked rice in the morning and another two ounces at night. Children and those too old to work received no allowance. There was almost no other food.

About the middle of February, the Christians were forbidden to rest or gather together for worship on Sundays. Spies were sent out who reported on those who refused to obey the command. The offending leaders were severely punished. One of our beloved Lisu preachers was punished by having his ears, nose and tongue cut off. An elder was beaten before the people of his congregation until he could not stand. It was the practice to beat and torture a leader in front of his congregation as a warning. Many, many believers went through a terrible time of suffering for Christ's sake. It was reported that one of the elders was skinned alive, and others were burned alive.

Oh! how our hearts ached for them. How many Christians in the free world could withstand such trials? For many Christians in the West the biggest problem with regard to their faith sometimes seems to be deciding whether or not to go to church, because it is too hot, or too cold, or may be raining. Oh, think well, dear friend, think well! Then fall on your knees, and thank God for your freedom to worship Him without persecution.

The political situation in Southeast Asia, and particularly in Burma, was in great turmoil, and we saw anew the needs and challenges of preaching the Gospel with intensified fervor. We heard that in spite of brutal attempts of border guards to stop them, thousands of refugees were escaping out of communist China from almost all the areas bordering on Burma.

✟

We continued to carry on our mission work. Russell sometimes taught in the Bible Schools held at Muladi, but the increasing need for medical care by the 80-100 people who came daily, gradually demanded more and more of his time. Usually, Eugene, Robert, LaVerne and I taught in the Bible Schools, where attendance averaged over 200.

Besides teaching in the Bible Schools, and going on evangelistic trips to various villages, Eugene supervised the building of a new house, beginning in the fall of 1958. While Russell tried to improve the health of the local people, Eugene was always trying to find ways to improve their living conditions, experimenting, and using locally available materials. So instead of the usual bamboo structure built either up on stilts or at ground level, this one had a foundation and floor of lime concrete. The walls were made by using bamboo strips woven loosely to form lathing, and this was then covered with lime plaster on both sides. Since building materials could not be bought locally, men had to be sent into the jungles to cut and saw lumber according to the desired length and thickness. Other men went and carried the lumber down to the village on their ox-carts. The cost of buying cement in Rangoon and transporting it by plane was prohibitive, so it was necessary to make lime concrete, using local materials. The lime was burned where the stone was found, then carried to a nearby village, and from there hauled by ox-carts to Muladi. It took many lengthy conferences and much patience to complete all these arrangements. It took almost a year to complete the house, but when it was finished, it was a pattern which others could copy.

✟

On February 10, 1959 we had another example of how the Lord cares for us. John McCoy, the tractor mechanic from Rangoon was in the back yard with David when they happened to look toward laVerne and Lois' kitchen house and saw the roof ablaze! He shouted immediately and all the nearby folks, as well as the students from the middle school and the 200 or so Bible School students all came running. Some cllimbed to the roof, pulling off bundles of burning grass, while others collected all available buckets, pans, and bamboo tubes with water and passed them up to those on the roof. The kitchen house was connected to the main house by a 10-12-ft. long runway, and because it was so close, the students carried everything from the house, and had it cleared out in a matter of minutes. The flames were fierce, shooting up in the air 5-6 ft. or more as the flames got down to the bamboo roof supports. Bamboo burns very quickly, and the timbers of the main house had been treated with earth oil, so it too, would have burned quickly. There was grain stored in the main house, and if that had cought fire, it would have burned for days.

It seemed as if the fire would never stop, but actually it was out in about 20 minutes, and in another 15 minutes the students were all back in their classrooms. There was enough usable grass and bamboo from their house and from Eugene's old house to do the necessary repairs, and by 4:00 p.m. everything was fixed up, ready to resume normal living.

We were all very thankful to God for keeping the fire confined to the one small building, and preventing what could have been a real disaster.

✟

In the year of 1959 our famillies were beset with health problems. On March 5 Betty went to Rangoon, where she was hospitalized and given blood transfusions for an anemic condition. I accompanied her and her two younger children. Lois and Marcia went at the same time, as Lois was to await the

370

birth of their second child there. Robert went later and took their two older sons with him. When Betty was strong enough, they took a short trip to Hong Kong, leaving the children with us in Rangoon. Upon their return, the whole family flew to Putao on May 4.

On March 15 we received a telegram from the family in Putao, saying Russell was ill and flying to Rangoon. We took him straight from the airport to the hospital. Tests confirmed the doctor's initial diagnosis of infected gall-bladder. He was so ill that it took almost two weeks of treatment before he was strong enough to undergo surgery on April 2 for removal of his gallbladder and appendix. Afterward, he made a remarkably rapid recovery. I was so glad I was already there in Rangoon and could be with him. By mid-May Russell was almost back to normal, so he and I left Rangoon by plane on May 14.

We were not sure if we'd be able to get all the way to Muladi, because the monsoon rains had started early. We had to wait over in Myitkina for a week, until the next plane was scheduled to go to Putao. On May 22, the next scheduled flight day, an unusual thing happened. We went to the airfield, all ready to fly to Putao, but when the plane arrived from Rangoon we were told that it would not fly on to Putao that day. The plane took off on the return to Rangoon, but a few minutes later was instructed to return to Myitkyina to pick up all the passengers there and take them to Putao. We were told, "This has never happened before. In the past, when service was suspended, it really WAS suspended! It is most unusual." I guess the Lord knew how much we needed to get home, and opened the way specially so we could get there.

On March 27 (their wedding anniversary), LaVerne joined Lois in Rangoon, where their second child, first son, Mark Russell, was born on April 14th. On June 4th they left for the U.S., for a one-year furlough, traveling by way of the Holy Land and Europe, and arriving on the east coast of the United States.

On May 2, Helen, her three boys and Margaret, along with Drema Esther and Sammy, and one Lisu girl helper flew to Myikyina, where they were delayed for a week before proceeding by train to Rangoon for medical and dental care. Eugene planned to join Helen and the children around the end of May, and then be on hand for the birth of their next child. However, he was delayed longer than expected, partly due to work on their new house, but also due to the fact that early arrival of the monsoon rains caused the plane service to Putao to be discontinued. Even though Eugene had to travel overland, he arrived in Rangoon on July 1, well before the birth of their second daughter, Marilyn Louise, on July 28, 1959. Drema Esther and Sammy completed their check-ups and left Rangoon on June 2. They, too, were able to fly all the way to Putao, on an unscheduled flight, in spite of the fact that it was during the rainy season and the plane service was "officially" suspended until after the rains.

Eugene and Helen and family spent the summer in Rangoon, and when the baby, Marilyn, was about six weeks old they started out overland by train, expecting to go as far as Myitkyina. However, upon arrival in Mandalay, they learned that the train service had been interrupted by derailment of a freight train. After a delay of several days, they decided to go ahead by train, knowing they would have to walk around the accident area, and board another train for the remainder of the trip to Myitkyina. They finally reached Myitkyina, and after another week's delay there, traveled 130 miles by jeep, and the remaining 80-85 miles to Putao on foot, arriving home in late October.

We were so thankful that the fire in LaVerne and Lois' house was so rapidly put out, and that it was possible to repair the house quickly.

Eugene and Helen and Drema Esther took Russell to the airfield when he got sick, and we met him in Rangoon and took him straight to the hospital.

Page from Naga Primer

Robert worked with the Naga students to formulate a trial script for their language. Then Robert, Eugene and Helen all worked hard and fast to finish making the books for the Naga students to take with them.

Zacharias and his wife were the first Lisu to go to the Nagas as missionaries. They lived among them and learned the language.

38
Education, and Evangelism

One day in late January, 1960, from deep in the jungles about ten days' journey to the west, three young men arrived in the village of Muladi. One of them was Jeremiah, son of the Lisu preacher Paul who gave his life in the Lord's service. Jeremiah had come to continue his schooling begun when he was staying with Robert and Betty. This time he brought with him two boys from the Naga tribe who also wished to attend school.

Jeremiah told us how he and several others had gone to a Naga village the year before, telling them about the "Jesus Way", and using phonograph records with Gospel messages in Kachin. The people became so interested that the chieftains of fourteen villages wrote a joint petition, signed with all their thumb prints, begging us to send a full-time preacher into their area. The two Naga boys, acting as their representatives, now presented the petition to us.

One Lisu preacher, Zacharias, the missionary preacher sent by the Muladi church to the Lisu Christian refugees from China, had been serving the Lisu congregations nearest the Naga area, and in response to this request, he and his family moved to a Naga village. Using an interpreter, he began preaching the Gospel to them. Surely our Lord works in mysterious and wondrous ways.

After talking with the two Naga boys, Robert learned that they had no written script for their particular dialect. Therefore, it seemed wise to try to reduce their language to writing.

Since the boys were to enter school, beginning in March, Robert felt there would be plenty of time to work on this project, with no need to rush. However, in April, after only three or four weeks of school, the boys decided they were too homesick to stay any longer. After considerable persuasion, they agreed to stay another two or three weeks, but no longer.

They stopped school at Muladi and went to Dukdang where Robert and family lived, so Robert could work more closely with them. After working with scarcely a break from early morning until late at night for two weeks, Robert had worked out an alphabet and, with their assistance, was able to prepare a simple primer containing the plan of salvation and four hymns.

Working at top speed, stencils were prepared, the material was mimeographed by Eugene and Helen, and the books were assembled and ready for the boys to take with them on May 6th, even though it meant working until 2:00 a.m. that morning to finish the work of collating and stapling.

✝

It was in 1951 that the first Lisu Christian Day School was opened in Muladi, under the supervision of the church elders, with a board of directors drawn from parents of attending children. That first year there were about 20 students and just one teacher, a local Christian young man who had studied in Myitkyina. By the second year there were 60 students and two teachers. Then, in order to provide for further progress and expansion, the mission assumed the financial support of the school. As a mission school there could be greater emphasis on the Bible and Christian training. Additional students and teachers could also be added year by year. Gradually the program was expanded, and Christian Day Schools were started in a number of Lisu and Rawang villages.

In June, 1957 the Putao Christian Day School, from kindergarten to fourth grade, was opened at Dukdang. This was something that would not have been possible a few years earlier. Until an addition could be built to the Dukdang school building, the fifth and sixth grades were taught at Muladi, in a new building which Eugene had designed in a new style, using different locally available materials. LaVerne was the supervisor, and he taught an hour each of Bible and English at Dukdang, and I taught the same at Muladi. Regular school subjects were also taught: reading, writing, arithmetic, history, geography, and five languages (Lisu, Rawang, Kachin, Burmese, and English). The Putao Christian School was the first of many such schools, and was the largest, serving the people of some twenty congregations. The school curriculum was compatible with that of the government schools, so the students could continue their education as they had opportunity.

Thirteen days walk away, the Rawangtang Christian School was opened. It served over fifteen congregations, and had an attendance of over one hundred fifty. Several other new schools were started later in other sectors of the field. The problem was to get Christian teachers. There was a Baptist Mission high school at Myitkyina, and we sent as many of our qualified Christian young people as we could for training there. But the needs always exceeded our ability to meet them.

Because of the previous lack of opportunities for education, many of the students in the higher grades of the Putao Christian Day School (as well as all the other newly opened Christian schools) were between sixteen and twenty-four years old. They often went out on week-end evangelistic trips, especially among the Shan and Kachin groups. Although the Lisu and Rawang had been evangelized extensively, there had been difficulty in reaching the Shan and Kachin because of the language barrier. The school was of infinite value in language training in Kachin and Burmese. It was possible to reach out to the Shans through these languages as well as their own.

Then in 1960 the Buddhist-dominated Burmese government changed the religious freedom clause of the Burmese constitution and made Buddhism the State religion. All students who took teacher's training were required to study Buddhism, and all government-supported schools were required to teach it. In one totally Christian Rawang village, when their village-operated school was turned over to the government aid program, a Buddhist school teacher was sent to replace the former Christian headmaster. The school refused government aid, and the Buddhist teacher left.

By not accepting government "aid", the Christian Day Schools still had the right to follow a Christian, Bible-based curriculum. By that time we had about thirteen Christian primary schools among the Lisu and Rawang churches. Most of them had been started and maintained by the Christians themselves, without government aid. So the North Burma Christian Mission schools refrained from asking for any government aid from then on. LaVerne worked hard to help the day schools get their proper books. While LaVerne was away on furlough, Robert served as supervisor, and taught in the Putao Christian Day School, which had about one hundred seventy students.

✝

During the winter and spring I had been visiting a number of churches in the Putao plains area, for this is the time when most people are not busy in their fields. My visit to Nam-hte-ku, about twelve miles from Muladi was typical. Imagine you are coming with me on this trip. First, we must get together a few necessary things such as a bed roll, and a ground sheet on which to place our bedding to protect it from the usual dirty bamboo or rattan bed, or else the floor. Then there must be extra clothes and shoes, medicines, a lantern, kerosene, enamel bowls, cups, spoons, salt, sugar, canned milk, coffee or tea, water canteen, tea kettle for boiling the drinking water, wash pan, umbrella, load covers for rainy weather, Bible — both English and Lisu, and any teaching charts. These must all be carefully packed into bamboo or rattan baskets to be carried by the Christians from Nam-hte-ku who were sent by the church leaders to carry our loads and act as our guides so we won't get on the wrong path. A young Rawang girl will accompany us and help fix our food.

The first part of the journey is along the ox-cart road across the Putao plain, then we turn off onto just a narrow trail. Sometimes there are logs put across the streams to serve as bridges, but sometimes we must wade. Soon after leaving the plain, the road leads down into a small valley. The road is very slippery because of a recent rain, but a friendly school boy going after wood offers a helping hand as we wade across the bridgeless stream. About noon we start to climb the steep mountain. The path winds back and forth across the face of the mountain. After about twenty minutes of steep climbing, we enter a forest. The trees are quite large and dense and block out the sunlight. After we have climbed some distance, it starts to rain. We must see that our plastic rain covers are put over the loads. The sound of the heavy tropical downpour is so loud that it is hard to talk. We must step carefully or we may slip, for the clay mud is very slippery.

See that large blood spot on your sock? It is where a leech sucked your blood until it was full and then dropped off. But your blood continues to ooze out until your sock is soaked. We must try to get the leeches off before they bite, if possible, for they make an irritating sore.

After about two hours of climbing, we get to the top of the mountain and can see many villages in the valleys far off in the distance. Away to the right is where Muladi is located. It is raining hard in that direction. Beyond the place where we are going is a very high, jungle-covered range of mountains. If we were to cross them, we would find ourselves in India.

As we descend the steep mountain through the over-hanging trees, it starts to rain hard again. There are many leeches clinging to the grass, so be careful! For another hour of walking, our path winds through the rice fields belonging to the Christians. When they see us, they stop their work and come over to shake hands and welcome us to their village. As we go across the last bridge, a crowd is waiting to shake our hands and lead us to the place which has been arranged for us to stay. It makes our hearts glad to see how happy people are to see us.

Are you tired? I am. Climbing the notched log which serves as a ladder, we enter our room, and are glad to sit down and rest a bit. Our host has a fire waiting for us, and a teakettle of water is soon hot. Our helper brings us some hot water with which we can wash our aching feet. After changing our wet shoes and drinking a cup of tea, we feel much rested. We are not allowed to rest for long, though. The preacher of the church has come to greet us and to talk about the services we are to hold. Also he tells us of problems in the church. Then some very sick people come for medicine, and others come to greet us. By that time our evening meal of rice and greens, and possibly some scrambled eggs, is ready. Fortunately we brought some cookies from home, and one of those is good for dessert.

It is getting dark, and as we are lighting our kerosene lantern we hear the gong being beaten to announce that it is time for church. About 200 Christians gather for the evening service. Their interest, and their gratitude for our coming warms our hearts. Plans are made for a full day of Bible study, classes and sermons on the following two days.

At the close of our visit we must once more pack up our things, bid farewell to our Lisu brethren, and set off to again climb the mountain and descend to the other side, and go on to visit some other churches before returning home. This is the way our lives go. We cannot follow a strict schedule, but try to meet the needs of the people as they arise.

✟

LaVerne and Lois returned from furlough in June, 1960. They flew directly from the U.S., with no stopover in Rangoon, and arrived in Muladi on June 6, 1960. During their year in the U.S. LaVerne had completed his year of graduate work and received his Masters degree from Cincinnati Bible

380

Seminary. Their third child, second daughter Cynthia Marie, was born at home in Muladi on October 2, 1960.

In August, 1960 Eugene and his family, and Russell and I left Muladi for a furlough in the U.S. Russell and I had a leisurely trip, visiting all along the way with dear friends and acquaintances. We finally arrived in California in October, and were met by Ruth Margaret and her four children. We spent several days with them, getting acquainted with her husband and our grandchildren, whom we had not met.

Eugene and Helen took a more direct route, because they needed to get settled before time for the boys to start school. They stopped in California only long enough to visit with Eugene's living link church, then went on to Tulsa, OK, where they visited some of the Morse relatives. Helen's parents met them there, and together they drove to Terre Haute, IN, where they spent the next several months, near Helen's parents, and her living link church. The three boys were able to start in school right away, and Eugene had the opportunity to visit and speak in quite a number of churches. Their third daughter, Frances Jeannette, was born on January 18, 1961.

While in the U.S., Eugene and Helen received many letters from Lisu and Rawang Christians, which kept on their hearts the urgency of getting back to Burma. One young man wrote, "When you are away, we are like children without their parents". A girl who had worked for them wrote, "Do come back quickly. Every time I see your house my tears come out." Another letter said, "Please hurry back. I am thirsty to see you, more than being thirsty for water when traveling in the hot sun." Such letters pulled at their heartstrings, and made them anxious to get back "home." In June, 1961, as soon as school was out, they started for California and final visits with supporting churches there.

39
Trials and Testings

It seemed that the year 1961 was to be a time of testing and trying for the missionaries at home and on the field. Not only those in Burma, but other fields also reported the many ways in which Satan was making it so difficult to carry on the Lord's work.

In February, 1961 Robert went to Rangoon with Betty, who was seriously ill, while Drema Esther stayed with their children in Dukdang Village, but made numerous trips back and forth to Muladi, to look after things at our house there. LaVerne had to go to Rangoon on pressing business, leaving Lois at Muladi. Spending the week days at Dukdang caring for Robert's boys, and weekends at Muladi taking care of mission work, plus other trips in between times took its toll on Esther. Early in March she suffered a complete breakdown and was unable to sleep. Excruciating pain from a carbuncle on her chin seemed to be the "straw that broke the camel's back", contributing to her sleeplessness. Lois cared for her and prayed for her, and finally she began to improve.

A strong testimony of complete dependence on prayer and how wonderfully the Lord answered is shown in the following quote from Lois's letter during Drema Esther's critical illness. Esther's condition was really very serious, and not responding to medicine as they hoped. Lois wrote of her vigil by Esther's bedside:

'...Minutes ticked slowly, slowly by. How I watched and prayed till 2:00 a.m. and pleaded with the Lord to give Esther the precious *gift of eight hours of sleep. Every time she stirred...I prayed the more fervently that the Lord would have mercy and keep her in a deep sleep. During those lonely hours, I felt the pulling hands of the rest of the family back home. I was positive they had gotten my cable and were praying even then, as I was. (How we were all praying!!) The Lord heard our united prayers and gave Esther not just eight but ten hours of sleep.'*

As soon as Robert and Betty returned, and Esther was able to travel, Lois, Marcia, Esther and Sammy went to Rangoon for medical treatment and rest. The day after their arrival, April 18th, when Lois was on her way to the hospital for minor surgery, she tripped and fell, breaking her arm at the elbow. Yet, even in the midst of these trials, they knew God was with them, as they experienced His answers to their prayers. As soon as we and Eugene and Helen heard about Esther's sickness and Lois's injury, we prayed, and also asked for special prayer in the churches where we visited.

LaVerne had returned from Rangoon to Muladi in March, when Esther was beginning to recover from her illness. He remained in Muladi when Lois, Marcia, Esther, and Sammy went to Rangoon. When he heard about Lois's accident he left little Cynthia with Robert and Betty, and, with son Mark, flew to Rangoon to be with her. He wrote of how God wonderfully answered prayer when her pain was most severe.

'On Saturday before the Monday I was to go to Rangoon, I went to the village of Sarkhumdam, about twelve miles from Muladi, to speak at the Rawang Easter Convention which was being held there. When I reached Dukdang, a telegram was handed to me which said that on Tuesday — the day after she went to Rangoon — Lois had broken her arm at the elbow! At the convention, I asked the 1,500 people who had gathered there, to pray especially for Lois. On Sunday morning, and again at about 2:00 p.m., the Christians at the convention had special prayer for her. When Mark and I reached Rangoon, we were met by Drema Esther, who told us that Lois had gone to the hospital for minor surgery. Hospital visiting hours prevented me from seeing her until the next morning. Then she told me how very, very much her

383

broken arm had pained her. Not only had the bone been broken at the elbow, but evidently a nerve had also been hurt, so that there was intense pain from Tuesday until Sunday. On Sunday morning, however, the pain had eased, and on Sunday afternoon the pain had gone away almost completely. I asked about what time Sunday afternoon the pain had specially eased. She said about 2:00 p.m. That was just the time when up at the Sarhkumdam convention, about 1,500 people had had special prayer for Lois. We truly thank God for His answering prayer.'

Then on April 28, 1961 LaVerne received unofficial word that their residence permits would not be renewed, and they were ordered to leave the country by April 30th. However, the OFFICIAL notification was not received until May 10th! Because of "extenuating circumstances" they were allowed a temporary extension, which gave them an opportunity to appeal the decision, and to return to Muladi to do necessary packing, and also to get their youngest child, who had been left with Betty and Robert.

When we learned of Betty's and Esther's illness, and Lois's injury, plus all the other problems those on the field were having, we decided to cut short our furlough. When we arrived in Rangoon in late June, we heard about LaVerne and Lois's visa problems. LaVerne was due to arrive in Rangoon on July 4th, so we waited there for him. The day after he arrived, he and Russell went to a conference of three Kachin State officials, who spoke encouragingly to them.

Many, many Lisu and Rawang friends sent petitions to the government. First, twenty-six headmen sent in one with all of their signatures. This was followed by a petition from one hundred thirty leaders, and another signed by 2400 people. Also several telegrams were sent. Finally, the churches gathered money to send five headmen to Myitkyina to petition the Kachin cabinet. Two of them went on to Rangoon.

On the following day Russell and LaVerne had an interview with a high-ranking military officer. He had just talked to the top Immigration Officer, who promised to give the permits, since the Kachin State officials, the military officials of our border area, and the people all wanted him. About mid-July Lois wrote to her parents, " It seems that we definitely will be permitted to remain in the country at least one more year." We surely praised God, and thanked all of our friends for their help and their prayers.

✞

By mid-July Russell and I felt relieved and free to take the plane to Putao, our mission home seven hundred miles north of Rangoon in Kachin State. We finally arrived at the Putao airport about 2:00 p.m. on July 17, 1961. Robert, Esther and the children, together with about six hundred Lisu and Rawang Christians were there to meet us. While Russell and I were shaking hands with the long line, two or three deep, the young people were singing hymns. It brought tears to our eyes. Esther said the pilot and crew were amazed, and didn't know what to think of such a reception for two old people!

The second evening home the Muladi church prepared a wonderful feast for Russell and me. It was so nice to see all of our old friends. We spoke a little at that time and then on the first Sunday both Russell and I spoke at the morning service to a crowd of about six hundred. At the close of the service, at the suggestion of one of the elders, the whole congregation stood and prayed, giving thanks for answered prayer for LaVerne's permit and for our safe return.

Eugene and Helen and family returned from furlough in August, 1961. In Hong Kong they met Robert and Betty and family, who were en route to the U.S. on furlough. There they had an opportunity to discuss needs and news of Burma. When Eugene and family arrived at Putao airfield with their six children on September 7, 1961 they, too, were welcomed by a group of several hundred people, including students from the Bible School and the Christian Day School. LaVerne met them with the tractor, so they had a nice leisurely, bumpy ride the seven miles from the airfield to Muladi.

40
A Dangerous Trip

From all directions, congregations were begging for Bible Schools for the different groups in their churches. There seemed to be a kind of desperation in the requests as if they sensed, as we did, that our time of being with them would soon be coming to an end, and they wanted to learn all they possibly could about the Bible while we were still there to teach them.

In November, 1961, a very urgent request came from some of the Christians living in the Nogmung area of North Burma. They wanted a member of our missionary family to come to their area to hold a Bible school. Eugene and I had held a school there about ten years before, while Russell was in the communist prison, but none of us had been back to that area since then, due to government restrictions. However, their preachers, elders, and other students had been attending our once-a-year Bible Schools. Although our family had been feeling a burden for that area even before the call came, we had been so busy with all of our other calls we had been unable to visit there.

For us to travel there, it was necessary to get a special permit from a high-ranking military officer usually stationed in Rangoon who occasionally visited Putao area. It was in God's plan that he should be in the area at that time, and thus we were able to get the needed permit.

The Nogmung area was a little beyond the fourteen mile limit to which we were restricted and our Muladi elders felt it would be unwise for any of the men of our families to go. However, they felt it would be safe for a woman to travel a short distance beyond the limits, so the decision was made that I should go. Just as I had felt the burden to teach those women in the thirty-five villages, I knew I *MUST* go to the Nogmung area. I was determined to make the trip, even though it might mean a life or death situation. I was sure God would help me through.

The military officer readily gave his permission, but did request that the military post be notified when my companions and I were ready to leave. Accompanying me was a young woman helper, together with Rawang preacher Peter, who spoke the language of that district, and the necessary carriers. The family escorted me and my girl companion in our little jeep across the Putao plain to notify the officer in charge of the military post, then our little group started out, walking, on our trek across the mountains.

We stayed the first night in the home of one of our elders, in the last village before starting up the mountain. After a long, hard climb the next day we finally reached the giant trees at the top of the mountain. On the third day we found the descent almost as difficult as the climb up, because the paths had not been cleared since the earthquake of 1950. But we did reach a rest house by evening.

Arriving at our destination fairly early on the fourth day, we were happy to find the customary long line of Christians waiting to shake our hands and welcome us. The pastor of the village church had arranged for us to stay at his house and had prepared two small bedrooms and a small kitchen for our use.

✝

About eighty church leaders arrived for the Bible School, which they were so very pleased to have in their area. Preacher Peter now helped with enrolling the students and in teaching half of the classes while I taught the rest. Peter had worked with Robert in the translation of the Rawang New Testament and was a fine teacher, one on whom I could depend.

Christmas convention time arrived when we were about half-way through our course. The Northern Baptists had some churches in that part of Burma and they sent an urgent invitation for me to come and speak at their Christmas program in a village four or five miles away. I felt that I should not take time out from our school, but the elders urged me to accept the invitation. I finally decided to accept after it was determined that we could walk to the village after our school closed in the afternoon and return by lantern light after the program was over. In that way, we would not have to miss any teaching.

Some of our students and my girl companion went with me. A very good friend of ours, a retired magistrate of that area, was an excellent interpreter for my talk. After some Christmas songs, they introduced me to speak. Following that the church presented a very good dramatization of the "Birth of Christ". The convention was attended by almost fifteen hundred people.

✝

On the way back we became aware of several soldiers who were following us some distance behind. Since we had always been treated with courtesy by any soldiers we had met, we thought nothing of it until they, too, turned into the yard of the home where we were staying. I was very tired after teaching, walking so many miles, then speaking, so I quickly retired.

I later learned that the soldiers stayed there the rest of the night and also that the preachers — Rawang preacher Peter and our host — had become suspicious and secretly called a number of the Christian men of that village together. They came and sat around the fire the rest of the night, in case some trouble developed with the soldiers. From hearing snatches of the soldiers' conversation, Peter felt sure it was their intention to arrest me early in the morning.

The preacher's wife tried to awaken me to take me to another place where I would be safe, but I was too fatigued to move and continued to sleep. About dawn she came again and shook me to awaken me.

"Mama, mama!" she whispered urgently. "You must get up and leave here at once. The soldiers stayed here all night, and we are afraid they will arrest you if you are still here when it gets light."

This time I accepted the warning, and after slipping quietly out of the back door, went with a guide to another house on the other side of the village.

Later that morning I received a message from the magistrate at the county seat, saying for me not to be afraid, but to come with the elders and some of the preacher students, and he and his wife would meet me half-way. They escorted me to their home near the military post in that area. I enjoyed a good rest that day waiting for the civil and military officials to take care of the situation. It seemed that the Putao military post had failed to inform the Nogmung military post of my permit to travel in that district. The officials were very embarrassed, and the soldiers, only recently arrived from Lower Burma, were transferred out of that area. We accepted the apologies of the friendly magistrate and said nothing, but we thanked God with all of our hearts for caring for us in what could have been a potentially serious and dangerous situation. I was glad I got to make that trip, but was very happy to arrive home again with no further trouble.

41
Unexpected Events

In February, 1962 Helen had to go to Rangoon for medical check-up and minor surgery. Of course, like everyone who made a trip to Rangoon for any reason, she had a long shopping list for all the mission members, with everything from medicines to bicycle parts to groceries to tractor parts. She was still in Rangoon when on March 2, 1962, Gen. Ne Win took over the Government of Burma in a "bloodless coup." Helen returned home a few days later, without incident.

For several months everything seemed to go along as usual, but gradually we began to hear of foreign businesses being closed down and their assets confiscated. There were reports, too, of foreign residents being ordered to leave without being allowed to take any of their belongings, and their valuables being confiscated. And little by little we began to feel the "pinch," as staple foodstuffs, such as salt, sugar, and oil began to be rationed, and there was more of a military presence in Putao. Those were also the days when resistance forces began to be formed in various parts of the country. Gradually we realized that the "Burmese Way to Socialism Program," which Gen. Ne Win was promoting, was really the way toward a communist-type government.

✞

When Isabel Dittemore left Burma in 1950, she had been unable to obtain permission to return to the mission field in Burma, so had been working near Osaka, Japan. Now, in July,

1962, she and her daughter were visiting Burma as tourists, and it was little short of a miracle that they were allowed to visit us at Muladi. We were so sure they would not be allowed to come to Putao, where we lived, that we had not even encouraged her in her efforts to secure a transit visa. Oh, we of little faith! But here they were, for three wonderful days of fellowship with all of us and hundreds of Christians whom Isabel had known in China and Burma. Some of them had fled from China into Burma along with the missionary group in 1949.

They were greeted at the Putao airport by Eugene, Jesse Chu (whom Isabel called "my son in the Lord"), and Daniel (son of Swami-pa), who had been her interpreter and friend in China. Climbing aboard the red jeep, they drove through Dukdang, then on to Muladi, where we gave them a royal welcome. As Eugene drove through town he told different ones to spread the news, then once he arrived home, he called out over the loud-speaker to tell the people across the river that Teacher Isabel had come. Isabel remarked, "This is such a thrill — like going to heaven early!"

The next day the church folks gave a big feast in their honor. Jesse and Daniel traveled all night just to find a Lisu outfit for Janet, and her old nurse, Amo, gave Janet her own beaded head-dress. But all too soon the visit ended, and they had to leave. Isabel expressed unlimited gratitude to God for allowing "this journey into Paradise."

☩

While Robert, Betty and family were in the States, both Robert and Betty attended Indiana University, in Bloomington, where Robert received his M.A. degree in linguistics on June 4, 1962. They arrived back on the mission field on August 13th, 1962.

Even while on furlough in 1962, Betty had been having trouble with what was finally diagnosed as gall-bladder trouble. She was told that sooner or later she would need surgery. After returning to Burma, she had increasingly frequent attacks, and suffered excruciating pain, until finally in January, 1963 she decided the time had come to do something about the problem.

In Rangoon, after examination and tests, she was admitted to the Seventh Day Adventist Hospital, where she underwent gall-bladder surgery. The doctor said it was no wonder she was having pain, because she had FORTY-TWO gall-stones! While the family was in Rangoon, and Betty was recuperating, both Stevie and Bobby had their tonsils out.

While Robert and Betty were in Rangoon, Helen was also there, to get treatment for her back trouble, and to get dental care for Tommy and Ronnie. While the others were there, Lois also had to make the trip to Rangoon for dental care. It was while all of them were there in Rangoon that the four of them were invited one evening to the home of some Indian friends. The man was quite a wit, and loved jokes. They also had some other guests that evening, and when our folks arrived, he very solemnly introduced them as Mrs. Morse, Mrs. Morse, Mrs. Morse and Mr. Morse. The other guests looked a bit startled, until the host explained that only Betty was Robert's wife, and the other two were sisters-in-law. After that they all had a good laugh.

☥

In February, 1963, following an extended trip among the various churches, LaVerne became quite ill. From his symptoms, we thought he might even have suffered a heart attack. In any case, he needed to go to Rangoon for check-up and treatment. Since Lois was pregnant and not able to travel at that time, we decided I should accompany him. In Rangoon, the doctors diagnosed his problem as bronchiectasis and high blood pressure, gave him some medication, and advised him to get more rest.

Whenever any of the missionaries went to Rangoon they always had long lists of supplies to buy for different families, but they also tried to take advantage of the time for getting needed printing done. It seemed some literature was always in short supply — Lisu or Rawang Bibles, primers, or hymnals, etc. On this trip LaVerne worked on proof-reading and correcting the Rawang Literacy Primer: Book II, as well as on the Life of Christ Visualized Books I and II in both Lisu and Rawang. The printers did not know any of the languages in which the various books were printed, so it was necessary to work very closely with them. Special type had to be cast for use with the Lisu or Rawang alphabets. And proof-reading had to be done very carefully to catch all the mistakes. We returned to Putao on March 18.

☥

About the last week in March, 1963 I started teaching Bible five to six hours a day to a class of fifteen Christian Naga boys who had traveled more than two weeks from their home near the Burma-India border, just to come study the Bible. We felt that we should give them all the Bible teaching we could. I taught in Lisu, which had to be translated into Kachin, so they could understand. I taught the life of Christ, from the four Gospels. It was a wonderful study, and the Lord blessed us. At the end of the "school" in mid-May, the boys returned to their homes in Nagaland. They had to travel for two weeks, westward to Pangsao, on the old Ledo Road, near the border of India. Lisu and Rawang missionaries had gone to teach among the Naga people several years earlier, and now the churches there had sent some of their prospective future leaders to study. We praised God that His Word was reaching even this hard-to-reach area.

Russell and I went to the airfield with Isabel Dittemore.

Some of the elders spent a whole night going from place to place to find all the parts for Janet Dittemore's Lisu outfit. Her old nurse, A-mo, even gave her own head-dress.

A group of Naga boys traveled almost a month from their homes in order to study the Bible. I taught them every day for about six weeks.

Drema Esther was married to Jesse Yangmi on April 15, 1962. Lois was matron of honor, David was best man; ring-bearers were Robert's son Stephen (L) and Drema Esther's adopted son Sammy (R); Robert's daughter Dede (L) and Eugene's daughter Margaret (R), were flower girls.

Daphne and Pesi Virjee, our dear friends from Rangoon who came specially for Drema Esther's wedding.

It was good to have all three sons working together with us. Eugene, Robert, and LaVerne all shared in the problems and helped bear the load of the mission work. ALL were under a lot of strain.

42
A Wedding Celebration

April 15, 1963 dawned bright and clear, a beautiful day for a wedding. And the one taking place that day was one that everyone in the village was going to attend. After all, it wasn't every day that one of the missionaries got married, but that day it was "Mama" (Lady Teacher) Esther. Yes, Drema Esther, our foster daughter, was being married to Jesse G. Yangmi, at 1:30 p.m. in the Muladi Church of Christ.

All morning everyone was busy with last minute preparations, even Mr. and Mrs. Virjee, our guests from Rangoon. Mrs. Virjee helped with arranging the flowers for the church, and made up the bouquets for the bride and matron of honor. Since the officials in Putao had been invited, Mr. Virjee took the jeep over to get any of them who could come. One group of village young people was busy decorating the church. Another group was finishing decoration of the shelter where the wedding dinner was to be served, while a third large group worked on preparing the meal itself.

By 1:00 p.m., there were around 1000 people gathered in the church for the occasion, including official guests from Putao, as well as a number of high-ranking military officials from the Army Headquarters at Muchambaw, about fifteen miles from Muladi. The ceremony, a combination of western and Lisu styles, began with congregational singing of the customary Lisu wedding hymns. This was followed by a solo, "Always", by Betty, singing first in Lisu, then in Englsh. So far as we know, that was the first time a love song had been sung at a wedding in Lisuland. In keeping with Lisu custom, Robert preached a wedding sermon. This was followed by recorded music, including songs by Helen, and the wedding march.

Esther, looking lovely in her white dress and short veil trimmed with baby rosebuds, was escorted down the aisle by her eldest brother, Eugene. Lois was matron of honor, and Sammy, Esther's adopted son, was a proud ringbearer, along with Stephen, second son of Robert and Betty. Margaret Elaine and Dorothy Drema, daughters of Eugene and Robert respectively, were the flower girls. David, the eldest son of Eugene and Helen, was best man. Robert conducted the double-ring ceremony according to American custom.

Following the ceremony, a wedding dinner of Chinese-style food was served to relatives and invited guests, while the 1000-plus guests from the villages were served leaf-wrapped packages of rice and meat, according to Lisu custom. Yes, that day, from before dawn to past midnight, was a hectic and memorable day for not only Jesse and Drema, but for all of us and for the entire village. After a brief honeymoon, the couple returned to Muladi — Jesse to complete his education, and Esther to continue her work with the mission.

✝

Visitors from "outside" were few and far between, and having Pesi and Daphne Virjee with us for the wedding was a special treat. The Virjees, though citizens of India, had for many years been residents of Rangoon, where Pesi was a well-known business man, the manager of an old English firm. Whenever any of the Morses were in Rangoon, the Virjees had been most kind, and helpful in countless ways. We prized their friendship, which they had proven on numerous occasions when true friends were needed. After the Virjees returned to Rangoon, they wrote to Russell's sister, Louise, in the U.S., describing their visit. I quote:

"There is a Burmese festival which comes around more or less

the same time of year as Easter. This year the two holidays ran concurrently, and so we had almost a whole week at our disposal. We took advantage of this, left the children in the care of Daphne's mother while both of us flew to Putao to spend the week with the Morses. As it turned out, at the end of the week the weather turned in our favour. A heavy storm developed, the clouds stayed low, and it rained so that the plane due in from Myitkyina could not come in on that scheduled flight. So we were, to all intents and purposes, 'marooned' in Muladi for a further four days.

"What a wonderful experience this holiday has been for Daph and myself. We spent the first afternoon and the night at Dukdang with Robert and Betty. They have such a lovely, quaint home. It is large and roomy, but built in keeping with the rest of the Rawang homes in the village. Betty's bedroom is probably the most lavish room in the whole valley. She is justly proud of it, and imagine the VIP treatment we got when they insisted we use that room while Robert and Betty camped on the sitting room rug!

"They have a delightful little woods just behind the house. Robert has built a tree house overlooking another valley, with a magnificent view of the snow-covered mountains in the west. What a glorious setting. That first evening the weather cleared to reveal those high mountains, their massive crags and snowy tops. I was thrilled when Robert explained that those mountains were actually Indian territory. He pointed out one of the crags on which he had been a couple of years before, and from where at night he could see in the eastern valley the lights of Putao (Burma), while from the same spot, in the west, he could see the lights of Ledo (in Assam, India), made famous by Gen. Stilwell during the last war (W.W. II). To me the sight of territory that was part of my home country was particularly thrilling, as recently when I wanted to go to India to be with my people for my sister's wedding, the Immigration Department refused to grant me a re-entry visa if I did leave the country. Ever since, we have felt like prisoners, knowing that we can no longer go and come as we please. It is galling and alarming!

However, to continue with our holiday, the next thrill came when I strolled out at dawn and discovered the pug marks of either a small tiger or a leopard. Each imprint was about 3½ inches across, and 4 inches long. The largest dog in the area is Bullet, Betty's Alsatian, and his paw prints didn't measure half that size.

Later in the morning, Eugene brought in the jeep from Muladi, and the whole lot of us trooped into it (it may sound unbelievable but we were often a round dozen in that jeep!), and off we went for a three or four mile jaunt. When we arrived at the top of the ridge overlooking Muladi, we stopped for a panoramic view of the village. It is difficult to describe, and no photograph seems to do it justice, but on that particular morning it was like a picture book version of a beautiful village. I believe Eugene has had a great deal to do with the original planning, the orderliness, and the layout. It would do credit to any Civil Engineer. I am sure many an Executive Engineer in this country wishes he could wear the honour of having "engineered" Muladi. Almost all the high-ranking civil and military dignitaries have, at some time or other, visited the village and have referred to it time and again as a pattern for imitation.

To attempt to describe the work done in the village for the uplift, the hygiene and the well-being of the community would require a great deal of space. I will not attempt it here, yet I cannot pass over it without specific mention of Eugene's achievements in getting water from a mountain stream across the river, and through an irrigation canal almost a mile long, into the village itself. Not only into the village, but through it, and out into the fields, where it will benefit around 300 acres of land. The bridge itself, a span of more than 400 feet, over the Muladi river, is an engineering feat on its own. It supports a pair of large pipes which in turn carry, by gravity flow, the water from a waterfall on the other side of the river to the canal on the Muladi side. The bridge is almost 100 ft. above the river.

Back to that panoramic view of Muladi from the ridge. The jeep was put into the four-wheel drive, and down we went along a slippery, slimy cow-path cork-screwing down to the village. Then a drive along the village main street, which in comparison was like Park Avenue, right up to the Morse residence.

The "residence" is a hive of activity. At the very entrance is a barn-like building housing the generator, the workshop, and the *engineering stores, including POL (petrol, oils, and lubrications), of which a year's supply must be bought at one time during the winter dry season. Going around it to the parking lot, you see tractors and trailers coming in or going out or under repair. This certainly is the community workshop, with David very much in command. And then, suddenly the two big houses hit you with quite an impact — Eugene's house, in which we all lived, and Mum and Dad's (Gertrude and Russell's), which is nearing completion. Eugene and Helen's house is, to all intents and purposes a community hall, a dormitory, restaurant, clinic, motel, granary, grocery and kitchen, concert hall, dog pound, nursery, chicken farm, lumber yard, library, and training ground for all and sundry, from helpers to preachers. There isn't a dull moment in that wonderful home. What wonderful fellowship, friendship and love emanate from it and touch the lives of hundreds of people who come for help and advice in the various fields of life. We were part of that household for eleven wonderful days of experiences. There were so many that at times Daph and I had to separate so as to cover as many activities as possible.*

Morning breakfast was a wonderful way of starting the day. This meal we shared with Daddy and Mother Morse, and with Esther and Ahpu (Sammy). The meal was always well done, with Esther and Mother attending to every detail, but above all, morning devotions from Daddy Morse seemed to set the pattern of the day. Just about that time, the sun would shine and a shaft of light would brighten his head and shoulders. It always worried him, but I sat opposite him at the table and never stopped admiring his countenance in that light. For that moment he looked — and behaved — every bit the patriarch of Muladi. During the meal we would draw out from Mother and Dad stories of their experiences in China, the Salween Valley, Tibet, and the war years. By the time the meal was over we would have most of the other children in the room, along with Lois and Helen.

The signal for the end of that part of the day always came with Mother leaving in a hurry to start her class for the day. What steadfast work she does with a group of 15 Naga tribal boys, putting in a full day's schedule of five to six hours of solid work with them each day. One morning we spent a while with them,

400

then went on to another class room across the road where LaVerne
was teaching typing to a group of 26 preachers and laymen. What
an earnest, industrious lot they were. What a fine job they were
doing.

Daddy Morse was always busy in the mornings attending to
the clinical needs of the village folk, some of whom came from distant villages three or four days journey from Muladi. I would
hang around until the last of these was attended to, and then without too much coaxing draw him away to the fruit trees and get
him to talk about his citrus "industry". I was interested, as maybe
when we leave this country in the very near future I will go back
home to Panchgani in India where our family owns some land,
and start a citrus orchard as Mr. Morse has done, and maybe in
another eight or ten years our village will reap as much benefit as
the various villages in and around the Putao sub-division have
gained from Dad's trees. Some believe that there might be as many
as 40-50,000 citrus trees in the Putao area having their origin
from Dad's trees. He himself is very modest about it all, but under
conditions as they exist in those remote and primitive areas, the
achievement is colossal.

More often than not, lunch was with Lois and the children.
Lois and LaVerne have the neatest little cottage I have seen anywhere. Its walls and floors are of timber boards and the roof is
thatch. The lovely petunias LaVerne grows in his window boxes
scintillate like jewels in some ancient setting. And as for Lois's
cooking! I am sure she gets the laurels of the village, nay, the plain
of Putao. We were privileged to spend several lovely evenings with
Lois, LaVerne, and the children.

But the most impressive part of our visit to Muladi was the
wonderful faith and fellowship that we noticed throughout this
Lisu village. Several mornings, as I strolled through the village at
dawn I was thrilled at the tunes the people were singing or
whistling while at work herding cattle or driving their carts. And,
almost without exception, everyone I met in the lanes of the village
would extend his or her hand and give a fine, firm hand-clasp
with a greeting. In the Orient a handshake is not common except
amongst the westernized urban people and so, finding it here in
remote areas amongst people we had thought of as being backward,

gave that greeting far more meaning than ever before. Truly, our hearts were touched as we came to know these Lisu Christians. It was a new experience to find a community in which spiritual values were more important than material ones."

✝

The next several months were filled with activities. About the first of June we moved into the new house which Eugene had designed and built for us. He spent several months supervising the construction, and making sure everything would be nice, and the way we wanted it. We specially enjoyed the lovely big porch, overlooking the yard with all Russell's fruit trees and Drema Esther's flowers.

Betty was in need of a medical check-up, and the different families needed various supplies, so it was decided that Betty should make the trip to Rangoon, where she spent three weeks. She was able to get the medical care she needed, and also to buy some much-needed medicines for Russell, as well as other supplies.

LaVerne had to make a trip to Myitkyina to register the Putao Christian School with the government. During the two weeks he was there, he also had a chance to visit several of the churches in or near the town. Then on July 15 LaVerne and Lois and their three children flew to Rangoon to await the birth of their fourth child. Lois Beth, their third daughter, was born on August 7, 1963. While they were in Rangoon, their son Mark had a growth removed from his back, which we were all very thankful was benign. They returned to Putao on October 8, in time for LaVerne to attend one or two of the seven Thanksgiving conventions held in different places.

Also in August, I helped Robert and Betty with a short Bible School for the women of their village, which had an attendance of one hundred forty. The women wanted to study longer, but troubled conditions made it seem unwise to do so.

It was about this time that we began to miss some chickens and eggs and suspected that a snake was the culprit. Then one of the Lisu helper girls saw one slither by, but was so startled at the size of it that she just stood there. We got Preacher Titus to come and shoot it, and found out it was a **nine-foot-long king cobra!** That is one of the most poisonous snakes there is, with a bite fatal within ten minutes. We certainly thanked the Lord for keeping us from that danger, for it was only a few feet from the path, which we used every day. We had never heard of king cobras eating chickens, but only other snakes, so we assumed it was after the snake that was eating the chickens. Evidently it had been successful, because we lost no more chickens or eggs.

✝

During the last two weeks of September, 1963 a "retreat" was held in Muladi, and it was a real blessing to all who attended. As Helen wrote, "The influence from the retreat extended all through the village. A number of the preachers' wives also attended the classes, as well as a few of the village girls who are interested in doing the Lord's work. It has been very difficult for any girl to have an opportunity for service because of local customs and prejudices. But we have been praying much about this, and now it seems the Lord is opening the way for them, too. At the final service four girls came forward, including the preacher's daughter and one of our former helpers. There has been a great conviction of sin among all the people. Old misunderstandings, resentments, and bitternesses have been confessed and forgiveness asked. Old debts from ten to fifteen years ago are now being settled. It seems a great cleansing is going on within the church. We feel it is the 'revival' which we have known was needed and for which we have long been praying. When misunderstandings and other sins are cleared up, then the Lord can bless."

✝

The year was climaxed by a special event. Robert and Betty were expecting their fifth child, and had planned to go to Rangoon for it, but had been told there would be no place for them to stay. So they were staying in Dukdang for the event.

However, they had made special arrangements with the doctor at the government hospital in Putao to call him when the time came. Betty had had no serious problems during the pregnancy, but as the time for delivery drew near, she had a number of "false alarms". Lois and LaVerne and Helen and Eugene, had made numerous trips from our home in Muladi to Dukdang, four miles away, thinking that the baby was going to be born. On the evening of December 30 Eugene and Helen decided just to visit them, and found that Betty was again in labor. As time went on it became evident that this was the real thing, and Eugene drove the jeep over to Putao to call the doctor. However, by the time he and the doctor arrived about 2:45 a.m., Helen (who is a nurse) had already delivered the baby. Once she decided the time had come, Martha Camille arrived in a hurry, and was born at 2:30 a.m. on December 31, 1963. She was a lovely baby, plump and rosy-cheeked, with light brown hair and blue-grey eyes, and was warmly welcomed by her three big brothers, and especially by five-year-old big sister Dee Dee.

43
Unexpected Visitors, and Political Turmoil

In early February, 1964 we were surprised and happy to have a visit from Mr. and Mrs. John B. Kuhn of the Overseas Missionary Fellowship (formerly the China Inland Mission). They had been fortunate enough to be granted a visa allowing them to stay two months in Burma, although resident missionaries were being denied permission to return if they left, and tourist visas were normally limited to only ten days, with no permission to leave Rangoon. Soon after this, even tourist visas were limited to only 24 hours. But they had come to Burma to hold a Bible School at the village of Goo-moo, about seven miles north of Myitkyina. Concerning their visit with us, Mr. Kuhn wrote:

"All during that month of blessed treasure hunting in the Word of God I kept wondering about a visit to Putao to see Mr. and Mrs. J. Russell Morse, whom I had known in China.

"On Monday, February 4th, we flew to Putao. LaVerne, the youngest of the Morse boys, came to the air-strip to meet us. We soon established contact in the midst of a hodge-podge, nondescript crowd of country folk who had come to flag the big event of the day — arrival of the plane from Rangoon. After LaVerne saw to an errand or two, we were off over the plain in the jeep and made our first stop at Dukdang, where second son, Robert and family live. Here we were accorded a most enthusiastic and heart-warming welcome. I had known Robert in his student days. All seemed to marvel at the strange working of Providence that brought us to their environs.

"*Then we were off again, over a beautiful plainland and through tall grass, until we crossed over a divide and faced the valley of Muladi. Here we laid eyes upon a recently opened countryside, populated on both sides of a gorgeous river by more than two hundred Lisu tribal homes. It was all virgin territory but a few years back. Now everything was green around the village of Muladi, which in itself was most attractive, having been orderly laid out by Eugene, the eldest Morse son. Most of the gardens adjoining the Lisu homes could boast at least one orange tree in them. The whole area appeared as a little paradise in itself. How our hearts thrilled as the jeep rolled down through main street and then was brought to a stop at the Morse plantation. J. Russell Morse said, 'This is a miracle', as he welcomed us. No one had visited them from the outside world for so long, and why and how could it be that the Kuhns should visit them?*

"*Well, the Morse family were missionaries to the Lisu, and we had come to visit them. Having known each other in China, and having been in Kunming when Mr. Morse was imprisoned there, I was specially interested in them. Lastly, curiosity took us there. We had heard of the phenomenal results they had reaped in the work. (We had been told that converts from the Lisu and Rawang tribal groups now numbered some 50,000 souls, and this we wanted to see.) Then, too, there was that 'still small voice' which said 'go'.*

"*Now we were being ensconced at the Morse home situated in their luscious citrus grove. Soon we were to learn that citrus fruit growing had been introduced to this area as a material contribution to the physical well-being of the people. It would build up vitamin C and give them stamina which otherwise they lacked. This cultivation had now developed to tremendous proportions, there being in the neighborhood of 50,000 fruit trees in the whole of this wide area. However, citrus fruit was not the heart of this work, but only a product. The Gospel message had taken root and the all-consuming concern of all the Morse family was the care and nurture of these thousands of precious souls — the spiritual harvest in the work.*

"*We were eventually introduced all around, and our 'listening in' became increasingly intense as we began to grasp the inside story of the whole Putao work right from the early evacuation jour-*

ney out of China in 1927 when the vision of the place and people was given, right through the change-over from China to Burma in 1949-1950, down through to the present. We were coming to see a very dear and unusual sight — eight members of the Morse family all heart and soul engaged in the Lord's work for the Gospel throughout the whole area. Here we were viewing the whole strategy of the harmony of gifts and ability within the fabric of a closely knit family which consisted of:

"FATHER AND MOTHER — J. Russell and Gertrude Morse — These two are the chief spiritual backbone to the entire work, having passed on the vision to the rest of the family which they have tenaciously held to and brought to accomplishment down through the years. Mrs. Gertrude Morse is the 'Mother in Israel' to the whole work, always keeping uppermost the spiritual needs and claims of the entire testimony. J. Russell celebrated his 66th birthday while we were there. He said our coming was his birthday present. He also carries responsibility for a fair portion of the medical work at the central station.

"EUGENE MORSE — The eldest son, Eugene, is an architect, a mechanic, and an engineer. This is seen in the buildings erected in the work, whether for residential purpose or for public worship, and in the layout of the village. The splendid church buildings speak eloquently of Eugene's skill and mastery of the basic principles of architecture. He is also a zealous evangelist.

"ROBERT MORSE — Second son, Robert, is a linguist with a splendid basic and working knowledge of Chinese and a mastery of the two main tribal languages with which he has worked — Lisu and Rawang. He is now engaged in the translation of the Bible into the Rawang tongue. He conducts literacy schools and shares in the regular affairs of the growing churches.

"LAVERNE MORSE — Third son, LaVerne, is an educator, but with heart and soul in the spiritual warp and woof of Christian growth. Schools have been established in the area which conform to Government standards, but which also are thoroughly Christian. The school at Dukdang is a model of Christian effort in each grade and every department.

"The noble and dedicated wives of these three sons are wholly

407

one with their devoted husbands in the work, taking their share of responsibility as well as faithfully overseeing the education and upbringing of their children.

"Our three-day visit was coming to a close. God was in the midst; that was most evident. Reasons behind our going to Putao were increasingly clear. In the midst of political unrest in North Burma, the Morse family was in a precarious position.

"Brother and Sister Kuhn, will you get others to pray for us on your return?'

"Yes, Russell, we'll do that very thing.'"

✟

On February 17, 1964, Drema Esther and Jesse Yangmi's first child, little Lucy Ruth, was born. Helen delivered the baby for Esther, as she had done for Betty about six weeks earlier when Martha Camille was born. They were both beautiful babies. Lucy was very small and dainty, had lots of black silky hair and a tiny rose-bud mouth. We called her our little Tibetan princess, since both Esther and Jesse had Tibetan ancestry in their family lines.

✟

The situation in North Burma became increasingly tense all during 1964. Our only contact with the outside was by air. Almost all canned goods were off the market, or too expensive, so we had very few groceries to fall back on for the coming year. We had to grow everything ourselves: rice, fruit, vegetables, as well as chickens and pigs for meat.

The Burmese Socialist Government had gradually been nationalizing all private business, industries, enterprises, and everything in lower Burma. But because of a well organized Kachin Independence Army and their strong resistance, the government had been unable to go ahead with their program of socialist "reforms" in northern Burma. As Robert said, "We are sitting on the edge of a razor blade and must not allow ourselves to become unbalanced on either side."

One day in April, Robert's children experienced real panic

when a special Burmese Army strike force, in battle array, guns at the ready, carrying full packs, wearing steel helments, and with grenades dangling from their belts, suddenly appeared and over-ran Dukdang village and came into their compound also.

The following day the strike force arrived in Muladi. At the upper end of the village, one crippled man protested when some of the soldiers entered his home, and they shot and killed him. They proceeded across the suspension bridge to Yichodi Village, opposite Muladi. There they engaged in random shooting to frighten people (although no one was hurt), burned ten houses, and took their leave. During the next several weeks, there was sporadic fighting in several places, but our village was not affected directly. However, many of the villagers, becoming disturbed about the over-all political situation, began to look for places to which they might flee in case of prolonged fighting. Some families even moved up in the mountains, and began doing their traditional slash-and-burn fields there, away from the villages, where there might be fighting.

In mid-June, 1964 LaVerne and Lois left on their furlough. They were expecting their fifth child, and Lois had not been well. Their furlough was due, but they had hesitated to leave, fearing they would not be granted a return visa. However, it had become increasingly hard to carry on the mission work, including the day schools, because of the fighting in nearby villages. So it seemed an opportune time for them to leave. Due to certain technicalities, they were delayed an unusually long time in Rangoon getting their departure permits. They finally left Burma the latter part of June.

44
Battle In the Village

On the morning of August 15, 1964 we awoke to find our houses, and in fact the entire village, surrounded with Burmese soldiers. We soon learned that they had chased a group of about 45 Kachin Independence Army (KIA) soldiers as far as Muladi, but the KIA soldiers had crossed the river and taken up positions at the bridge, which made it impossible for the Burmese to cross the river there without considerable loss of life. So the 200 or so Burmese were settled in on our side of the river to try to drive out the KIA, who were very firmly dug in on the other side of the river, which was in flood. The Kachin men have been noted for their fighting abilities, and the Kachin Rifles unit of the British Army was instrumental in keeping the Japanese out of the northern tip of Burma during World War II. So the Burmese knew these KIA soldiers would put up a stiff fight, even though out-numbered.

On a hill overlooking our village the Burmese mounted their mortars, and kept up a steady barrage toward the other side of the river. Machine gun "nests" were set up all along the river front, including one only about 100 yards from Eugene and Helen's house. Helen said, "Every time we sit down to a meal, they find something to shoot at, so we have 'music' with our meals." Recoilless rifles were also set up, which made a terrific noise.

After about ten days, when all these measures proved ineffective, the Burmese forces brought in planes, and bombed and strafed the bridge-head for three successive days.. They came in low over our houses as they made their approach, with guns blazing. Although we were not in any real danger, being on the same side of the river as the Burmese soldiers, some of us did decide to stay in the church during the day for a couple of days, to be more out of the line of fire. But sometimes the planes came before everyone got there, and one day when that happened, 13-year-old Tommy was real excited to have two empty shells fall at his feet as the plane went over.

Villagers from both sides of the river gradually moved out as the battle continued, and sought safety up in the mountains where they had made their fields. Some of those who remained came and stayed with us, and together we prayed constantly for the safety of the Christians across the river, for those who had fled into the mountains, and for the mission compound and village and those of us who remained. During the two weeks of fighting, many of the Burmese soldiers were killed, including one of their officers. On the other hand, not even one Christian or villager was hurt in any way. This seemed to us to be an overwhelming testimony to answered prayer, and God's power to keep those who put their trust in Him.

Because we were foreigners in the country, the Burmese government was responsible for our safety, and the soldiers were friendly. They had asked us to leave "for our own safety", but as Eugene told them, "If we were to leave now, many of the villagers might not come back, but if we remain, we can help persuade them to return." So we remained. Often, after the fighting was over for the day, some of the Burmese soldiers would change into civilian clothes and come talk with Russell.

It was one of these soldiers, a lieutenant, who told about what happened when, after two weeks of fighting, the Burmese soldiers finally crossed the river on rafts and went into Old Muladi village. He said they noticed smoke coming from one of the houses, and thinking it was some of the KIA soldiers, they surrounded the house, and fired into it from all sides.

Finally the lieutenant called out, "If there's anyone in there still alive, come out!" To their great surprise — and mortification! — a partially crippled little old lady, the only occupant of the house, hobbled out. When he asked how she had escaped being shot, she just pointed up, and he knew she meant that God had protected her.

That same lieutenant told us of another amazing incident which happened as some of the Burmese soldiers landed in Old (South) Muladi. He said the soldiers found one Lisu man, and thinking he must surely be part of — or at least a supporter of — the KIA, they were going to execute him there at the riverside. One of the soldiers pointed his rifle at the man and pulled the trigger, but the gun didn't fire. He tried a second time, but still nothing happened. As he tried the third time, and the third bullet failed to go off, the lieutenant came on the scene.

"What are you doing?", he asked. "No civilians are to be harmed! Put down your guns."

"We caught this man here," they replied, "and thought he was with the KIA force. But we tried three times to shoot him, and none of the bullets would go off. There's something strange going on here."

The lieutenant then took the three bullets which had failed to go off, put them back into the same gun and fired up into the air. All three went off as expected.

When the lieutenant told us about the incident, he said, "Surely your God is protecting His people."

These were very difficult days for us, because many of the soldiers among both the KIA fighters and the Burmese were Christians and were known to us personally. So we were caught in the middle, with friends on both sides, and had to be very careful and "walk a tight rope" so as not to offend either side.

✝

Twelve-year-old Stephen, Robert and Betty's second son, had an encounter with a cobra. Here he tells of the experience in his own words:

"We have seen many animals out in the jungle and have had many of their babies for pets. We've taken care of monkeys and apes, deer and goral, leopard and civet cat babies, plus many kinds of snakes and other animals.

"Snakes are about the easiest pets to raise, but the favorite of our whole family was a mongoose whose name, of course, was Rikki-Tikki. Rikki-Tikki was really brave and would attack any snake he saw, even our pet python, which was twelve feet long. If you keep reading, you'll understand why I wished for a snake-killing mongoose the other day.

"I was in the kitchen peeling a pineapple when I heard a squeak like a frog. I remembered the local saying that if you save a frog in trouble it will bless you, so I went outside to rescue it. When I got there I saw that two big chickens were pecking at a baby rat. I bent down and picked it up, but my terrier, Rickety (her name is Rickets because that is the disease she had when she was a puppy), snapped it out of my hand and started playing with it. I was watching when suddenly there was a loud 'phuuu' sound in back of me. I turned around and saw a big cobra with its hood expanded and its head waving in the air about a foot off the ground. "Our Alsatian, Bullet, saw it too, and got between me and the cobra, just about two feet away. Suddenly I got real scared so I thought of calling Mommy. She was in bed with Asian flu, so I ran in, waking her up yelling 'A cobra! a cobra!" She jumped up, looking around, and said, 'Where? Where? I told her it was just outside, so she said to hurry and get a machete (big knife). When I told her it was too big to kill with a knife, that she would have to shoot it, she told me to get the gun. But when we got outside the snake was gone.

"The dogs sniffed under the wall, and we heard the loud hissing again, this time coming from inside the house. Mommy told me to go in and open the storeroom door, so I did, and threw some rocks to try to chase it back out so that Mommy could shoot it. It didn't go out, but pretty soon I saw it. It was dark inside and we could barely see something shiny moving under a basket about twenty feet away. There was only a two-inch opening, but I had hope, because Mommy and Daddy are known as the best rifle shots in Putao. We

413

thought we saw it jump, and then it moved out of sight, but Mommy shot again, just in case. We threw some rocks but it didn't hiss, and when we poked with long sticks, we couldn't find it, so we didn't know whether she had hit it or not. We didn't know what to do because Daddy wasn't at home, and we didn't dare sleep in the house that night if we weren't sure it was dead.

"Finally I went back to school and got some of the teachers and students to come help us hunt. They all had big sticks and poked everywhere, but couldn't find it. They found a couple of dead rats that the cobra had bitten. The little rat I found must have been running away from the snake when the chickens saw it and pecked it. We thought it was interesting that the cobra would leave the rest of its dinner behind and chase after the one that got away.

"After a while, my friend was looking in another room and almost stepped on the cobra, which was lying on its back. Mommy was really happy when she saw that she had hit it, but it was still alive. I killed it and skinned the hood part which has an O mark on it. Imagine, Mommy had a fever of 102 degrees, but she managed to kill a cobra.

"Well, I learned a good lesson that day. What if we hadn't discovered that the cobra was around, and had gone to sleep with it still in the house? Many people are bitten in their sleep. We all need to learn that it is always good to help animals in trouble, because even though it wasn't a frog in trouble, still I got a blessing when I thought it was and went out to help!"

45

A Case of Tetanus, and a Trial By Fire

Early in May of 1965, Stephen, one of our older Lisu preachers who was the pastor of a church near us, brought his 10-year-old son to us for medicine. He told us only that the boy's chest and throat hurt, and that it was hard for him to swallow. We noticed that the child seemed to be having slight convulsions. Then we noticed a cut on his foot, and on inquiring found it had happened exactly one week earlier. Putting all the facts and symptoms together, we were almost certain it was tetanus. We all felt he should be rushed to the government hospital at Putao, hoping that the doctor there would have the antitoxin.

We fixed a Lisu-style bed across the back of the jeep for the child to lie on, and he was taken to Putao, even though it was after dark and we didn't usually travel then. When the doctor saw the boy, he confirmed our diagnosis of tetanus and said there was almost no hope for him. Even under the best conditions, he said, only about three out of a thousand get well. And our conditions certainly were not the best!

The doctor's medicine was out of date, but he said he would do what he could for the child. Helen had gone along to speak to the doctor, and when she returned and told us all, we determined to ask the nearby churches to pray for him. We felt that if God restored him it would be a great witness to the many non-Christians in the hospital. Besides, we all loved the child. So the churches and all of us prayed. Also, we sent a telegram to Rangoon for some more medicine, which was received on the very next plane, two days later. The child was VERY ill for several days, but little by little he began to improve. Gradually he was able to take liquids, then solid food, and after a month or so, to be out of bed and move about. Six weeks from the time he was taken to the hospital, he was discharged and taken home. How we did thank the Lord for undertaking in this case. Every time we saw the boy, we were reminded again of God's power to answer prayer.

✟

In spite of the troubles surrounding us, we held two Bible schools during March and April. One, for the elders of the many churches in the Putao plain, lasted eight days, with one hundred thirty-five students. The elders were appreciative, and wished it could have lasted a month. Following that was a one-month school, for the preachers, assistant preachers, and interested young people ("potential" preachers), with over three hundred students. It seemed as if the Lord brought those that should study, for some of the preachers said they were already on their way to Muladi, when they received the letter telling about the school. They said God had called them to come. The Lord seemed very near to all of us, and He kept everything peaceful so we could study. Nearby churches helped supply the food for the students, too. We and the students all wished it could have been for three months, but because of the unsettled conditions it seemed best to close after just one month.

For more than a year, Eugene and Helen's oldest son, David, had needed to have his eyes checked and get new glasses, but unsettled conditions had made it inadvisable to make the long, 700-mile trip to Rangoon. Then Tommy developed an abcessed tooth which needed attention, so it was finally decided that Helen should go and take the two boys. It took about two months to obtain a permit to leave the Putao area, but they were finally able to leave on May 20, 1965. Then when they arrived in Myitkyina, they learned they had to apply for additional permits to travel on to Rangoon, which took another five days. It was while they were in Myitkyina that Helen received the sad news of the death of her father, Oscar L. Myers, who with her mother, Julia, had helped represent the mission in the U.S. It was a great shock, and it was very hard for Helen to be away from the rest of the family at that time.

Upon arriving in Rangoon, Helen talked with some of the other missionaries about getting glasses for David. They were very pessimistic, and said it often took up to three months to get glasses, even after you had your prescription, and it usually took weeks to get a dental appointment.. So everyone was really amazed when she was able to get David's glasses in less than twenty-four hours, and Tommy was able to see the dentist the very next day after their arrival. Also, she encountered no difficulty in getting their new passports, which had to be gotten in person. She and the boys were back home in Muladi by June 10. Truly, God undertook for them.

✝

The rambling bamboo house in which Robert and Betty had been living at Dukdang was about to collapse through sheer decay. Houses made of bamboo and other jungle materials do not last very long in that tropical climate. So they decided to go ahead and build a new house, in spite of the troubled situation all around them. They designed and Eugene supervised the building of a nice two-story house, with wooden floors, bamboo walls and thatched roof. By the first week in July, 1965 the upstairs wooden floor, beautifully planed and smoothed by Eugene's power planer, had just been finished, they were half moved in and ready to tear down the old house. However, the thatched roofs of the two houses were still side by side, almost touching when their "trial by fire" occurred. Here are excerpts of Betty's and Robert's accounts of that shocking and traumatic experience:

BETTY: "Sometime after midnight, July 4th, we were awakened by a blood-curdlIng scream from Joni, 'Mommy! Daddy!' We jumped up, grabbing our flashlights, and my heart seemed to stop beating. I feared the years of hidden dread of communists' threats against the children had materialized. Joni, Ahkey Bobby (Robert, Jr.), and some of the helpers were still sleeping in the old house, so Robert hurried over there while Stevie and I ran onto the porch to see what was happening. Joni's voice had seemed to come from down by the fence toward the village. Then, from the upstairs porch, where we had gone to get a better view, we could see that the old house was on fire! All I could think was — 'Oh, thank God! It's only the house on fire! Thank you, God!'

"Stevie and I immediately got the two school girls and Dee Dee and Camille out, and I ordered him to stay with the girls so they wouldn't panic. Rushing back upstairs, I tried to tear away the grass of the old house roof where it joined the new house at the balcony. The last thing I had asked the workers Saturday afternoon was to take off that part of the roof, and they said, 'First thing Monday'. It seemed I was there an eternity before the students and teachers got there with buckets of water, but it must have been only a few moments. Then I saw the very corner of the new house catch fire. Until that instant I had felt we could save the new house some way, but as the flames crackled from the new roof, I realized that all was hopeless.

"Then I began yelling outside to ask if Ahkey and the others who had been sleeping in the old house had gotten out safely. When I was assured they were all safe I dashed up to my new study to try to save something. Mangutaq Duh came and I asked him to get out what he could. I grabbed my writing files and typewriter and threw them out the window. The stairs and den seemed so bright by then, so I grabbed the radio and the Tiliwago church painting, along with a few other things and went down the stairs. I wanted to go back for my Bible, our Daily Light and our shoes, but Stevie was screaming hysterically and Joni was frantic for me to get out so I grabbed a Lisu skirt to put over my gown and went.

"Robert dashed up at that time from his study, which was completely gone by then. He had gotten his most important translation files out, but couldn't get his personal typewriter, the Butoba recorder or tapes, and lost ALL of his life-long stamp collection. His head and one hand were badly burned. He had held his breath

while getting what he could, and we all marvelled at his endurance.

"It amazed us how quickly the whole thing was over. The house was gone in ten or fifteen minutes. If Robert had not gone straight for the translation material, he wouldn't have saved a thing because that part of the house went first."

ROBERT: *"We have seen a lot of excitement and activity, but the experience of almost getting burned to death in your own home, and of losing all your earthly possessions and cherished belongings in an eternity of stress and terror compressed into a few short minutes, was a new experience to us. We hope we don't have to repeat it! But I'm sure the traumatic experience will prevent us from ever accumulating so much again.*

"I suppose there's nothing so combustible as bamboo and thatch, well cured by ten years of dry rot. Anyhow, it went up fast and furious, melting everything it didn't consume. We had no time to try and get out our most precious writings and books, most of which are nothing but a memory now; also Betty's nicest dishes, all the children's hobbies and toys, my stamp collection, and our library of study and reference books (some 3000 volumes).

"We have really marveled, though, at some of the things that did get out 'by accident', through somebody having grabbed it and throwing it out. Betty's sewing machine was thrown from her second-story window and didn't break up. The typewriter she threw out was found in a tree and was somewhat askew, but David took it apart and put it together again, and I am using it now. Joni personally yanked out our yellow porcelain washbasin and handed it down, minus a plug. He took one last look around, grabbed up a crystal glass teardrop design flower vase, and jumped off the second floor balcony with it. He then came to Betty and said, 'I'm going to have this for my own keepsake of what I rescued from the fire.'

"All of our children's birth certificates and other important papers, plus about $700 in cash, were burned, and yet our passports, recently renewed in Rangoon, were saved! A slightly ironic feature about it all is that we had been preparing for just such an emergency for almost two years, and had long ago sorted out most of our important things and put them aside, where they would be

419

*instantly available. If we had had even twenty minutes we proba-
bly could have saved them all.*

    *"Well, the Lord had prepared a place for us — a big, hollow,
40' x 60' shed on the grounds, and we're living in this, dormitory
style, practicing 'togetherness' in a big way. Twelve persons are
sleeping in two rooms, with another big area serving as kitchen-
dining-living-den-study-sewing-guest room combined. We're cooking over an open fire on the ground, with utensils given us by the
villagers and other local Christians."*

That tragedy brought all of us so much closer to the
Christians. Hundreds of Lisu and Rawang Christian families
had been burned out that year, mostly due to the fighting, and
we had always tried to help them. Now, it was those same poor
people who were helping Robert and Betty. The village people
came in a constant stream all week with gifts of food, money,
tins of milk, fish, and household utensils. Betty said one of the
sweetest notes came from a Lisu boy who expressed his sorrow
and wondered what he could do to help "now that you all have
become poor like we are". He sent a cotton blanket and a head
strap for a carrying basket.

✝

The first we in Muladi knew of the disaster was at dawn on
July 5 when we were awakened by a messenger bringing the
news. Right away we started getting together things we
thought they might need. We and Eugene's family got together
sheets and blankets, mosquito nets, some cooking utensils,
foodstuffs such as flour and sugar, home-made bacon, canned
milk, etc., and children's clothes, which Eugene's children were
happy to share with their cousins. As soon as possible we were
on our way to Dukdang to see what we could do to help.
Helen described our feelings when we arrived there:

    *"When we arrived at Dukdang we felt like crying. The place
looked so bare! Everything was gone — old house and new. We
found Robert and Betty in the big work shed (formerly it had been
used for storage and wash house), with the things which had been
salvaged piled up in little heaps here and there. When Robert came*

420

out to meet us, wearing a pajama shirt and old longyi, barefoot, with gentian violet smeared liberally on his burned hand and head, with a 2-day beard, and minus his front tooth, he really looked like his namesake, Job! (In both Lisu and Rawang his name is Yo-be, or Job).

"But through it all, Robert and Betty have shown a wonderful spirit and have been a marvelous example to everyone. I know that the loss of some of their things has hurt them a lot. But they have not shown any bitterness of spirit at all. Truly the Lord has helped them in this difficult time."

Although things were very difficult for Robert and Betty, they thanked God that all their family was safe, that at least some of Robert's sixteen years of research was saved, and that the Bible translating work** could continue. The translation had been going rather slowly, but they were now 'fired' with new determination to work harder than ever to complete the New Testament

---

**(Robert finally completed the Rawang New Testament translation seven years later while in prison in Mandalay, as described in "Exodus to a Hidden Valley.")

46
End of an Era

As the autumn and winter dry season of 1965 came, the fighting continued between the rebels who wanted independence for Kachin State, and the government, which had nationalized and socialized every aspect of life. Almost nothing was available by then except from government stores. Many people had not been able to get either salt or cooking oil for months. Withholding essential supplies seemed to be a form of punishment to villages which refused to co-operate as fully as the government thought they should.

As foreigners, we were "officially" out of favor, but the local people remained friendly. We were not allowed to buy any medicine at Putao. We could get things like salt and cooking oil only with ration cards. If we wanted to travel we had to wait for permission from state officials at Myitkyina, over two hundred miles away. We could get very little gas for the jeep, but when we could, the government soldiers would demand rides. Then the rebels would threaten to shoot if they saw soldiers in our jeep again. Both groups came and wanted us to surrender any guns we had, but we had none to give either side.

Such pressures, not so gently applied, had caused many missionaries to give up and leave Burma. With God's help, we were desperately trying to hang on. There was no one to whom we could look for help and safety. The government soldiers became wild and unruly when out on operations. Officers and men were often drunk, even on duty. The rebel soldiers treated dissidents harshly, too, so it was like walking a tight rope.

✝

We all were aware that our days in the Putao area might be numbered, but felt impressed that we should go ahead with the Bible School in September as planned. We were glad we did. About seventy preachers gathered, coming from all parts of the field. We had first planned to continue through to Christmas, but many of the preachers felt they should get back home to harvest their fields, so we closed at the end of October, planning to hold another school in January or February. But that was not to be.

On December 3, 1965 we received the official order which we had been dreading, a letter from the Revolutionary Government of the Union of Burma. Subject: Presidential Order and Instruction to Leave the Country. This document came directly from the Rangoon headquarters, bypassing the usual channels through local officials. It ordered us to leave Burma by December 31, 1965, which gave us only three weeks to "wind up" the work, and dispose of the equipment and personal goods accumulated in the course of fifteen years of living and working with the people we loved.

The next three weeks were a time of frantic activity. We all needed to go through all our belongings and decide what we should take with us, what we should give away, and to whom it should be given, what should be thrown away, and what we would have to just walk off and leave.

The news that we had been ordered to leave spread rapidly, even to areas several days' walk away. Soon we had people coming almost all day long, wanting to have a final visit and to bid us farewell. It was very hard to do any packing or work when people wanted us to talk with them. So it turned out that we had to do most of our sorting and packing at night, after people had left — usually between midnight and 2:00 or 3:00 a.m.

To complicate matters, Drema Esther's little Lucy developed chicken pox, and Robert's 6-year-old daughter Dee Dee came down with mumps. Besides this, Drema Esther was expecting her second child and was in the last month of her pregnancy. We checked with the airlines, and they said none of these conditions would be accepted on the airlines. We had applied for an extension of time through the Security Council in Putao, and had been refused. We had also sent an appeal to the American ambassador in Rangoon, asking that he intervene and try to obtain an extension for us. We were awaiting a reply to that effort.

Meanwhile, we had been trying to complete all government formalities in preparation for leaving. We had completed all the necessary procedures for clearance with the police and immigration departments — had been fingerprinted, and had filled out multiple copies of forms, and had even taken, processed, printed, and submitted pictures for each person, including the children. Everything was in order, and the only thing remaining was to fill out the final forms in Rangoon at the time of actual departure.

✞

Many of the Lisu there in north Burma had escaped from the communists in China, and to them the expulsion of the missionaries sounded very much like the communist procedures. Having no desire to be caught again under that kind of government, many, many Lisu families had already left the Putao plains area and headed up into the mountains to join with the families who had moved out at the time of the battle. Some of the men had come and talked to our men-folk, saying that if we couldn't get an extension of time, and couldn't get on the plane, they would be very happy if we'd come out and join them in the "jungle". In fact, they said, since they were hoping to go across the border into India, they would really like to have us come along and talk on their behalf, and explain to the Indian government that they didn't want to be under a communist government again. They said there were plenty of people who would be glad to come and carry loads for us if we

424

decided to go that way. All we would need to do would be to let them know.

The more we talked it over, the more we thought maybe alternate preparations should be made for an overland evacuation through India. So we all began packing loads of things which we would need for overland travel if it became necessary for us to take such a journey.

On December 21 our grandson David drove the tractor to Putao to get the mail and came back with a telegram from the American ambassador, informing us that his efforts to obtain an extension of time had been fruitless. That was the word that clinched matters. Early the next morning messengers were sent to inform our Lisu brethren up in the hills that carriers would be needed and we would be joining them on their trek toward the Indian border.

On the evening of December 22, 1965 as we were making final arrangements for leaving, a group of officials and soldiers came from Putao, wanting to take an inventory of our houses. Eugene and Robert pointed out to them it was much too big a job to do in just an evening, and convinced them it would be much better to wait until the next morning. That night, carriers came and picked up all the loads we had prepared, and at midnight we turned out the lights and left our houses, to begin the "exodus" into an unknown future. The account of that pilgrimage under the Lord's care and guidance, and the events of the next six years in an area we called "Hidden Valley" is another story, told in the book "Exodus to a Hidden Valley", by our son Eugene.**

** The book, "Exodus to a Hidden Valley", by Eugene Morse, can be ordered from Mrs. Art Bitts, P. O. Box 4074, Terre Haute, IN 47804. Price is $5.00 plus $1.95 postage

Out of all our years of missionary work, we feel that the years in North Burma were our "Golden Era", especially the time from Russell's and my return in 1953 until about 1963, when the effects of the Socialist government take-over became evident. All three of our sons and their families were working with us in a heart-warming and spiritually fulfilling endeavor. We carried the Gospel to farflung places where it had never been heard and the response was wonderful. The transformation which took place in thousands of lives was truly thrilling. We knew that whatever had been accomplished was by God's enabling, not in our own strength. It was almost overwhelming to see"what God hath wrought."

In looking back over all the years on the mission field, I feel we can never thank God enough for His tender care over us through all the serious situations when each member of our family, at one time or another, has been near death. He has been with us every step of the way, from that first trip from Kunming to Batang, when Eugene was a baby and we were threatened by robbers and kidnappers, all the way to the present time. He wonderfully protected Russell on his long trip through robber-infested country on his way to the dentist at Kunming. Then on that seventy-day trip through the jungles from China to Myitkyina, across snow mountains over 12-14,000 ft. passes, He was with us and strengthened us; and when carriers threatened to run away in the freezing weather and leave us stranded, He caused the sun to shine, then took us safely down. He protected us as we crossed turbulent streams over flimsy bridges or in tiny canoes. He kept us in times of severe illness when we had no other source of help, guided us in travel over dangerous mountain trails, and protected us in times of danger from local political uprisings. He kept and rescued us at the time of flood, when He saved the children and me from being swept away. He preserved us in time of war, making it possible for Russell and the boys to serve Him and our country at the same time. He has always been there to comfort us in times of sadness, as when our hearts ached over the parting with loved ones. He brought Russell through the terrible tortures in the Chinese prison, and guided LaVerne and me to Hong Kong at the exact time of his release. He saved us numerous times from the communists. He saved Robert, Betty and their children when their house burned; kept all of us through the years in Hidden Valley; and brought us all safely back to civilization.

Now we rejoice in the fact that not only our children, but many of our grandchildren also are serving the Lord as missionaries, preachers, or other Christian workers. We pray that they will continue faithful, and that THEIR children also will grow up to love and serve our loving, living Lord, Jesus Christ.

"Now unto Him that is able to do exceeding abundantly above all that we ask or think....be glory...throughout all ages, world without end. Amen." (Eph. 3:20-21, KJV)

"To the only wise God our Saviour, be glory and majesty, dominion and power, both now and ever." (Jude 25, KJV)

Map of the Salween River Valley

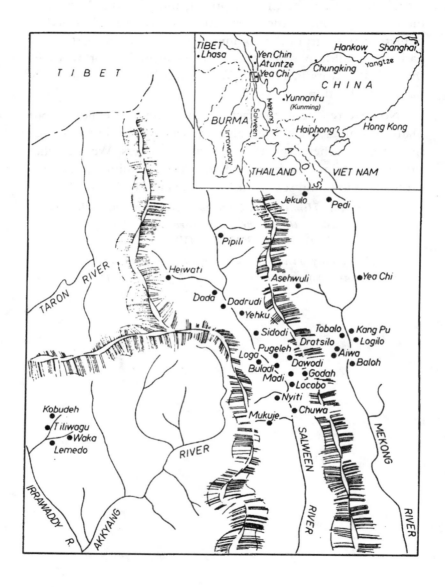